A Theology of Nonsense

A Theology of Nonsense

Josephine Gabelman

FOREWORD BY John Milbank

PICKWICK *Publications* · Eugene, Oregon

A THEOLOGY OF NONSENSE

Pickwick Publications
An Imprint of Wipf and Stock Publishers
199 W. 8th Ave., Suite 3
Eugene, OR 97401

www.wipfandstock.com

PAPERBACK ISBN: 978-1-62564-553-1
HARDCOVER ISBN: 978-1-4982-8598-8
EBOOK ISBN: 978-1-5326-0189-7

Cataloguing-in-Publication data:

Names: Gabelman, Josephine. | Foreword by Milbank, John.

Title: A theology of nonsense / Josephine Gabelman.

Description: Eugene, OR: Pickwick Publications, 2016 | Includes bibliographical references and index.

Identifiers: ISBN 978-1-62564-553-1 (paperback) | ISBN 978-1-4982-8598-8 (hardcover) | ISBN 978-1-5326-0189-7 (ebook)

Subjects: LSCH: Faith and reason—Christianity. | Paradox—Religious aspects—Christianity. | Philosophical theology. | Nonsense literature. | Philosophy in literature.

Classification: BT50 G112 2016 (paperback) | BT50 (hardcover) | BT50 (ebook)

Manufactured in the U.S.A.   09/07/16

For Lambie, my dearest apostate

Contents

FOREWORD

Theology as
Anastrophe _____

CHRISTIANITY IS FOUNDED ON unimaginable disaster: the death of God himself in the death of a man. But from the outset it was re-founded on the overturning of even this catastrophe. Unsurprisingly then, it has proved well able to undercut and survive every later twist of fate. Over the last two centuries its finality and even its truth have been denied and it has been increasingly denounced as a fiction, as foolishly incoherent, as a failure of human maturity, and a refusal of political responsibility. Yet as the current book explains, with an unprecedented scope and unpretentious directness, the most subtle Christian apologists within this era—often literary and often British—have simply accepted these denunciations, but overturned their apparent implications. Yes, Christianity is a fiction, is nonsense, is childlike and anarchic. But thereby it is all the more true, rational, human, and socially harmonious. In this way Christianity has come to be seen with a new intensity as not merely mysterious and symbolic, but also paradoxical in a strong and irreducible sense. In effect then, the cultural Golgotha now faced by the church has also proved the occasion for a spiritual resurrection involving nothing less than a deepened apprehension of the heart of the gospel.

Christianity is indeed "made up," but then fiction alone is able to complete our enigmatic world through speculation. Fiction alone is able to probe the limits of our apprehensions of reality and to expose the ways in which every such apprehension is itself fictionally limited, the ways in which our given reality may itself be a shadowy story, and to suggest that more ultimate reality may involve a coincidence of truth with myth or fairy-tale. Much has already been written upon the new sense of the importance of the imagination for religion, ever since Schelling and Coleridge.

Josephine Gabelman supplements such reflection, but more centrally focuses upon the less well theologically-explored issue of nonsense. This permits her to see a profound theological significance in the writings of Lewis Carroll (as much as in the more "romantic" imaginative fictions of his friend George MacDonald) and to engage with his teasing questionings of the bounds of sense and logic. For Gabelman, nonsense can be considered with respect to human theory, to human practice, and to the phases of humanity both in time and in relation to eternity.

In relation to theory she provides a comprehensive account of the ways in which nearly all the main Christian teachings concerning Trinity, creation, fall, redemption, and eschatology seem to exhibit strong instances of paradox. She robustly defends the case of Chesterton and others (Kierkegaard and Péguy, for example) that these instances cannot be reduced to merely apparent paradox. Instead, they exhibit "real contradiction"—ultimately traceable, one could argue, to a pure but not pantheist monotheism, which sees God as irreducibly all in all, and yet (incomprehensibly) able to admit an "other" alongside of himself. The otherness of this other, the freedom of this other, the distance of this other, and the separateness of this other, even within the incarnate union of God with the other to God, cannot after all be seen as denying the equal identity of this other with God, nor her command by God, nor her absolute intimacy with God, and nor finally the personal identity of Christ's manhood with his divinity. To deny these things, in accordance with a theological rationalism, is demonstrably to enter into heresy, as Gabelman lucidly insists.

Thus it turns out that orthodoxy has always been nonsense. In the face of atheist accusers, we have turned back to the Scriptures and occasionally the church fathers, and discovered that, while they insist of the reasonableness of Christianity, they have equally insisted upon its folly. This implies, as Gabelman argues, that reason and its opposite, unreason, are themselves paradoxically at one. Again it seems that theology is, as Nicholas of Cusa first realized, "dialetheic"—committed to the truth of certain outrightly contradictory statements. This implies a rejection of the coincidence of the rational with the real and a priority for the latter. The radical realism of Christianity suggests that aspects of the real can only be felt, intuited, or imagined. Or even invoked through nonsense—statements that may be at once unsettling in a purgative way and yet equally propositional in a manner that logic fails to grasp.

Here Gabelman gently locates an ambiguity within postmodern thought. Its recognition of the paradoxical hovers between a negative deconstruction that removes the possibility of the seriously meaningful with a kind of manic laughter on the one hand, and a positive embrace of the "impossible" as indeed one aspect of the real on the other. If this be the case (as is more allowed by the new spirit of "speculative realism" currently in fashion) then, as "radically orthodox" thinkers like Catherine Pickstock (much cited by Gabelman) have insisted, it must also be the case that the impossible analogically manifests itself—as paradoxically at once close and distant—through the possible, if it be, as real, more than a mere sublime horizon. Thus, for Gabelman the luring horizon of nonsense at once evermore beckons and evermore recedes, up to and including the beatific vision itself.

To see this is, for her, also to see that only Christianity outplays the reign of the serious. For a secular person, the "serious" insertion into a random, meaningless world of human sense and of human justice is, understandably, the first and last word—and an inevitably political word. But if, for faith, the original given and unfallen world (which is still more truly there than the fallen world, as Gabelman "Platonically" affirms, after Berdyaev) is pure gift, pure abundant play without any further sense, point, or purpose, then levity is more serious than the serious, more grave than the grave. Thus, as Gabelman puts it, with great acuity: "For the Christian it is a duty not to take reality too seriously, but from a secular point of view, deconstructing the seriousness of a subject could be taken as a devaluation of meaning" (189). Just for this reason, one could add, the postmodern is ambivalently caught between a tragic skepticism and an irresponsible ludicity. Theology, by contrast, can offer a ludic responsibility, or rather, lucid grounds for the non-necessity of the responsible, in any ultimate terms.

This book then offers a trenchant account of the irreducibly dialetheic character of Christian thought. There exist strong paradoxes of sense and not merely of language, in the end because the finite depends upon the infinite, which alone fully exists, even though the finite (somehow) also exists in participatory dependence upon it. The consequent paradoxicality of finite existence itself is indicated by the primacy of the temporal, for which an ordered, consequent logical sequence itself depends upon the "impossible" co-inherence of past, present, and future moments. Christian teaching records and intensifies these intra-temporal paradoxes also: we are fully in Christ and yet ourselves; salvation is both already and not-yet; in Christ we are fully innocent and yet remain sinners. (One can note here how any merely "imputational" account of grace is precisely a rationalist attempt to reduce paradox.) The Christian stress on salvation by the preached word also underscores, as Gabelman argues, a paradoxicality of language, rather than sense that is yet itself irreducible to linguistic appearance: namely the way in which words are at human command and yet always command us. Therefore, even, or even most of all, Christian words turn out to mean more and sometimes the opposite of what was first intended. Language thereby also reveals a controlling surplus of the infinite at the very heart of finite freedom—not as thwarting it, but as strangely confirming it.

But if nonsense is theory then it is also—as in the *Alice* books—practice. The anti-practice of anarchy. As Gabelman argues, Christian anarchy does not mean either an assertion of individual autonomy, nor of ontological disorder, because such secular theories remain normative and therefore not genuinely anarchical. Instead, Christianity opens out the only possible creed of anarchy as linked to a suspense of law and an interval between different legal orders. Through a fine defence and elaboration of Berdyaev, Gabelman argues that the true anarchic condition is to live between the relativization of the law of Caesar on the one hand and the coming of the kingdom of Christ on the other. As she rightly argues, the Russian sage was not here proposing (at least at his best, as she allows) a gnostic retreat into a private space in default of the final polity's arrival, but rather saw "anarchy" as paradoxically distilled within the mingling of an always lingering Caesarian law on the one hand and the new law of the gospel on the other. Since all human law is deluded in its claim to have found a remedy against sin, and the violence of human law only compounds such sin, there can be no doubt that, for the gospel, secular legitimacy is in a sense "over." Yet equally, as for Paul, a certain legitimacy for the law persists in time as long as the effects of the fall, while the other order, the disordered order of the gospel polity, is now but partially intuited and exercised. Indeed its operation of purely positive joy is paradoxically only exhibited through the suffering and endurance of the old order, whose privacy and ultimacy is yet refused—hence the levity of the martyrs.

For Gabelman the church is the social occupancy of this "anarchic moment wherein the supreme reign is not visibly constituted, in a world where the ruling power is not actually ruling" (123). Just for this reason its liturgical celebrations always exceed in purpose any mere "purpose"—even if this be the rescuing of the poor and the securing of social justice. To subordinate the latter to the former would be to intrumentalize present individuals and to deny the ultimacy of fulfilling play beyond the necessary but still too serious work of making amends and remedying defects. Thus, in contrast to secular expectations and continual sacrifice of the present, the church is the anticipation of the kingdom as paradoxically fully present now in its mere rumouredness.

Within time, human life has its phases, and especially the growth from childhood to maturity. But if nonsense has a certain Christian priority over sense, then the time of babbling, of infancy, has also a certain priority over adulthood. Only since George MacDonald and others has the astounding gospel demand that we become again like children been more fully explored. Childhood is no mere human phase, but the crucial phase, and even coincides with the human span as a whole, since pure wonder is more crucial than critique, grateful reception than ordering command, original simple initiation than development and creativity than theoretical detachment. In conscious agreement with Barth and Moltmann, Gabelman insists that we are first of all children and not autonomous adults in relation to God and that only a non-consideration of the Trinity would regard this view as patriarchal oppression on an ontological scale. For if one takes the doctrines of the Trinity and the incarnation together, then one sees that God is in some way eternally a child, even eternally a baby. God is only the initiating, commanding Father because he is also and to the same extent the receptive, obedient and trusting Son. The key paradox is that it is in this original trust and reception that there is also original outgoing, original creation, establishment, and affirmation. For God the Father has no word to utter before the Word of the Son and yet that word is from the outset pure response and pure loyalty. Impossible to understand! But as Gabelman argues, this gives the most radical meaning to Christian anarchy. In the beginning was *not* the beginning, not the voice or will of cosmic command, but always already the word, the interpretative response, that which comes *after* the beginning, the *an-archic*. Thus, paradoxically in the very (thereby denied) beginning there was the infinite plurality of unlicensed creative response. Before order there was a harmonious disorder; before sense an unrestricted sense-making nonsense.

Throughout this book, Gabelman continuously grasps that ontological paradox has been entirely overlaid by contingent historical, ethical paradox. All we know of the world is its untrue, fallen aspect. Therefore we know it only as false nonsense. But this false nonsense always poses as true, restricted sense, and indeed this is the devilish essence of the world's lapse. So apparent sense must be exposed and mocked as derisory nonsense—as by Alice, the child confronted by multiple fools, unlike (as Gabelman points out) the many actors confronted by one fool in Renaissance plays. But it can only be adequately mocked in the name of the true, infinite nonsense as we pass from a spirit of satire to that of pure hilarity. So a certain nonsense must be exposed and refused; a certain other nonsense must be embraced as therapy and exposure of the arbitrariness of conventions; but finally this other nonsense must be teleologically embraced as at least an intimation of a higher propositional truth, beyond the law of contradiction. As ceaseless *anastrophe* (as in Christ's overturning of the tables in the temple), following Gabelman's suggestion, or re-ordering of sentential, temporal, and ontological sequence: a kind of ceaseless and "randomly" redone *anakaphalaiosis*.

Once again, the most ultimate response of secularity to Lewis Carroll's nonsense has to be serious: has to undo it, has to see it as an indirect therapeutic means to further finite sense. But this is to see no difference between the fool and the lunatic, as Gabelman explains, after Jean-Yves Lacoste. The fool does not fail lunatically to reach, but intentionally breaches the normative bounds of the finitely serious in the name of the uncontainable sense of the infinite. And what is more, following the paradox of linguistic usage itself, nonsense renders this witness, even without intent, in such a way that it cannot fail to be theological, even without the intervention of the theologian.

This book begins with an invocation of Jane Austen at her wittiest, on the matter of balls and boredom, as the reader will shortly find. One might say that Josephine Gabelman has more boldly suggested than anyone hitherto that the Christian life, if it is true to the Christian vision, should be more like a ball than a conversation—however fascinating. As she says, "Christianity has an ontological warrant for thinking and acting in a manner of extravagant frivolity" (189).

John Milbank

Acknowledgements ———

LIKE ANYONE WHO HAS ever had the supreme good fortune to be supervised by Gavin Hopps, I am indebted to him for his wisdom, dedication, erudition, and matchless scholarship. I am grateful to Trevor Hart and Simon Oliver who made the experience of my doctoral examination both stimulating and enjoyable; their perceptive comments have greatly assisted the transition from thesis to book. I am also grateful to have received generous advice from John Milbank. I would like to thank the Master and Fellows of Pembroke College, Cambridge for hosting several study visits, which provided an enchanting space in which to research and write.

After a decade of trips to Tuscany, I am obliged to Charlotte Horton for her provocative conversation and anarchic intellect. I have been greatly supported and encouraged by my wonderful Grandparents, Geoffrey and Mary. To my dearest parents, who expect nothing but to whom I owe everything, thank you for your profound and unending love.

Finally, I thank my wonderful husband Danny, a brilliant scholar, Master of nonsense, and love of my life, who leads me further up and further in to the land from where the shadows fall.

Less Rational, But More Like a Ball ___

Has God not made foolish the wisdom of the world?

1 Corinthians 1:20

At first glance, *A Theology of Nonsense* sounds illogical. Why would one seek to align Christian beliefs with Lewis Carroll's preposterous wonderlands, if not with the intent to falsify faith? Yet, this book seeks both to support Christian theology and to promote a correspondent incredulity, believing that the skeptic's perennial refrain—"you can't seriously believe [this nonsense]"[1]—speaks a profound, but largely unembraced, religious truth. The apologist who overlooks the absurdity of faith in order to advance a strictly rational apologetic misrepresents Christianity. He is like Jane Austen's Caroline Bingley who declares: "I should like balls infinitely better if conversation instead of dancing were made the order of the day." To which her brother consents it would be "Much more rational [but] rather less like a ball."[2]

The comedy here arises from our understanding that dancing is essential to the nature of balls, and whilst Caroline Bingley may indeed desire

---

1. A phrase used by the character Charles Ryder inquiring into his friend's Catholic faith in *Brideshead Revisited*. Charles begins this discussion by saying: "I suppose they try and make you believe an awful lot of nonsense." Waugh, *Brideshead Revisited*, 84.

2. The same parallel is discussed by C. S. Lewis in his essay: "Priestesses in the Church," from *God in the Dock*, 255.

an evening of rational conversation, she cannot simply alter the definition of "ball" to accommodate her disposition. In a similar way, it is poor theology that distorts the nature of religious truth to make it congruent with the desires of a particular audience. The intention of this work is not to impose an alternative framework on Christian theology or to manipulate the statements of Christ to make them seem absurd or nonsensical. Rather, it is an attempt to articulate orthodox faith honestly, and, if it is found that it has more in common with the jovial frenzy of a dance than with rational discourse, then let us not shy away from saying so.

The major problem confronting any apologetic account of Christianity is that certain crucial tenets of the faith seem to carry us the other side of reason. It is of course true that Christianity has always had a sense that its claims will appear foolish from a certain perspective, yet despite this, a dominant strand of its traditional self-exposition has sought to demonstrate its conformity to Western standards of reason. As a result, the importance of "a-rational" modalities of faith has been significantly downplayed. In response to this widespread under-emphasis, this book calls for a corrective balance of reason with unreason, logic with paradox, skepticism with credulity, as well as the recovery of a number of other biblical themes sidelined by the rationalistic tendencies of modernity. In sum, the hypothesis explores the idea that in certain crucial ways Christian teaching runs counter to the customary secular practices of reason. The primary method by which this is articulated is through an ongoing dialogue with nonsense literature, focusing on the work of Lewis Carroll. In this way, I hope to demonstrate that some of the structural devices used in literary nonsense share a deep resemblance with and cast new light on traditional modes of religious thought.

Part One discusses the character and the role of the imagination in Christian belief. Three aspects of this are seen as central: the paradoxical, the anarchic, and the childlike. The first chapter considers a range of apparently incompatible claims within Christian doctrine and suggests, in view of this, that paradox is an essential feature of the Christian imagination. The areas examined include the epistemological paradox of transcendent and immanent knowledge; paradoxical accounts of time and space within Christology; the logical problem of the incarnation; the traditional numerical conundrum of the Trinity; and the relationship between freewill and grace. These puzzles are customarily seen as a result of linguistic limitation (where the claim is accepted) or as a way of deflecting attention away from empty premises (where the claim is rejected). In contrast, I offer a description of these tensions as "theoretic"[3] paradoxes, which convey an accurate

---

3. W. D. Hart distinguishes between linguistic or "semantic" and "theoretic"

description of essential "illogicalities," acknowledging their importance as tenets of Christian faith, whilst recognizing that this represents a departure from the commonly upheld law of non-contradiction. The aim of this section is to show how thinking in paradoxical terms is a vital component of the Christian imagination since it allows the believer to hold these contraries in a meaningful tension.

The second chapter concentrates on the interval of suspense between Christ's defeat and his reign to come. In particular, the focus is on the implications of the teaching that the kingdom of God is situated both in the "now and the not yet," and the correlative belief that Christ is absolutely sovereign even though his sovereignty has in some sense not yet come into its fullness of divine rule. The term I use to describe the experience of living in this epoch of "eschatological suspension," between Christ's victory and the final establishment of his kingdom, is "anarchy." The aim of the section is to show how during this "in-between time" the Christian must develop an anarchic imagination in order to live faithfully in this era of dual temporalities.

The third part of the project seeks to recover the "childlike" as a category of the religious imagination. I discuss the significance of the Gospel declaration that only those who change and become like children can enter the kingdom of heaven and ask whether the term "childlike" is a necessary description or merely an analogy of peripheral significance to Christian faith. In essence, I consider this injunction to "change" to involve an imaginative re-orientation towards a childlike mode of relating to God as Father. There are several qualities that this transformation seems to demand: a simplistic approach to the world and the self, the ability to trust, the capacity to wonder, and an impulse for make-believe and play. On the basis of this I conclude that the childlike is not simply a phase of being before God, but the ongoing ideal of that relationship. The aim of this section is to show how the adoption of a childlike posture fosters a mode of imaginative play that opens up the possibility for a genuine encounter with God. In general, I suggest that this attitude, though born in the imagination, may nevertheless involve real development and transformation. The childlike, together with the anarchic and the paradoxical, I believe, go some way to describing the necessary role the imagination plays in Christian faith and its divergence from the dominant Enlightenment model of rationality.

In Part Two, after considering how each of these aspects of the religious imagination comes into conflict with a secular construal of reality, I

---

paradoxes, suggesting that in the first instance there is an *appearance* of the paradoxical, conceding that the contradiction is ultimately solvable. In the case of "theoretic" paradox the core of the conflict is a logically irreconcilable tension. For an initial outline see Hart, *The Evolution of Logic*, 67.

develop a counter-theology of nonsense, and explore the theoretical, practical, and evangelical implications of associating nonsense literature with
Christian faith. Of particular concern is the response of the non-believer to
the apparent unreason of religious claims. I suggest that "nonsense" has the
potential to be a peculiarly useful descriptor in the communication of the
Christian message, since, in accepting the atheist's application of unreason
the believer necessarily challenges the presumption that because faith is unreasonable it is therefore untrue. Prompted by the work of G. K. Chesterton,
I conceive of the fall as "the condition of being born upside down" and in
this light consider an imaginative reordering of our notions of the possible
as a vital aspect of faith. This provides the underlying warrant for offering
"nonsense" as an illuminating and hitherto unexplored way of conceptual-
izing Christian theology.

INTRODUCTION

A Brief History of
Faith and Reason _____

Every man is stupid and without knowledge.

JEREMIAH 10:14

IN A GENERAL SENSE, this project is concerned with the longstanding opposition between faith and reason—the conflict, reconciliation, or deconstruction of which has been an abiding concern throughout Christian history. Thus, in order to contextualize the investigation it will be helpful to begin with a short overview of the development of this antagonism within the journey of religion. An obvious place to begin is with the wisdom of the Greek philosophers, with *philos sophia*, the love of reason, which seeks to understand the nature of how things are.

Traditionally, the philosopher's elevation of reason presupposes a faith in its ability to discover and reliably describe that which is. A central feature buttressing this faith in reason is the law of non-contradiction—a fundamental precept of classical logic, which is, for the most part, presented as an undisputed arbiter of sound reasoning. The modern philosopher and theologian James Anderson serves as exemplar of this assumption; he affirms: "what is deemed unacceptable is for some person to speak against or deny some proposition *whilst also affirming* that same proposition. Such a practice is invariably viewed as the height of irrationality."[1] Nearly two and

---

1. Anderson, *Paradox in Christian Theology*, 108.

half thousand years earlier Aristotle articulated the same rule: "if whenever an assertion is true its denial is false and when the latter is true its affirmation is false, there can be no such thing as simultaneously asserting and denying the same thing truly."[2] Logician J. C. Beall observes likewise: "that no contradiction is true remains an entrenched 'unassailable dogma' of Western thought."[3]

Although the Greek philosophers did not have the Judeo-Christian concept of a relationship with a personal god, this period is nonetheless indispensable in charting the interaction between faith and reason, as Paul Helm observes: "the classical period provided the tools of reason which are applied to faith and have been ever since."[4] Ultimately, Aristotle along with Plato sought to show how religious sensitivity evolves from rational inquiry. Plato believed it was the *rational* aspect of his tripartite theory of the soul that yearned after truth and that alone could discover the real. Furthermore, Plato claimed, "it [is] appropriate for the rational element to rule, because it is wise and takes thought for the entire soul."[5] So we find in the Hellenic period both a sensitivity to spiritual truths but also the foundations of rationalism with an ultimate emphasis on the primacy of reason. Accordingly, when the teachings of Christ and the apostles arrived in Athens there was much that St. Paul found in common with Greek philosophy, but also a substantial amount that did not accord with the superior wisdom of the Greeks.

The biblical confrontation of issues of faith and reason is of course an area of enormous complexity and my aim here is only briefly to sketch an outline. But even a cursory summary, however, should recognize that the New Testament presents truth both in accordance with classical reason and also as its antithesis. According to the book of Acts, Paul *"reasoned* [. . .] from the Scriptures, *explaining* and *proving* that it was necessary for the Christ to suffer and to rise from the dead."[6] Here the emphasis is on Christianity's reasonability; those who believed "were *persuaded."*

---

2. Aristotle, *Metaphysics*, 1008.a.34, 14.

3. Beall "Introduction in *The Law of Non-Contradiction*," 2–3. It is worth noting that scholars tend to recognize three versions of Aristotle's description of the law of non-contradiction: an ontological variant, a doxastic or psychological form, and a semantic version. For the purpose of our investigation the ontological version—the statement: "it is impossible to predicate contraries simultaneously" (Aristotle, *Metaphysics*, 1007.b.17, 12)—will take precedence, since this tends to be the most common application of the law, and indeed, provides the greatest potential for hostility to statements that seem to oppose the law.

4. Helm, *Faith and Reason*, 3.

5. Plato, *The Republic*, 138.

6 Acts 17:2–3, my emphasis.

On the other hand, Paul gives equal emphasis to the view that Christianity appears as folly to the wisdom of the Greek philosophers. In his letter to the Corinthians, he writes: "Christ did not send me to baptize but to preach the gospel, and not with words of eloquent wisdom, less the cross be emptied of its power."[7] Here, Paul seems to caution against the presentation of religious truths in synthesis with a contemporary understanding of good reason. Instead, Paul associates the gospel message with foolishness, and yet at the same time undercuts this emphasis by preaching that "the foolishness of God is wiser than men."[8] Given these two contrasting attitudes, then, how can we accurately characterize the approach of the New Testament to the dialogue between faith and reason?

The biblical teaching that God alone is wise has often led theologians to downplay or sidestep the reality of this foolishness, perhaps because wisdom seems the more appealing characteristic, especially if the theologian is engaged in apologetics. But the truth that Paul teaches clearly entails a dual dimension: Christianity is both supremely wise *and* supremely foolish. The wisdom that the world does not understand not only seems like folly, but indeed it *is* folly by the world's standards. Festus is thus in a certain sense correct when he tells Paul that he is out of his mind, and yet Paul is also correct in his affirmation that he is not mad but speaking rationally.[9] Therefore, an accurate depiction of the biblical attitude to issues of faith and reason seems to involve a direct challenge to Aristotle's law of non-contradiction in order to uphold the affirmation that faith is both rational and also a scandal to reason.

Broadly speaking, the Christian conjunction of reason and faith seems less complicated in the patristic period that followed, or rather less strikingly paradoxical, as this era by and large can be characterized by Augustine's desire "to understand what we believe,"[10] an idea that forms a central part of his work *De Libero Arbitrio*, written between 387 and 395. Augustine's influential thought established a clear order: faith is primary; reason is always a secondary aid to theological reflection since belief comes before understanding. On the one hand, Augustine defines theology as "reasoning

7. 1 Cor 1:17. "Eloquent wisdom" is the translation of σοφία meaning clever and wise. See also note below.

8. 1 Cor 1:25. Here, Paul draws on the classical concepts of wisdom and folly (*moros* and *sophos*) but inverts their roles by applying a different standard of wisdom that has the outward appearance of *moros*.

9. "Festus said with a loud voice, 'Paul, you are out of your mind; your great learning is driving you out of your mind.' But Paul said, 'I am not out of my mind, most excellent Festus, but I am speaking true and rational words.'" Acts 26:24–25.

10. Augustine, *Free Choice of the Will*, 7.

or discussion about the Divinity,"[11] and describes the Christian God as "a God who gives blessedness to the rational and intelligent soul."[12] We cannot therefore dismiss the importance Augustine places on human reason. And yet, elsewhere, in his work *City of God*, Augustine rebukes "the unbelievers" who "demand a rational proof from us when we proclaim the miracles of God." He observes that "since we cannot supply this proof of those matters (for they are beyond the powers of the human mind) the unbelievers assume that our statements are false."[13] Here Augustine does not deny that certain acts of God seem unlikely or impossible, but impresses upon the reader the reality of the limitations of his own reason, suggesting that we should not expect to be able to understand all aspects of divinity in a rational manner. Indeed, Augustine interprets rationality as a gift from God that is itself beyond human understanding.[14]

By the sixth century, Pseudo-Dionysius had laid a greater stress on the *via negativa* and with this emphasis came the idea that religious revelation can seem contrary to common sense. "The man in union with truth," he writes, "knows clearly that all is well with him, even if everyone else thinks that he has gone out of his mind."[15] Denys' desire to provide a faithful theological account leads him to describe God using paradoxical expressions such as "brilliant darkness."[16] One of the advantages Denys saw in using paradox to speak of God is that it prevents the individual from fixating upon any single attribute or manifestation; God can be praised in the same breath for his meekness and for his majesty. Denys' commitment to paradox is such that he even undercuts his own apophatic method by maintaining that in addition to being "beyond every assertion," God is also "beyond privations [and] beyond every denial."[17] Denys' paradoxical account of God seems to imply therefore that strict obedience to the law of non-contradiction cannot provide a satisfactory description of the divine. The principle that God is beyond all assertions cannot logically be held together with the notion that God is equally beyond all privations; a thing that is fully meek cannot not also be supremely majestic, unless of course it is accepted that paradoxical statements can provide an accurate means of describing reality.

11. Augustine, *City of God*, 298.

12. Ibid., 299.

13. Ibid., 971.

14. "It is in no trivial measure that a man understands and knows God, when he understands and knows that this knowledge and understanding is itself the gift of God." Ibid., 721.

15. Pseudo-Dionysius, *The Divine Names*, 110.

16. Pseudo-Dionysius, *Mystical Theology*, 135.

17. Ibid., 136.

Whilst the medieval theologians never lost sight of Denys' practice of speaking paradoxically in an attempt to signify the divine, the significant landmark in the dialogue between faith and reason in the Middle Ages was, of course, the rediscovery of Aristotle, and by the latter half of the thirteenth century the re-integration of Greek logic into Christian dialogue was firmly established. The masterful assimilation of Aristotelian reason into Christian theology by Aquinas (1225–74) has come to be seen by many as the beginning of a deeply rationalized Christianity and the prioritization of reason over mystery.[18] Whilst there is without doubt an element of truth in this, it is easy to misunderstand Aquinas' view of reason on account of its distorted reflection in Enlightenment theism. As Rowan Williams points out, for Aquinas "*intellectus* [. . .] is a rich and comprehensive term which is totally misrepresented if understood as referring to the discursive intellect."[19] Thomas' extensive application of reason always finds its genesis in his prayerful contemplation of the transcendent deity. And, whilst he defends the use of rational argument in theology on the grounds that reason is a gift from God, he is clear to affirm that "philosophy should be subject to the measure of faith."[20] Moreover, in the event of an antagonism found between faith and reason, Aquinas believes it is always the result of faulty reasoning, rather than the exposition of some falsehood in Scripture.[21]

It could be suggested that what Aquinas' work most significantly reveals is that the great quarrel between reason and faith had not yet arrived.[22] In fact, Aquinas goes so far as to say, "it is impossible that those things which God has manifested to us by faith should be contrary to those which are evident to us by natural knowledge."[23] Chesterton describes Aquinas as

18. Whilst it is extremely apparent that Aquinas in no way primaced reason over faith, he could be said to have exalted the role of reason in matters of theology by maintaining firmly "both kinds of truth are from God." Aquinas, *Super Boethium de Trinitate*, q. 2, a. 3.

19. Williams, *The Wound of Knowledge*, 125.

20. Aquinas, *Super Boethium de Trinitate*, q. 2, a. 3.

21. "If, however, anything is found in the teachings of the philosophers contrary to faith, this error does not properly belong to philosophy, but is due to an abuse of philosophy owing to the insufficiency of reason." Ibid.

22. John Milbank recognizes a similar falsity in distinguishing a strong antagonism in Aquinas' understanding of faith and reason, writing: "this dualistic reading of Aquinas is false." Milbank argues that the Thomistic tension between *divina scientia* and *sacra doctrina* ought to be reconsidered as "a single gnoseological extension" and interpreted together as a sacred unity in pursuit of divine knowledge. *Truth in Aquinas*, 19.

23. Aquinas, *Super Boethium de Trinitate*, q. 2, a. 3. The impossibility of disagreement stems from Aquinas' belief that both faith and reason are gifts from God, and that it is not congruous with God's perfect nature to be an "author of error."

"belong[ing] to an age of intellectual unconsciousness, to an age of intellectual innocence,"[24] and perhaps this, more than anything, characterizes the medieval response to issues of faith and reason. Certainly, there was a strong urge to systematise Christian theology and demonstrate its inherent coherence, but without the modern distinction between the theologian and the philosopher, the objectives of philosophy were met and satisfied in Christian metaphysics.[25] Paul Helm describes the reintroduction of Aristotle into theological thought as "a synthesis and not a take-over,"[26] and one of the principal reasons that Helm's hypothesis seems true and that Hellenic discourse did not usurp medieval piety is that scholasticism always remained skeptical about the role of reason, using it as a means of *interacting* with an already established faith, not by way of primary justification for that belief.

Throughout the work of Anselm, the father of the scholastic tradition, we can further trace the medieval sense of harmony between rational argumentation and meditative devotion. In his *Proslogion* (1077–78) Anselm writes: "I give thanks to You, since what I believed before through your free gift I now so understand through Your illumination."[27] In this sentence, we again witness the acknowledgment that both belief and illumination—faith and reason—are gifted from God to the individual. This supports the case that many medieval philosophers did not see faith and reason in antagonism with each other, but believed like Augustine that both were gifts from God. In Anselm's work we observe not just the medieval *sanction* that faith may be investigated with reason, but rather what one might call the medieval *obligation* that seeking rational justification for belief is the duty of a believer. John Wippel concurs with this conclusion, writing: "For Anselm the dialectician to find necessary reasons for that which one already believes is part of the task of an enlightened faith."[28]

Yet, alongside the development of a "rationalized" scholasticism, the medieval period is also known for its embrace of mystical theology,[29] many aspects of which defy rational exposition. The law of non-contradiction, for example, is famously and explicitly overturned in the writing of the

24. Chesterton, *St Thomas Aquinas*, 234.

25. John Wippel agrees with this characterization of Aquinas. He believes "throughout his career Aquinas would remain true to his conviction that there should ultimately be harmony between faith and reason and hence, when they both are correctly practiced, between theology and philosophy." Wippel, *Mediaeval Reactions*, 32.

26. Helm, *Faith and Reason*, 85–86.

27. Anselm, *Proslogion* , 89.

28. Wippel, *Mediaeval Reactions*, 7.

29. Some of the great mystics date from this period, such as Meister Eckhart (*c.* 1260–1327) and Lady Julian of Norwich (*c.* 1342–after 1416).

Christian mystic Nicholas of Cusa (1401–64), in particular in his development of the "coincidence of opposites." In the introduction to Cusa's works Bond reminds us that "by its very nature mystical theology assumes the task of outstripping reason and intellect. It presumes to see what reason excludes as impossible."[30] Bond reflects accurately Cusa's own admission that in order to experience God it is "necessary" to "admit the coincidence of opposites, above all capacity of reason, and to seek the truth where impossibility confronts me."[31] Cusa's teaching of the "coincidence of opposites" is a patent overhaul of the rule of non-contradiction since he strives to comprehend divine paradoxes such as the Trinity and the incarnation "without violating the integrity of the contrary elements and without diminishing the reality or the force of their contradiction."[32] Cusa's mystical writing, full of language embracing impossibility, venturing beyond thinking and transcending rational discourse, is radically divergent from the scholastic theology we claimed previously characterized medieval Christianity. There is another important medieval institution that likewise unsettles our picture of the sedate synthesis of faith and reason: the tradition of holy folly.

John Saward remarks on the unlikely juxtaposition of folly with the schoolmen and asks "why was it that the golden age of the fool coincided with the age of scholasticism?"[33] Saward answers his question by suggesting that "in the late Middle Ages there is an unselfconscious revelling in mirth, joy, and good humour of life in Christ."[34] Saward thus gestures to an important feature of this "intellectually innocent" age, which is the idea that scholastic endeavor could co-exist happily with mystic ecstasy and foolish revelry because there was an implicit understanding of the interwovenness between reason, folly, and mystery.

However, Mark A. McIntosh in his book *Mystical Theology* tells a different story altogether. He describes how "during this period of the rise of scholastic theology there were also shifting trends in Christian spirituality that made it harder for the two realms of life to communicate, let alone nourish each other."[35] For example, he believes that there is an awareness throughout Lady Julian's writing that her mode of theological engagement as a mystic was unlikely to be respected. McIntosh believes that this is because "the ecclesiastical and academic culture of her era was already less

30. Bond, *Nicholas of Cusa*, 33.
31. Cusa, *De Visione Dei*, 9.36.
32. Bond, *Nicholas of Cusa*, 22.
33. Saward, *Perfect Fools*, 81.
34. Ibid., 80.
35. McIntosh, *Mystical Theology*, 63.

than open to the insights of someone situated far from the impressively authoritative halls of the university."[36] Here we are faced with the suggestion that far from an era of "intellectual innocence," the later Middle Ages were in fact an epoch dominated by an intellectualized Christianity, which rather than embracing the words of fools and mystics, inhibited this avenue of spiritual discourse. "The real tragedy," McIntosh writes, "is that by the later Middle Ages fewer and fewer saints, mystics and theologians still knew how to knit spirituality and theology together in their own life and work."[37]

It is hard to decide, given the complexity of the issue, whether McIntosh or Saward offers the more realistic portrayal of the character of medieval theology. In a sense there is no fundamental disagreement since Saward is referring to the High Middle Ages up to around 1300, whilst McIntosh is mainly addressing the attitude during the Late Middle Ages. They are, then, in a narrower sense, both right and there was something of a later medieval shift to demarcate spirituality from scholarship. Certainly during the following period—the Renaissance and Reformation—any remnants of the medieval synthesis of faith and reason were largely abolished by the establishment of a divide between God's revelation and man's rationality. Some element of this divide we can assume stemmed from the scholastic flourishing of the medieval church and the extensive influence of Aristotelian logic.

As we move into the first half of the sixteenth century, a dominant figure in the discussion between faith and reason is, of course, Martin Luther (1483–1546). Luther argued that reason outside of grace is bound by sin and that reason therefore can never form the sole basis from which religious truth is articulated.[38] Within the history of faith and reason, Luther presents a strong case against the elevation of reason, arguing instead for the primacy of faith. He cautions the Christian in strong terms: "away with reason, which is an enemy to faith."[39] Luther's more extreme denunciations of reason as "impious and sacrilegious"[40] or most famously as "the Devil's bride"[41] are frequently quoted, though the impression they encourage leaves out the

---

36. Ibid., 13.

37. Ibid., 63.

38. Alister McGrath describes how "Luther's fundamental point is that 'the Fall' is first and foremost a fall from faith." McGrath, *Christian Theology*, 155. The implication of this belief for Luther is the understanding that atonement requires, above all, faith and that to seek God's justification through any other means (such as rationalized argumentation or the practice of indulgences) is wrong. As a result, Ephesians 2:8–10 became a central verse for Luther's teaching.

39. Luther, *Commentary on Saint Paul's Epistle*, 94.

40. Luther, *Bondage of the Will*, 106.

41. Luther, "Second Sunday in Epiphany," 126.

nuances of Luther's dialogue with reason; for it is not that he is hostile to reason in all its manifestations. Indeed, in his response before the Diet of Worms in 1521 he states: "Unless I am convinced by the testimony of the Scriptures *or by clear reason* [. . .] I cannot and will not retract anything."[42] Here it is evident that Luther trusts the conviction of his own reasoning, which might suggest that when he speaks antagonistically it is because he believes reason is in a particular instance being used in a manner other than that which God intended.

Generally speaking, however, Luther did see reason as an inadequate and impoverished method of comprehending divine matters. "Reason," he writes, "interprets the Scriptures of God by her own inferences and syllogisms [. . .] how foolish she is in tacking her inferences onto the Scriptures."[43] The gospel, by contrast, Luther explains, "leadeth us beyond and above the light of the law and reason, into the deep secrets of faith, where the law and reason have nothing to do."[44] Faith and salvation for the reformers were seen as gifts that cannot be attained through human reason, and it was during the popularization of their views that the concept of faith underwent a distinct shift from *fides* to *fiducia*, from faith *that* to faith *in*.[45]

By the beginning of the seventeenth century the extreme volatility of the Reformation period had largely abated. Yet growing incompatibility between scientific and religious claims brought about a different set of circumstances whereby faith and reason again came into conflict. The Galileo controversy concerning the geocentric model of the solar system engendered a greater schism, whereby church leaders saw certain advances in science as heretical, and scientists such as Galileo found religious authorities intolerant and ignorant. John Lewis believes that the most prominent effect of the Galileo affair, in particular his trial and imprisonment, was that it "helped in no small measure to create that perceived separation of faith from reason, of religion from physical sciences."[46] Certainly, it was during the seventeenth century that the establishment of the modern polarity between science and religion took root. Science started to be perceived as the authoritative voice in matters of the phenomenal world, and as a result, religion began to be confined to the territory *beyond* the physical. However, as one historian observes, "the great scientists of the seventeenth century, including Kelper,

---

42. Quoted in Donald K. McKim (ed.), *The Cambridge Companion to Martin Luther*, 182, my emphasis.

43. Luther, *The Bondage of Will*, cited in Helm, *Faith and Reason*, 140.

44. Ibid.

45. For a further discussion on the different interpretations of faith in the Reformation period see McGrath, *Reformation Thought*, 115–37.

46. Lewis, *Galileo in France*, 15.

Galileo, and Newton, had pursued their work in a spirit of exalting God not undermining Christianity,"[47] and so it is not totally accurate to characterize the seventeenth century as the establishment of the radical schism between religious faith and scientific reason. Nevertheless, the scientific revolution of the seventeenth century inevitably gave weight to the religious skepticism that arrived with the Enlightenment in the century that followed.

Within the history of faith and reason, the Enlightenment is the high water-mark of rationality; although it is important to note, as McGrath does, that "the Middle Ages was just as much an 'Age of Reason' as the Enlightenment; the crucial difference lay in the manner in which reason was used, and the limits which were understood to be imposed on it."[48] Enlightenment thinkers such as Kant (1724–1804) wanted to see theology develop within the limits of reason alone and, arguably, as a result, lost sight of the careful qualifications maintained by the pre-moderns. Kant declared instead: "The *public* use of reason must at all times be free, and it alone can bring about Enlightenment among men."[49]

The Enlightenment recast rationality in its own image, the guiding sentiment of which Isaiah Berlin describes as the conviction that "all principles of explanation everywhere must be the same."[50] This of course extended from practices of law, politics and science to philosophy and religion. Hence, religion for many believers became an "Enlightenment theism," which according to McGrath had two major consequences: "First, Christianity was in effect *reduced* to those ideas which could be proved by reason [. . .] and second, reason was understood to take priority over revelation."[51] Gavin Hyman, who argues that atheism is "roughly contemporaneous with the birth of modernity,"[52] also describes how one of the major differences between medieval and modern theism was modernity's dissatisfaction with abstract theology and the desire for a more normative and rationalized religion. Hyman believes "Hume and Kant demonstrated how their frameworks disallowed, in principle, any substantive metaphysical knowledge of God."[53]

The chief sentiments of the Enlightenment thus expanded into the modern period; scientific advancement in biology and geology continued to broaden the gulf between reason and faith; evidentialism and verificationism

47. Spielvogel, *Western Civilisation*, 514–15.

48. McGrath, *Christian Theology*, 87.

49. Kant, "What Is Enlightenment?" 59.

50. Berlin, *Three Critics of the Enlightenment*, 279.

51. McGrath, *Christian Theology*, 214.

52. Hyman, *A Short History of Atheism*, 2.

53. Ibid., 45.

gained popularity as the accurate means of testing the validity of a statement; empirical proof was the stipulation of many rationalists and religious
truths simply could not satisfy these new demands. For this reason, Hume's
essay disparaging the miraculous basis of Christian belief in 1748 was taken
seriously, as was Locke's earlier request for faith to show itself in accord
with reason. "Faith," Locke taught, "can never convince us of anything that
contradicts our knowledge."[54]

Whilst some believers greatly supported the Enlightenment task
of bringing religion in line with modern rationalization, others reacted
strongly against this. Johann Georg Hamann (1730–88), for example, one of
the fathers of German Romanticism, wrote passionately against the attempt
to redefine faith in accordance with this strict application of rationality.[55]
In his essay, "Metacritique on the Purism of Reason," Hamann argued that
"analysis is nothing more than the latest fashionable cut, and synthesis nothing more than the artful seam of a professional leather or cloth-cutter."[56]
At the time, Hamann's rebuttal did not pose a significant hindrance to the
rationalists. Berlin believes that this was because Hamann was one of few
vocal dissenters against the swift imperialization of reason.[57] In the year of
Hamann's death, however, an influential ally in the revolt against the supreme rationalization of thought was born.

Arthur Schopenhauer (1788–1860) was among the first of the nineteenth-century philosophers to dissent from the belief that the universe is
ultimately rational. Instead, he developed a proto-Nietzschean rejection
of the ultimacy of reason and introduced a pre-Freudian emphasis on desire and drive as what constitutes the knowing of the self. Schopenhauer
was critical of Kant and Hegel[58] for their belief that reason is the founding

54. Locke, *An Essay Concerning Human Understanding*, 529.

55. Matthew Bagger highlights Hamman's refusal to accept the principle of non-
contradiction as an abiding maxim: "responding to Enlightenment criticism of orthodox Christianity, the influential Prussian thinker Johann Hamann gives paradox a very
different valuation [. . .] he adopted the medieval mystical notion of the coincidence
of opposites, gave it his own interpretation and claimed to prefer it to the principle of
non-contradiction." Bagger, *The Uses of Paradox*, x.

56. Hamann, *Writings on Philosophy and Language*, 217.

57. Berlin, *Three Critics*, 279. "He [Hamann] attacked the entire outlook in every
particular; and feeling himself a David chosen by the Lord to smite this vast and hor-
rible Goliath, he marched into battle alone."

58 Although Hegel argued for a supremely rationalized noumena, in order for this
rationality to be effective in society he believed that the individual must abstract from
the realm of phenomenal experience since within everyday reality he claimed there is a
"law of contradiction" operative. So, although Hegel gives fuel to the Age of Reason, he
nevertheless raises a specific objection to the law of non-contradiction by stating that
the phenomenal is in a state of becoming and constant flux.

principle of a just society, and their reliance upon logic as the way of reaching this truth. Like Hamann before him, Schopenhauer sought to dethrone reason from its imperial reign: "He argues that rationality confers on us no higher moral status than that of other sentient beings."[59]

Schopenhauer is an interesting figure to consider from a theological perspective, since on the one hand it would seem in the interests of religion to qualify the claims for an entirely rational justification for belief. Yet on the other hand, his work argued for the possibility of achieving moral excellence without religion and so he is in this sense an unlikely ally for the church. His book *On the Basis of Morality* is concerned primarily with critiquing the Kantian dependence upon God as the only possible postulate for moral behavior. Instead, Schopenhauer argues, gallantry, selflessness, and compassion are "universal and occur irrespective of religion."[60] The separation of the religious from the moral led Schopenhauer to associate religion with the irrational and with superstition. This interest in the sociological and psychological explanation of religious belief was continued after his death, culminating at the turn of the century in Freud's declaration that religious belief compensates the need for a father-figure.

Freud (1856–1939) expressed the view that while religion had once been beneficial to the civilization of humanity, the rational development of the human race meant that there was no longer a social need to believe in religion, and that those who tried to maintain its importance did so for psychological reasons and acted neurotically. Freud sided with the empirical atheism of his age when he spoke of the inevitable demise of religious belief driven by a heightened rationality. "In the long run," he wrote, "nothing can withstand reason and experience, and the contradiction which religion offers to both is all too palpable. Even purified religious ideas can not escape this fate, so long as they try to preserve anything of the consolation of religion."[61] Freud's ideas contributed to the spread of secular modernity by attempting to reduce religious belief to a psychological phenomenon, and by continuing the subjection of religious ideas to criticism set within the limits established by the Enlightenment.

Of course, not all nineteenth-century thinkers accepted the need to acquiesce to the demands posited by the empiricists. Kierkegaard's existentialism, for example, recalled the pre-modern delimitations: "human

---

59. Janaway, ed. *The Cambridge Companion to Schopenhauer*, 6.

60. Schopenhauer, *On the Basis of* Morality, 201.

61. Sigmund Freud quoted in O'Neil and Alchtar (eds.), *On Freud's "The Future of an Illusion,"* 60.

reason," he cautioned, "has boundaries."[62] In the face of the preoccupation with rationality Kierkegaard (1813–55) described belief as a leap and faith as a risk, claiming "the absurd and faith are inseparable."[63] Kierkegaard's conjunction of absurdity and Christian faith shares obvious parallels with the pairing of literary nonsense and theology, which we will be discussing in greater detail in the final chapter. For the present, however, it is worth noting that Kierkegaard is a central figure in the dispute against the universal validity of the law of non-contradiction for the chief reason that he held paradox as a logically baffling but integral part of Christian faith. Yet, perhaps the most important nineteenth-century figure who railed against the narrow scope of Enlightenment rationality was Nietzsche (1844–1900), whose general thrust was oddly parallel to Kierkegaard, although it stemmed from entirely different criteria.

Nietzsche, heavily influenced by Schopenhauer, proposed a significant and direct challenge to classical logic and in particular to the law of non-contradiction. In *The Will to Power* he describes the law as "*coarse and false.*"[64] He describes it as "a subjective empirical law, not the expression of any 'necessity' but only of an inability."[65] As Michael Green points out, "Nietzsche does not argue that the principle of non-contradiction should be abandoned. He does, however, argue that an acceptance of the principle is not demanded by the nature of the world."[66] Nietzsche provides a profound objection to the ontological validity of the rule of non-contradiction, urging us to recognize that the avoidance of the unity of contraries is a psychological desire and not a universal imperative. At a fundamental level Nietzschean thought is an attack upon the stability and scope of philosophical reasoning; even the basic components of logical formulae such as subject, object and attribute are not accepted as a "metaphysical truth."[67] Instead, he argues, "these distinctions have been *made*."[68]

Nietzsche's description of the artificiality of logic is a close echo of Hamann's criticism of rational analysis as "nothing more than the latest fashionable cut," and it is in this capacity—as an enemy to the staunch rationalists—that some recent theologians instead of being offended by Nietzschean atheism, have discovered that his work may be used to support their case.

---

62. Kierkegaard, *Journals and Papers*, 5.

63. Ibid., 7.

64. Nietzsche, *The Will to Power*, 32.

65. Ibid., 30.

66. Green, *Nietzsche and the Transcendental Tradition*, 56.

67. Nietzsche, *The Will to Power*, 28.

68. Ibid., 54.

Gavin Hyman describes Nietzsche as "the last thinker of modernity or the first thinker of postmodernity,"[69] and it is particularly amongst postmodern theologians that Nietzschean thought has been embraced rather than rejected. Among others David Tracy, Graham Ward, and David Deane have argued that when Nietzsche announced the death of God, he killed the god *of modernity*, the deity who "could not fit what counted as rational."[70] By suggesting that human logic is not the ultimate arbiter of truth, postmodern theologians argue that he did not succeed in killing the biblical, pre-modern, or medieval deity; rather, the god that died was an idolatrous god.[71] Thus, even though it would have to await the outworking of modernity, Nietzsche's work, in spite of its author's intentions, helped to open the way for something of a recovery of the Thomist and Augustinian ordering of faith and reason, where reason does not exercise superiority over faith. The breakdown of the sovereignty of reason had begun and the circumstances in the latter half of the nineteenth century were ripe for a less rationalistic apologetic.

It was in this context that figures such as G. K. Chesterton (1874–1936) were prompted to declare with boldness that in certain crucial ways Christian truth departs from what is commonly constituted as rational. "While we are being naturalists" he writes, "we can suppose that Christianity is all nonsense; but then, when we remember that we are Christians, we must admit that Christianity is true even if it is nonsense."[72] Chesterton's conviction has the potential to disarm the religious cynic who believes that once the illogicalities of faith are pointed out religion loses its credibility. What Chesterton reveals is that the authority of faith does not rest on human conceptions of rationality. This suggestion calls into question the ability of logical descriptions to convey the full reality of the Christian message.

Chesterton is famed for his frequent appeal to paradox. As a result, much of his writing offends those rationalists who hold the law of non-contradiction as unbreakable. Chesterton's use of the paradoxical is so pervasive that critics have suggested he uses paradox simply to shock his reader, to create humor, or to shroud Christianity's logical flaws in the more romantic trappings of mystery. However, Chesterton declares at the beginning of *Orthodoxy*: "I know nothing more contemptible as a mere paradox; a mere ingenious defence of the indefensible."[73] When he uses paradox he does so because he believes that there are instances in Christian doctrine

69. Hyman, *History of Atheism*, 176.
70. Tracy, "Fragments," 171.
71. See Ward's Introduction to *The Postmodern God*.
72. Chesterton, *St Thomas Aquinas*, 106.
73. Chesterton, *Orthodoxy*, 15.

that cannot accurately be expressed without deviating from the law of non-contradiction. It is not that Chesterton rejected common-sense logic for the sake of it; indeed, he believed that reason is central to theology and tells us an enormous amount about the way the world is. But he emphasized that reason does not tell us *everything*, and sometimes that which seems quite unreasonable might in fact be a closer representation of the truth.

The wider context in which Chesterton was speaking was a particularly tumultuous time in the history of faith and reason. His sparring partners H. G. Wells and George Bernard Shaw were in many ways representative of mainstream Victorian views, since, following the industrial revolution and the popularization of German philosophy there had been an explosion of skepticism. And yet, this growth of secularism was juxtaposed with a fervent religious revival across the denominations. Along with Chesterton, one of the central figures preaching the validity of Christianity's seeming "mass of mad contradictions"[74] was John Henry Newman (1801–90). His defense in *Grammar of Assent* (completed in 1870) argued that logic did not meet the challenges of real life. "As to Logic," he wrote, "its chain of conclusions hangs loose at both ends [. . .] it comes short both of first principles and of concrete issues."[75] The significance of Newman's work is that he not only suggested, like Kierkegaard, that faith should not be assessed within the boundaries of logic, but he also attempted to show the shortcomings of secular rationality and how religion, assessed internally, is in fact natural and plausible. This was in part an argument against the law of non-contradiction, since Newman, like Chesterton, exposed paradoxical realities and observed how reason was inadequate to account for such phenomena. "It is plain," Newman argued, "that formal logical sequence is not in fact the method by which we are enabled to become certain of what is concrete."[76] In sum, the Victorian period exhibited a splintering of religious ideas due to the rise and respectability of agnosticism and skepticism, yet it also coincided with a powerful orthodox religious revival. It was in this complex and contested period that Lewis Carroll (1832–98) lived and wrote.

In the twentieth century, the writings of Darwin and Freud remained central to the attack on faith by reason; secularism became widespread and scientific advancement, no longer hindered by theological authority, gained increased prestige and importance. Science and religion grew further apart and yet, perhaps due to the antagonism of the proceeding century, a mood of tolerance arose in certain circles and with it a strong desire for a more

74. Ibid., 162.

75. Newman, *Grammar of Assent*, 272.

76. Ibid., 276.

pluralist approach to knowledge. Wittgenstein's concept of language games satisfied the concern for a more relativistic assessment of meaning, although this was met simultaneously with opposition by strong evidentialitsts such as Flew and Clifford, who wanted to assess all claims of faith from the presumption of atheistic values. Ronald Nash explains how according to Clifford "[i]t is always the believer's responsibility to produce reasons or evidence to support his belief."[77] The effect of this extreme emphasis on verification via empiricism meant that for Clifford, Flew, Ayer, and their followers: "there is never sufficient evidence or proof to support religious belief."[78]

However, the non-religious world was by no means governed by staunch evidentialism. In fact, alongside the increasing popularization of logical positivism among philosophers, scientists began to undercut the infallibility of the evidentialist's claim. As certain aspects of theoretical physics became more advanced, greater skepticism accompanied its observations. Heisenberg's uncertainty principle in 1927, along with growing evidence in support of "chaos theory," began to throw some doubt on the universal reliability of reason.[79] The twentieth century is therefore very difficult to summarize in terms of a general reaction to issues of faith and reason since alongside evidentialism and verificationism, this period also witnessed the arrival of such things as pluralism, quantum theory, Dadaism, and deconstructionism.

The end of the Second World War instigated the meltdown of a whole variety of conventional beliefs and standards. The basic principle of absolutism was railed against in a host of contexts from politics, religion, and society to art, morality, and science. During the 1960s one of the most significant figures contributing to the deconstruction of absolutist ideas was Michel Foucault who challenged historical conceptions of madness and sought to depict unreason in a more positive light. In *Madness and Civilisation* Foucault addresses the historical "fear of madness" and the "dread of unreason."[80] He traces the history of society's response to cases of madness and insanity, and comes to the conclusion that madness is associated with art and can be understood as a tool or expression by which "the world is forced to question itself."[81] I shall return to this issue in the chapter on the

77. Nash, *Faith and Reason*, 72.

78. Ibid., 71.

79. In 1947 C. S. Lewis in his book *Miracles* makes a similar observation: "Science itself has already made reality appear less homogenous than we expected it to be: Newtonian atomism was much more the sort of thing we expected (and desired) than Quantum physics." Lewis, *Miracles*, 41.

80. Foucault, *Madness and Civilisation*, 211.

81. Ibid., 288. "Through madness, a work that seems to drown in the world, to

anarchic, in which I consider a similar function of nonsense, which, like the madness described by Foucault, has a marginal presence and through it, I suggest we are able to reflect critically upon the phenomenal world. Like Foucault, I examine the history of folly and observe a close connection between lunacy and wisdom. However, the aspect of Foucault's work that is most valuable for our present discussion is his recognition of "the great theme of the madness of the Cross."[82]

In *Madness and Civilisation*, perhaps unintentionally, Foucault provides a brief but brilliant Christology of madness. He coins the phrase "Christian unreason"[83] and describes how Nietzsche and Dostoevsky pave the way for its rediscovery following its exile by the militant seventeenth-century pursuit of reason. He characterizes this period as the wait "for Christ to regain the glory of his madness, for scandal to recover its power as revelation, for unreason to cease being merely the public shame of reason."[84] Foucault's interest in the value of madness and unreason is indicative of the return to a less empirical-based philosophy that blossomed in the second half of the twentieth century. Although Foucault's focus is primarily socio-historical, his work was nevertheless significant in the decline of the popularity of logical positivism and the rise of its philosophical nemesis: deconstructionism.

By any account, the work of Jacques Derrida (1930–2004) had, and continues to have, a major impact on the fundamental assumptions of Western philosophy. His influence is pervasive and extremely controversial, and although it is possible here to give only a very brief and limited overview of a particular aspect of his work, his importance to current debates on metaphysics can hardly be over-emphasized. Thinkers such as Lyotard, Deleuze, Nancy, and Marion are all deeply indebted to Derrida's work, as are whole movements such as postmodernism and post-structuralism.[85]

---

reveal there its nonsense, and to transfigure itself with the features of pathology alone, actually engages itself with the world's time, masters it, and leads it; by the madness which interrupts it, a work of art opens a void, a moment of silence, a question without answer provokes a breach without reconciliation where the world is forced to question itself."

82. Ibid., 78.

83. Ibid., 79. "Christian unreason was relegated by Christians themselves into the margins of a reason that had become identical with the wisdom of God incarnate."

84. Ibid.

85. The historian Donald Yerxa explains: "The theoretical origins of postmodernism are primarily located in the post-structuralist philosophy that emerged in France during the latter 1960s and blossomed in the 1970s." Yerxa lists Foucault and Lacan alongside Derrida as the chief thinkers associated with the movement's genesis. Yerxa, *Recent Themes in Historical Conversation*, 69.

Like Nietzsche before him, Derrida launched an attack on the general application of and strict adherence to the law of non-contradiction. However,
before we consider this attack in more detail, it will be helpful to situate this
aspect of his thought within the context of his work more generally, which
is antagonistic of the wider metaphysical assumptions embedded in the history of Western thought.

It is of course a difficult task to propose a starting point of Derrida's
philosophy, given its contestation of origins, but there are several critical
components to his theory of deconstruction with which it might be useful
to begin. At base, deconstruction criticizes the Platonic idea, perpetuated
by Western metaphysics, that the essence of a thing is more significant than
its appearance, since essence is transcendental and therefore its meaning is
fixed and definite. In this sense, both metaphysics and language are *logocen-
tric* and give primacy to the signified over the signifier. What Derrida refers
to as "the absence of the transcendental signified,"[86] however, calls into
question this monolithic conception of essence and attempts to destabilise
binary oppositions within both metaphysics and language by focussing on
the marginal *aporias* of meaning.

Throughout his work, and particularly in "Plato's Pharmacy" and
"Dissemination,"[87] Derrida demonstrates how binary oppositions are both
arbitrary and unstable and have no fixed transcendental origin.[88] Instability
occurs because "meaning is nowhere punctually *present* in language [. . . ,]
it is always subject to a kind of semantic slippage."[89] In other words, Derrida
insists that there is never a perfect unity of signifier and signified. Therefore,
metaphysical assumptions, which rely upon the stability of meaning, undercut themselves and meaning is set free from the security of transcendental
attachment. It is important to note in this connection that the sign in a sense
is *self*-deconstructing; Derrida does not approach a text with a set of external maxims that seek to undo the fixed meaning. Rather, Derrida draws
attention to an inherent and already existing instability within the system
and thereby reveals the radical interdeterminacy of its signs.

We are now perhaps in a better position to suggest more specifically
how Derrida contributes to the argument against the infallibility of the law of
non-contradiction. In order to contain the discussion, I am going to focus on
two aspects of his work that specifically require acceptance of a "both/and"

---

86. Derrida, *Of Grammatology*, 50.

87. Both essays can be found in Derrida, *Dissemination*.

88. He begins *Of Grammatology* by announcing "the de-sedimentation, the deconstruction, of all significations that have their source in that of the logos," 11.

89. Norris, *Derrida*, 15.

logic: the trace and *différance*.[90] When Derrida refers to the "trace," he is indicating "an absence that defines a presence."[91] Derrida believes every present event contains traces or spectres from the past and anticipations of the future. "It is not absence instead of presence," writes Derrida, "but a trace which replaces a presence which has never been present, an origin by means of which nothing has begun."[92] In other words, every experience is both its own unique event and at the same time present in repeatable future moments and marked by past occurrences. These non-present elements are, according to Derrida, in some real sense present, though marked by an absence—an absence, which because it is nonetheless present troubles the law of non-contradiction. Aristotelian logic, by contrast, would maintain that something within an event is either present *or* absent—hence, there cannot be both presence *and* non-presence, as is the case with Derrida's concept of the trace.

Différance also confuses the law of non-contradiction, for Derrida insists on the reality of difference within identity—that is to say, that within the identity of the thing is also contained its difference. In *Aporias* he writes, "The identity of a language can only affirm itself as identity to itself by opening itself to the hospitality of a difference from itself or of a difference with itself."[93] Here, we see how Derrida opposes the Aristotelian insistence on a univocity of meaning by playing with identity and suggesting that there are differences within the same essence. It is important to appreciate that in speaking of *différance* Derrida is not simply opposing univocity with polysemia but suggesting that the singular only exists as a playful movement between multiple identities and that identity even within itself is polysemous.

At this stage, we can begin to see how Derrida's ideas relate to the nonsense literature of Lewis Carroll. The following example from *Alice Through the Looking-Glass* is a helpful clarification of the contrasting logic of *différance*. The White Knight tells Alice the name of a song, but Carroll, in a proto-Derridean fashion, facetiously suggests that a single signifier cannot fix the identity of a song:

'The name of the song is called "*Haddock's Eyes*."'

---

90. There are of course a variety of other importance instances where Derrida seeks to expose the fallibility of the law of non-contradiction. One such example concerns his commentary on Rousseau in *Of Grammatology*, in which he elaborates on Rousseau's unification of the contradictory aspects of the process of articulation. He concludes that "it does not suffice to understand Rousseau's text within the implication of the epochs of metaphysics or of the West." Ibid., 246.

91. Mullarkey, *Post-Continental Philosophy*, 228.

92. Derrida, *Writing and Difference*, 372.

93. Derrida, *Aporias*, 10.

'Oh, that's the name of the song, is it?' Alice said, trying to feel interested.

'No, you don't understand,' the Knight said, looking a little vexed. 'That's what the name *is called*. The name really *is* "*The Aged Aged Man.*"

'Then I ought to have said 'That's what the *song* is called?' Alice corrected herself.

'No you oughtn't: that's quite another thing! The *song* is called "*Ways and Means*": but that's only what it's *called*, you know!'

'Well, what *is* the song, then? said Alice who was by this time completely bewildered.

'I was coming to that,' the Knight said. 'The song really *is* "*A-sitting On A Gate.*"'[94]

The extract seems comically to differentiate between what the song "is"; what it is "known as"; what it is "called"; and what its "name" is called. These proliferating signifiers "*Haddock's Eyes,*" "*The Aged Aged Man,*" and so forth are ludicrously divergent, and yet all relate to the identity of the song, and so the meaning of the song as a whole appears to be located playfully in the inter-relationship between the perpetually shifting signifiers. As with Derrida's theory of *différance*, each of these names gestures to a single identity, which thus appears to contain within itself a multiplicity of differences, which in turn suggests that no signifier contains the identity uniquely, "*A-Sitting On A Gate,*" for example, does not encapsulate the essence of the song; it is simply another signifier. In this way, Carroll, like Derrida, demonstrates that there is no single fixed identity, and although Alice keeps attempting to grasp the meaning, the White Knight, playing a Derridean role, presents a playful proliferation of signifiers, which points towards a perpetually receding signified.

Our commentary on Derrida thus far has suggested that he may be an ally to this project to the extent that his ideas contest the universality of the law of non-contradiction. However, it is also clear that Derrida's relationship to the theological imagination is somewhat hostile. He insisted, for instance, "the age of the sign is essentially theological,"[95] and with the deconstruction of *logocentricism*, in many ways sought the undoing of Christian theology. Yet, despite his ambiguous relationship to the religious, for certain theologians such as John Caputo,[96] Derrida opens the way for the recovery of

94. Carroll, *Alice Through the Looking-Glass*, 186–87. Hereafter referred to as *LG*.

95. Derrida, *Of Grammatology*, 14.

96. For an extensive inquiry into the presence of the religious within Derrida's work see Caputo, *The Prayers and Tears of Jacques Derrida*.

pre-modern conceptions of the possible by drawing upon the impossible. Caputo states "Deconstruction is a passion and a prayer for the impossible, a defense of the impossible against its critics."[97]

Here we see how Derrida might be of service to religious thinking since the critics against whom Derrida defends the impossible are those who perceive Enlightenment rationality as absolute. Derrida believes that traditional logic limits meaning to the confines of the possible and by doing this makes the articulation of an idea such as hospitality or forgiveness not "worthy of the name,"[98] since forgiveness, logically speaking, can only be applied to that which is forgivable. However, for Derrida (and for Christianity) true forgiveness entails forgiveness of the unforgivable or it is not forgiveness at all, hence the only true or possible meaning of forgiveness is impossible. This is one of the reasons that Caputo seems justified in stating that "being impassioned by the impossible, is the religious, is religious passion."[99]

Whilst Derrida never described himself as a postmodern, his deconstructive ir(religion) has nevertheless been adopted, as we saw with Nietzsche's philosophy, by postmodern theologians as a way of returning to a less secular metaphysic by embracing the collapse of the onto-theological conception of God. Ian Edwards, for example, believes that the "boundary-less space" of unknown possibilities (and impossibilities) is one area where Derrida and theology intersect. Edwards explains: "what can happen within a boundary-less space is unlimited. It is here where Derrida finds a kinship with negative theology. Both deconstruction and negative theology [. . .] attempt to assert what cannot be asserted."[100] Of course we cannot simply assume that when Derrida unsettles certain delimitations imposed by reason this is automatically of value to faith. Yet, in a sense, Derrida provides a negative warrant for the present thesis by exploring and vindicating a territory beyond the conclusions of classical logic, which as we have seen throughout this introduction are often at odds with Christian beliefs. The particular merit of Derrida's thought is that from a non-religious perspective he fulminates against the same foe as St. Paul, Denys, the medieval mystics, Luther, Kierkegaard, and the other propagators of truth claims that carry us the other side of reason.

---

97. Caputo, *Prayers and Tears*, xx.

98. Derrida, *The Beast and the Sovereign*, 309. By contrast, Derrida believes we are required "to think the *possible* [. . .] *as the impossible.*" Derrida, *Paper Machine*, 79.

99. Caputo, *Prayers and Tears*, xx.

100. Edwards, "Derrida's Ir(religion)," 144. It is of course important to recognize that whilst différance and apophaticism share similar passions there are, nevertheless, significantly distinct from each other.

Contemporary
Cognate Projects _____

IT WILL BE HELPFUL to conclude our brief history of the dialogue between faith and reason with a discussion of the various cognate contemporary projects, in order to determine to what extent the current project relates to or is distinct from adjacent and overlapping work in recent research. Mark Taylor's "a/theology" is an early response to Derrida's thought and significant for our study since he uses postmodern philosophy to draw out and comment on what he sees as marginalized and subversive aspects of Christianity. Like this book, Taylor begins his deconstructive theology by charting the history of Enlightenment thought and in particular observes how the Enlightenment brought about "the renewed confidence in human reason."[1] The manner in which this is highlighted suggests that the author is interested in deviating from the rational security of the Enlightenment, and indeed fairly swiftly Taylor emphasizes that his a/theology will "invert established meaning and subvert everything once deemed holy. It will thus be utterly transgressive."[2]

With this agenda it is possible to see how Derrida's thought could be of great value to Taylor's work, since Derrida likewise approaches Christianity with the intention of deconstructing its established meaning. Taylor observes how "it is just this antithetical association with theology that lends deconstruction its 'religious' significance for marginal thinkers."[3]

1. Taylor, *Erring*, 3.
2. Ibid., 6.
3. Ibid.

However, for our investigation, whilst we can appreciate that an attempt to discuss religion through the principles of nonsense may seem like a similarly transgressive endeavor, the aim of this thesis is paradoxically to reveal the truly conservative core of such "transgressive" theology. Thus, although this project is in many ways assisted by Taylor's creative and counter-intuitive theology, I want to question whether his programmatically "errant" theologizing doesn't end up creating its own boundaries, and ask if one can be both marginal and orthodox at the same time.

Though less well known in theological circles, the concept of "dialetheism" is an important parallel development in the field of analytical philosophy that closely corresponds to the breakdown of the certainty of the law of non-contradiction. Given the context of its emergence, it offers perhaps the most surprising challenge to the laws of classical reason, and in particular to the principle of non-contradiction. Dialetheism [literally *di aletheia* (two truths)]—which was coined by Graham Priest and Richard Routley in 1981—refers to the possibility that certain logically contradictory statements are accurate descriptions of reality, or as Priest summarizes: "The view that the LNC [law of non-contradiction] fails, that some contradictions are true is called *dialetheism*."[4]

What was in the 1980s an obscure and somewhat far-out suggestion has now gained widespread support and respect among many leading logicians. Michael Resnik, for example, introduces dialetheism thus: "For centuries logicians have held that contradictions cannot be true. This has been a fundamental principle of every system of logic capable of expressing it or a reasonable approximation thereof [. . . .] But today, thanks to forceful and astute criticisms by the dialetheists, we can no longer take this dogma for granted."[5] Briefly, dialetheism takes its cue from "paraconsistent logics,"[6] a philosophical method of determining statement veracity that allows for inconsistency-tolerant conditions and is able to support a sentence whose negation and affirmation both hold true. The significance of the dialetheist's challenge to the dialogue between faith and reason is that dialetheism comes from within the analytical tradition known for its harsh criticism of religious statements for failing to conform to the standards of Western metaphysics and, like postmodernism, shows these standards to be less stable than is commonly assumed.

---

4. Priest, "What's So Bad about Contradictions?" in *Law of Non-Contradiction*, 29.

5. Resnik, "Revising Logic," in *Law of Non-Contradiction*, 178.

6. The term was first used in 1976 by Francisco Miro Quesada.

Perhaps, therefore, it is surprising that dialetheism is seldom included in theological discourse.[7] James Anderson mentions the concept in his treatise on religious paradox, but discounts its relevance, claiming, "dialetheism only saves rationality at the expense of trivializing orthodoxy."[8] However, it is worth paying attention to the objective of Anderson's argument, which is to support religious paradox and yet "avoid denying or revising the law of non-contradiction or any other classical rules of logic."[9] He believes firmly that "the more exalted the epistemic status of Christian doctrine, the better equipped it will be to deal with epistemic challenges such as those raised by the problem of paradox."[10] Yet, as we have seen, the laws of classical epistemology are themselves being called into question by logicians, and in many circles adherence to the laws of reason is no longer considered a necessary measurement of intellectual rectitude. The diversity of thinkers involved in the challenge to the imperial reign of reason seems to demonstrate that the opposition is not simply a distortion serving the particular agenda of one ideology, but an important objection to heed. As we have seen, the history of protest belongs not only to advocates of deconstruction or nihilism, as one might anticipate, but also to analytical philosophers and orthodox theologians.

The philosophy of Gilles Deleuze provides a revolutionary approach to metaphysics, exploring significant correlative trajectories, such as the commonplace acceptance of Aristotelian and Husserlian logic. In particular, his book *The Logic of Sense* contains strikingly adjacent material to this treatise since he uses nonsense literature as a way of interacting with ontological concerns. What is especially interesting is that from a position of atheism Deleuze sees a need to speak of nonsense in order to describe that which is. As with Nietzsche and Derrida, we find in Deleuze the suggestion that

---

7. Although it is only an isolated footnote to the main treatise, Fronda, in *Wittgenstein's (Misunderstood) Religious Thought* identifies a point of sympathetic unity between Dialethism and theology: "One may then suppose that the logic underpinning the Pseudo-Dionysian discourse may be better accounted by non-classical logics such as *dialetheism*. Its development is motivated by the realization that certain contradictions are true. While the motivations that led to the development of these logics differ, they intersect at certain points, the most noteworthy of which is their rejection of the absolute applicability of the law of non-contradiction; there are, they hold, some contradictions [. . .] that are true [. . .] he [Graham Priest] argues that the law of non-contradiction is an Aristotelian dogma that can and should be challenged—an attitude reminiscent of Nicholas of Cusa," 5, n. 24.

8. Anderson, *Paradox in Christian Theology*, 126.

9. Ibid., 219.

10. Ibid., 156.

atheism is not coextensive with rationality, and that to speak truly of that which is one must be prepared at a certain point to let go of logic.

Obviously, a comprehensive discussion of Deleuzian philosophy is beyond the scope of this introduction. However, an indication of his views on the subject of sense and nonsense will help to contextualize our concerns. There is an ongoing attempt within Deleuze's work to undo Russell and Frege's assumption that truth and sense are necessarily conjoined and that sense provides a firm veridical basis. In *The Logic of Sense* Deleuze seeks to demonstrate the instability of sense and its co-presence with nonsense.[11] He suggests that sense is not its own origin, but is a product of various non-sensical components, claiming that sense is merely one type of effect produced at random out of the metaphysical flux of meaning and is thus connected to and stabilized by nonsense. "Reason is always a region carved out of the irrational," writes Deleuze, "not sheltered from the irrational at all, but traversed by it and only defined by a particular kind of relationship among irrational factors. Underneath all reason lies delirium, and drift."[12]

Deleuze turns our basic conception of sense upside-down, implying that the very foundation of sense is nonsense.[13] This intimate connection between sense and nonsense is effectively a disturbance of the law of non-contradiction and the erection of a paradoxical ontology in its place. Jean-Jacques Lecercle likewise identifies "the Deleuzean logic of unholy mixtures, an AND rather than an INSTEAD OF logic,"[14] and it is this characteristic that is of obvious relevance to our concerns since it is a further demonstration that the inherited laws of logic do not necessarily hold in every circumstance, even before we say a word about God.

Since his philosophy is launched from a position of atheism, it unwittingly gives credence to the similar theological questioning of principles of Western logic. Deleuze's own attempt at disarming staunch rationalism and scientism assists a religious endeavor to do the same. "What I'm interested in," he writes, "are the relations between the arts, science and philosophy. There's no order of priority among these disciplines. Each is creative."[15] Perhaps the ultimate significance of Deleuze for this book is that, like Schopen-

11. For a further discussion on this theme see Parsons, *Touch Monkeys*. She describes how for Deleuze "sense is co-present with nonsense," 20.

12. Deleuze, *Desert Islands and Other Texts*, 262.

13. Lawlor comments on Deleuze's phrase "the foundation can never resemble what it founds" and explains: "This Deleuzian principle, which is perhaps *the* defining principle of all of Deleuze's philosophy implies that the foundation of sense is nonsense." Lawlor, *Thinking Through French Philosophy*, 132.

14. Lecercle, *Deleuze and Language*, 53–54.

15. Deleuze, *Negotiations*, 123.

hauer, he attempts to show that the status of sense is not as secure as is often assumed, and that any accurate evaluation of reality must begin by calling this status into question.

Postmodern theology shares many of Deleuze's central objectives and within this field, the status of sense and logic is unashamedly called into question. John Caputo and Michael Scanlon amongst others have mounted an explicitly theological inquiry into the value of unreason. They associate secularization with modernity and see a desecularized return to religious thinking as a product of postmodern, deconstructive theory. There have been significant recent advances in the theological recognition of the value of the non-commonsensical, or to use the language of Caputo and Scanlon, "of what the 'old enlightenment' declared impossible."[16] They look to the "*new* enlightenment [. . .] which is given over to dreaming of the *impossible*."[17] Caputo and Scanlon's objective seems to be an important step in retrieving a pre-modern balance of the mystical with the evidential by allowing for the experience of "impossible" ideas that cannot be interacted with on a purely rational level. That is not to say that the rational is wrong—this project does not call for the usurpation of reason, but seeks to give space to, or to share court with, alternative methods of theorizing. To this extent, the task before us is properly postmodern in that it is not a rejection of reason, but the denial of reason's *universality*.

In *After the Death of God*, Caputo associates the kingdom of God with paradox, anarchy, and Lewis Carroll, all of which play a major part in the current book. Although it is only a brief reference, mainly in response to Deleuze's *Logic of Sense*, Caputo writes: "the divine madness of the Kingdom of God described in the New Testament, where the event provokes the most sublime effects, a veritable 'sacred anarchy', whose parables and paradoxes are easily the match of any of the tales told by Lewis Carroll."[18] Here Caputo encourages in his reader the idea that the kingdom of God might have some analogous connection to Lewis Carroll's nonsense worlds. Although Caputo does not devote any time to exploring what is specifically entailed by this analogy, it is nevertheless useful to discover such a close connection to this project within recent postmodern theological thought.

Carroll's nonsense stories have been revisited by many philosophers and linguisticians who draw upon semantic and hermeneutical devices, which they see as anticipating central themes of postmodernity such as the freeplay of language, the collapse of certainty, and the deferral of meaning.

---

16. Caputo and Scanlon, *God, the Gift and Postmodernism*, 3.

17. Ibid.

18. Caputo and Vattimo, *After the Death of God*, 60.

Jean-Jacque Lecercle's influential text, *The Philosophy of Nonsense*, is at the center of this exploration and will be discussed in further detail, but thinkers such as Gabriele Schwab,[19] Robin Lakoff,[20] and Alan Lopez,[21] all find within Carroll's nonsense worlds a prophetic herald of the postmodern age.

A highly interesting contemporary monograph by the visual artist and theorist Ted Hiebert links postmodernity to the nonsensical through identity and visual culture. Reflecting on the conclusions of postmodernity, Hiebert considers how the breakdown of the way in which we verify certain ideals is held in tension with an inability to uphold the method of deconstruction in any affirmative sense. "If the tenets of postmodernism hold," he writes "the (sometimes contested) declaration that 'postmodernism kills truth' finds a counterpart in the paradox of its own methodological procession, in this case a simultaneous death of falsity."[22] According to Hiebert, the effect of this is not an artistic horizon of "rhetorical nothingness," but a horizon of "the imaginative possibilities of nonsense,"[23] a fluid and playful artistic framework that he claims comes more naturally to the "children of post-modernism" than a canvas of fixed boundaries.[24] Although Hiebert does not address literary nonsense, he is of great benefit to this project insofar as he establishes the nonsensical (paradoxically) as the logical mode of artistic and philosophical progression in a world where rational thought is "insufficient to grasp the paradoxes and complexities of postmodern living."[25]

We have now arrived at the contextual birth of this book and it is worth pausing for a moment to clarify the two separate claims. Firstly, we have looked at recent theological thought that suggests postmodern philosophy recovers elements of pre-modern Christianity. Secondly, we have seen how non-theological theorists believe literary nonsense anticipates aspects of

---

19. "Carroll's break with the mimetic tradition anticipates many new literary techniques developed later during the proliferation of multiple forms of experimental literature . . . to the manifold simulacra of postmodernism." Schwab, "Nonsense and Metacommunication," 157.

20. A proto-postmodern questioning of the very possibility of certainty: truth, identity, authority, reason, and finally reality itself are revealed in the Alices as no more than convenient constructs—not eternal verities. Lakoff, "Lewis Carroll," 385.

21. Following a close reading of Lecercle, Lopez remarks in depth on the "anticipated or missed encounter between Carroll and postmodernism." Lopez, "Deleuze with Carroll," 102.

22. Hiebert, *In Praise of Nonsense*, 6.

23. Ibid., 3.

24. "For a postmodern generation it is simulation that is more familiar than reality, contingency more familiar than truth, doubt more familiar than conviction, and nonsense that is more familiar—much more familiar—than sense." Ibid., 5.

25. Ibid., 7.

postmodern philosophy. These two contentions are fairly well established in current scholarship: literary nonsense speaks forward to postmodernity; postmodernity speaks back to authentic Christianity, but the final side of the triad connecting nonsense to Christianity has not been addressed. What this book aims to explore is the potential connection between literary nonsense and orthodox faith, and for this we will need to bring the theologians together with the nonsense theorists in a union that has been hitherto unexamined in any depth.

It might be assumed, given the current postmodern dissatisfaction with inherited conceptions of the possible, the theological tradition would be more widely amenable to the postmodern movement as a deliverance from the imposition of non-religious standards of reason, and indeed we have witnessed some significant research into this area. Yet some of the strongest arguments in support of Aristotelian logic still come from within the field of theology, where rationality is often given ontological significance. This idea underlies Nicholas Wolterstorff's dictum: "When the theist believes nonrationally, he acts in violation of the will of the very God in whom he believes."[26] Many theologians firmly uphold the principles of Western metaphysics and formulate their apologetics in accordance with these rules. Geisler and Brooks, for example, maintain, "if logic is a necessary precondition of all thought, then it must also be necessary for all thought about God."[27] Despite the many attempts to show that logic is not a *necessary* precondition of all thought, the persistence of Enlightenment assumptions remains dominant in contemporary Christian theology, even though the resurrection it affirms is considered an empirical impossibility.

A defense of religion reliant upon tenets of logical reasoning assumes that if theological precepts can be articulated in accordance with logic then religious belief can be insulated from rational repudiation.[28] Logicians, however, rarely hold this view, and should they interact with theology at all will frequently use logic as a means by which they *disparage* religious belief. Anthony Kenny in his lecture series *Faith and Reason* typifies this view: "I conclude, then, my inquiry into the rationality of faith with the conclusion that faith is not, as theologians have claimed, a virtue, but a vice, unless a

---

26. Wolterstorff, "Can Belief in God be Rational?" in Plantinga and Wolterstorff (eds.), *Faith and Rationality*, 156.

27. Geisler and Brooks, eds., *Come, Let Us Reason*, 16.

28. As one author demonstrates: "Whether in a discussion between Christians on a matter of interpretation or in a debate with a non-Christian, no one could prove any point without the laws of rational inference. These tools of the theologian are all kept in the logician's toolbox." Geisler and Brooks, eds., *Come, Let Us Reason*, 16.

number of conditions can be fulfilled. One of them is that the existence of God can be rationally justified outside faith."[29]

This reliance on logic as the arbiter of veracity has led certain thinkers, such as D. Z. Phillips, to seek to relocate theological inquiry outside of the type of foundational rationalism that Kenny insists is compulsory for belief. Phillips describes his dissatisfaction with the "post-Enlightenment conception of rationality and its notion of sovereign reason" as a "philosophical scandal."[30] "We are asked to accept," Phillips complains, "as the only appropriate philosophical method for establishing the rationality of religious belief, a method which actually distorts the character of religious belief."[31] We are thus faced with a radical and seemingly incompatible divergence among theologians. On the one hand, we are urged to uphold a logical account of faith, a "rational belief," one "which does not violate our noetic obligations."[32] On the other hand, theologians seem to be celebrating religion as "the unassimilable other of Enlightenment modernity."[33] We find ourselves forced into a perplexing dichotomy: Christian faith, it seems, is either supremely rational *or* it transcends all rational inquiry.

This is in many ways an unhelpful dichotomy and some theologians have recognized the inadequacy of this either/or approach, calling for an encounter that has a more paradoxical flavor, allowing for a richer combination of reason with its antithesis. Prompted by a dialogue between Slavoj Žižek and John Milbank, in which both express a certain desire to "go beyond the impoverished Enlightenment view of reason,"[34] Creston Davis acknowledges the need for theology to avoid creating a dichotomy between rationality and faith: "the return to the theological in our time," Davis writes, "may be a call, once again, to strike a balance between reason and myth, between belief and faith [. . .] and between the divine and the human."[35] One way to accomplish this is to synthesize faith with rationality, as we have seen in Anderson's treatise.[36] An alternative method, however,

29. Kenny, *Faith and Reason*, 84.

30. Phillips, *Faith After Foundationalism*, xiii.

31. Ibid., 12.

32. Wolterstorff, "Can Belief in God be Rational?" 144.

33. Tracy, "Fragments," 171.

34. Davis, Introduction to Slavoj Žižek and John Milbank, *The Monstrosity of Christ*, 10.

35. Ibid., 5.

36. Anderson creates a model for understanding theological paradox which he calls "RAPT"—Rational Affirmation of Paradoxical Theology, "according to which Christians can be entirely rational in believing certain apparently contradictory doctrines." Anderson, *Paradox in Christian Theology*, 218.

would be to re-evaluate the status of the irrational, and rather than trying to circumvent or explain away moments of logical conflict within theology, one might instead countenance the theological validity of unreason.

This does not seem to be an approach that has been significantly explored. George Mavrodes, for example, in response to the atheist's objection to faith on the grounds of irrationality suggests there are "three alternatives by way of setting the record straight." He explains: "we could simply assert that the faith is rational, or we could produce a positive argument in support of its rationality, or we could undertake to refute the atheist's argument."[37] Mavrodes does not consider a fourth alternative, however, which this book proposes—and that is to agree with the atheist, but to transvaluate the language of unreason by demonstrating its ability to describe the nature of that which is. Indeed, it will be a central part of the argument of this book that there are certain aspects of reality that are best described by means of "nonsense."

On the whole, terms such as "irrational," "absurd," and "nonsense" still belong to the skeptic, and form part of his arsenal. Such descriptors are rarely accepted or favored by religious believers, and perhaps with good reason. Within the symbolism of philosophical logic, Neil Tennant explains "$\perp$ is, logically, as horrific a conclusion as one can possibly get. Indeed, $\perp$ is *so* bad that, funnily enough, nothing *can* really follow from it the way the absurdity rule would otherwise maintain. $\perp$ is like a logical black hole: no possible thought that makes any sense could ever escape from it."[38] This work is concerned with whether there are any moments within orthodox Christian teaching that lead to the conclusion $\perp$, and if so, whether this makes such claims redundant, or if, on the other hand, absurdity might in some sense itself be a revelation of truth.

The history of faith and reason that we have sketched indicates that our normative ways of discerning reality are structured by the principles of logic. This manner of perceiving the world is both instructive and necessary, but, as we have seen, at the same time it also prejudices, leaves out and discounts what has become the other of logical discourse—the a-linear and the nonsensical. Since our intention is to explore the theological value of these alternative ways of interacting with and regarding the structure of reality, we will use nonsense literature as a point of comparison with the religious imagination.

---

37. Mavrodes, "Jerusalem and Athens Revisited," in Helm, *Faith and Rationality*, 204.

38. Tennant, "An Anti-Realist Critique of Dialetheism," in *The Law of Non-Contradiction*, 358. [$\perp$ is the logical symbol representing absurd or absurdism.]

Michael Ward, commenting on the use of fantasy literature as a method of religious teaching, writes: "As an apologetic strategy, it only makes sense to meet people where they are. Where else, indeed can they be met?"[39] Ward's statement helps to indicate why exploring theology through nonsense literature could be a valuable pursuit; it allows us to begin by listening to the skeptic and ask if some measure of irrational credulity is required in order to accept Christian faith. This project is not in any way set up to discredit the innumerable, vital and rational defenses of Christianity, but to seek a restoration of the Pauline balance of reason with a delight in unreason and wisdom with a reverence for folly.

There are of course many questions to ask and qualifications to be made, but at this initial stage, in the view of secular misgivings about the laws of human reason, there seems to be a warrant to explore the possibility that moments of logical discord within Christian theology are not necessarily adequate grounds for dismissal. Certainly Stenson means to discredit Christianity when he suggests that "if [. . .] no theist can give satisfactory criteria for establishing the truth or falsity of such statements even in principle (let alone practice), then these expressions must be like Lewis Carroll's nonsense verses, statements which seem to be genuine assertions, but which, like the Jabberwock poem, have no cognitive significance at all."[40] The question posed by the current book, however, is: what implication might it have for theology if we accepted the analogy Stenson makes with nonsense, but disputed the assumption that it has "no cognitive significance"?

---

39. Ward, "The Good Serves the Better and Both the Best," 68.

40. Stenson, *Sense and Nonsense in Religion*, 19.

PART I

Christian Unreason

CHAPTER 1

The Paradoxical _____

NONSENSE AND PARADOX

THE HISTORY OF FAITH and reason summarily sketched recognizes that our customary ways of discerning reality are structured by the principles of logic. This manner of perceiving the world is appropriate—and our normative posture—and I do not at all wish to deny its value or our fundamental need of it. However, it is also clear from the previous section that for many thinkers this approach does not exhaust, and sometimes distorts, the nature of human experience. I will therefore consider a range of a-rational ways of describing reality, not as an *alternative* to the exercise of reason, but in an attempt to preserve or retrieve what Enlightenment approaches often leave out or obscure.

Having found from our survey that logic does not always lead to an accurate description of reality, I intend to experiment with the nonsensical to see whether in worlds such as Lewis Carroll's Wonderland a faithful apprehension of the real may paradoxically be achieved by recourse to the surreal or anti-real. I begin by simply seeking to define the character of the nonsensical imagination, which will involve exploring central structural devices of nonsense fiction which require imaginative participation on the reader's behalf. Since this project is concerned with a religious worldview, these key descriptors will then be brought into dialogue with Christian faith. In creating a connection between faith and nonsense it is important to conduct the study by commencing with nonsense rather than theology in order to demonstrate that our main areas of examination are genuinely significant features of the nonsensical imagination and not merely one-off instances that happen to be suggestive of theological maxims.

Alongside the nonsense stories of Lewis Carroll, I will draw these central characteristics from a variety of nonsense theorists. Perhaps the three most important commentators on literary nonsense are Elizabeth Sewell (1952), Wim Tigges (1986), and Jean-Jacques Lecercle (1994). Having already established the law of non-contradiction as a foundational precept of common-sense logic, the most conspicuous contravention of this principle is the idea of paradox—a contradiction that is true.[1] The idea that paradox is a consistent and important dimension of nonsense literature is recognized by Sewell as "the game of nonsense," which she describes as "the mind's employing its tendency towards order to engage its contrary tendency towards disorder."[2] Tigges defines literary nonsense as "a genre of narrative literature which balances a multiplicity of meaning with a simultaneous absence of meaning."[3] And Lecercle argues, "the genre is structured by the contradiction [. . .] in terms of a dialectic, between over-structuring and de-structuring, subversion and support."[4] More specifically, he describes *Alice in Wonderland* as "a text so paradoxical that it destroys itself."[5] Each of these thinkers insists upon the presence of contradiction and dialectic as fundamental to literary nonsense.[6]

Paradox is a central feature of Lewis Carroll's fictional worlds. Peter Heath in *The Philosopher's Alice* provides excellent commentary on the logical inconsistencies of Wonderland. Referring to the absurd Caucus race in which the Dodo declares: "*Everybody* has won, and *all* must have prizes,"[7] Heath describes this as a paradox in breach of the law of non-contradiction since "winning logically entails that some contestants do better than others."[8] Either somebody has won *or* they have all drawn; the contestants cannot

---

1. By "true" I do not mean that the contradiction corresponds to some existential reality, rather, I mean that within the parameters of a particular grammar both sides of the tension are necessary and cannot be dissolved.

2. Sewell, *The Field of Nonsense*, 48.

3. Tigges, *An Anatomy of Literary Nonsense*, 47.

4. Lecercle, *A Philosophy of Nonsense*, 3.

5. Ibid., 124.

6. Susan Stewart, although lesser known, has an important treatise on nonsense: *Aspects of Intertextuality in Folklore and Literature*. In her work she also refers to paradox as a central characteristic of literary nonsense; she writes: "the social use of nonsense is paradoxical; nonsense presents the uncategorizable category, the context that cannot be contextualized." Ibid., 207.

7. Carroll, *Alice in Wonderland*, 23. Hereafter referred to as *AW*.

8. Heath, *The Philosopher's Alice*, 32.

both draw and not draw as the Dodo proposes. Cases, then, where the law of non-contradiction appears to be breached will be accepted as instances of nonsensical paradox. It may be helpful, however, to distinguish three separate types of paradox in which the majority of all nonsense contradictions find root: paradoxes of speech; paradoxes of sense; and paradoxes of time. I will begin with a summary of the paradox of speech.

The first type—linguistic paradox—involves an apparent contradiction, which is utilized to comic effect by nonsense writers. Lecercle summarizes it as follows: "I speak language, in other words I am master of the instrument which allows me to communicate with others, and yet it is a language that speaks: I am constrained by the language I inhabit to such an extent that I am inhabited or possessed by it."[9] Carroll delighted in this linguistic paradox, and a prominent cause of nonsensical wit in the *Alice* books centers around the problem that words aren't entirely in our control and often fail to convey what the speaker means.

Through the character of Humpty Dumpty, Carroll demonstrates the resultant nonsense of attempting to avoid encountering the paradox of speech. In the following well-known extract, Alice tries to engage sensibly in Humpty Dumpty's absurd reasoning, which results in her complete bewilderment:

> 'When *I* use a word,' Humpty Dumpty said, in rather a scornful tone, 'it means just what I choose it to mean—neither more nor less.'
>
> 'The question is,' said Alice, 'whether you *can* make words mean so many different things.'
>
> 'The question is,' said Humpty Dumpty, 'which is to be master—that's all.'
>
> Alice was too puzzled to say anything; so after a minute Humpty Dumpty began again. 'They've a temper, some of them—particularly verbs: they're the proudest—adjectives you can do anything with, but not verbs—however, *I* can manage the whole lot of them! Impenetrability! That's what *I* say!'
>
> 'Would you tell me, please,' said Alice, 'what that means?'
>
> 'Now you talk like a reasonable child,' said Humpty Dumpty, looking very much pleased. 'I meant by "impenetrability" that we've had enough of that subject, and it would be just as well if you'd mention what you mean to do next, as I suppose you don't mean to stop here all the rest of your life.'[10]

9. Lecercle, *Philosophy of Nonsense*, 25.

10. Carroll, *LG*, 162–63.

This exchange seems to suggest, contrary to Humpty Dumpty's approach, that true mastery of language involves relinquishing the desire for total control over meaning. Effective communication seems to have to acknowledge the imprecision of language but speaks as if it were precise. To use the formula of non-contradiction, this paradox reveals that in one sentence an individual can both say and not say precisely what he intends. In everyday use, this is for the most part a dormant paradox; we tend to know what is meant even if the words are approximate. However, through the process of deconstruction Derrida brings this inconsistency to the surface, explaining how words always convey "more, less, or something other than what [we] mean."[11] This is what the nonsense author brings gently and playfully into view, provoking the reader to recognize the subversive and ungovernable feature of his own speech.[12]

The second main type of nonsense paradox involves the co-dependency of nonsense and sense, an idea particularly associated with Deleuze though taken up and explored by Lecercle. In the introduction to *The Logic of Sense*, Deleuze outlines why paradox is intricately linked to a discussion of both sense and nonsense: "we present here a series of paradoxes which form the theory of sense. It is easy to explain why this theory is inseparable from paradoxes: sense is a nonexisting entity, and, in fact, maintains very special relations with nonsense."[13] Perhaps this union is inevitable given Carroll's dual life as an Oxford logician and nonsense writer.[14] Good nonsense, it seems, is reliant upon strict sense, and in fact, it is Carroll's brilliant logic that gives birth to some of his most ingenious moments of nonsense. Lecercle observes a similar phenomenon: "Lack of sense here is always compensated by excess or proliferation of sense there. This [. . .] is the central paradox or contradiction of the genre."[15]

It is paradoxical because one would anticipate that the more strictly one adheres to sense, the more it should correspond to sound reason, yet

---

11. Derrida, *Of Grammatology*, 158.

12. Lecercle goes into great depth about this phenomenon which he deems as "the central paradox of language." He explains: "On the one hand, language is based on the impossibility of saying everything [. . . ;] on the other hand, there is nothing that cannot be said. [. . .] This paradox, a genuine one, for we must maintain both propositions, and they are incompatible" *Philosophy Through the Looking-Glass*, 65.

13. Deleuze, *The Logic of Sense*, ix.

14. During his career he published various academic pamphlets specifically concerning paradox, such as: "Hypotheticals and Paradox" (1893) "Logical Paradox" (1894) and "Barbershop Paradox" (1895). Lecercle certainly feels that "there is a profound similarity between the author of logical paradoxes and the author of literary nonsense." Lecercle, *Philosophy Through the Looking-Glass*, 104–5.

15. Lecercle, *Philosophy of Nonsense*, 31.

as literary nonsense reveals, it is sometimes the very strictness of the adherence to logic that results in absurdity.[16] As the following dialogue demonstrates, much of the Hare and Hatter's nonsense is derived from their
pedantic demand for clarity.

> 'I'm glad they've begun asking riddles.—I believe I can guess
> that,' she added aloud.
>
> 'Do you mean that you think you can find out the answer to
> it?' said the March Hare.
>
> 'Exactly so,' said Alice.
>
> 'Then you should say what you mean,' the March Hare went
> on.
>
> 'I do,' Alice hastily replied; 'at least—at least I mean what I
> say—that's the same thing, you know.'
>
> 'Not the same thing a bit!' said the Hatter. 'You might just
> as well say that "I see what I eat" is the same thing as "I eat what
> I see!"'[17]

G. K. Chesterton in *Orthodoxy* dedicates a chapter to "The Maniac,"
whom he describes as possessing "the combination of an expansive and
exhaustive reason with a contracted common sense."[18] This indeed seems
to be an accurate description of the Hare and Hatter in their conversation
with Alice, as they demonstrate a sort of unreasonable logic in exhibiting a
concern for precision that is out of all proportion; indeed, we might say they
have lost everything *except* their reason. The law of non-contradiction tells
us that if something is fully irrational it cannot also be rational, but as we
have seen it is not the Hare and Hatter's irrationality but their strict rationality that renders their dialogue nonsensical.

Such nonsense reveals to us that in everyday communication sense
and nonsense flow into one another and that the staunchest sense touches
the strictest nonsense. What we take to be "sensible" Carroll reveals to be
the happy balance of sense and nonsense, as opposed to strict reason, which
often results in absurdity.[19] Such an example can be found in the ludicrous

16. This is why Lecercle describes nonsense (paradoxically) as a "conservative-
revolutionary genre." Lecercle recognizes that in everyday life we must be lax with our
adherence to certain laws of logic, since, as Carroll demonstrates, if they are pursued
too rigorously they produce absurd results. Ibid., 2.

17. Carroll, *AW*, 55.

18. Chesterton, *Orthodoxy*, 36.

19. This second paradox in many ways parallels deconstructive philosophy as there
is the explicit demonstration that "sense" has no transcendental signifier that guaran-
tees its meaning. It is the nonsense characters who are occupied with fruitless attempts
to fix and tie down meaning, whereas the rational Alice is happy to accept a degree of

judicial system of Looking-Glass land. As Alice admits, there is nothing exactly at fault with the Queen's logic, and yet the conclusion is supremely unreasonable:

> 'There's the King's Messenger. He's in prison now, being punished: and the trial doesn't even begin till next Wednesday: and of course the crime comes last of all.'
>
> 'Suppose he never commits the crime?' said Alice.
>
> 'That would be all the better, wouldn't it?' the Queen said
>
> [. . .] Alice felt there was no denying *that*. 'Of course it would be all the better,' she said: 'but it wouldn't be all the better his being punished.'
>
> 'You're wrong *there*, at any rate,' said the Queen. 'Were *you* ever punished?'
>
> 'Only for faults,' said Alice.
>
> 'And you were all the better for it, I know!' the Queen said triumphantly.
>
> 'Yes, but then I *had* done the things I was punished for,' said Alice: 'that makes all the difference.'
>
> 'But if you *hadn't* done them,' the Queen said, 'that would have been better still.'[20]

The steps of the Queen's argument are perfectly legitimate but the contention is still irrational; it is all sense yet no meaning. Nonsense logic, as we can see here, often produces a perversion of sense via a perfection of reason and it is this second type of paradox that creates much literary nonsense wit.

The third type of paradox dominant in nonsense literature concerns time. Susan Stewart describes how literary nonsense "stands in direct contradiction to the remaining three laws of Husserl's 'lived experiences of time.'" These include: "That different times can never be conjoint; that their relation is a nonsimultaneous one; and that there is transitivity, that to every time belongs an earlier and a later."[21] It is easy to find a multitude of nonsense examples that flout Husserl's laws and give way to paradoxical expressions of temporality. In Carroll's worlds, several days come at once;[22]

---

semantic slippage. Deleuze notes likewise that nonsense "lends itself only too readily to deconstructive manoeuvring and a Derridean reading." Lecercle, *Philosophy of Nonsense*, 163.

20. Carroll, *LG*, 151.

21. Stewart, *Aspects of Intertextuality*, 146.

22. "Alice was puzzled. 'In *our* country,' she remarked, 'there's only one day at a time.' The Red Queen said 'That's a poor thin way of doing things. Now *here*, we mostly have days and nights two or three at a time, and sometimes in the winter we take as many as five nights together—for warmth you know.'" Carroll, *LG*, 195.

time can stand still for a few individuals whilst speeding up for others;[23] and the ordinary sequence of events is distorted so that future events can take place in the past or present.[24]

The three different types of paradoxes identified testify to the extensiveness of Carroll's usage of contrary logic. His paradoxes are temporal and also spatial; they are concerned with reason and speech, personal identity, and imaginary objects; they are physical, literal, moral, and metaphysical. Alice is herself even described as possessing a paradoxical character, "simultaneously Wonderland's slave and its queen, its creator and destroyer as well as its victim."[25] Having established that paradox is indeed a pervasive theme in Carroll's nonsense, we can now consider the effect or significance of such paradoxes.

Within the sphere of the imagination, one of the effects of this type of paradoxical play is that it nurtures a cognitive flexibility. The presence of paradox within nonsense requires the imagination to perform the critical role of envisaging the "impossible" or thinking outside the parameters of logic. We know that days come one after another, and yet Carroll prompts us to conceive of the event of having several Tuesdays at once. This activity of imaginatively overstepping the boundaries of the possible resonates with the various theological deviations from Aristotelian logic that were chartered in the historical survey of the relationship between faith and reason. Garrett Green explains how followers of the Kantian tradition "hesitate to use the *term* imagination to describe religion, even though it would seem appropriate. To modern ears it simply sounds too much like admitting that religious belief is imaginary."[26] However, if we are dissatisfied with the Kantian limitation of religion "within the bounds of reason alone," then the imagination, and in particular the nonsensical imagination with its flagrant defiance of the rational, could become a force for the theology of "the new enlightenment."

---

23. "Now if you kept on good terms with him, [time] he'd do almost anything you liked with the clock. For instance, suppose it were nine o'clock in the morning, just time to begin lessons: you'd only have to whisper a hint to Time, and round goes the clock in a twinkling!" *AW*, 56. This appears in contrast with the Hatter's experience of reality: "He [time] won't do a thing I ask! It's always six o'clock now." *AW*, 58.

24. "'Living backwards!' Alice repeated in great astonishment. 'I never heard of such a thing!'

'—but there's one great advantage in it, that one's memory works both ways.'

'I'm sure *mine* only works one way,' Alice remarked. 'I can't remember things before they happen.' The Queen then tells Alice that her clearest memories are 'things that happened the week after next.'" Carroll, *LG*, 150–51.

25. Auerbach, "Falling Alice, Fallen Women, and Victorian Dream Children," 49.

26. Green, *Imagining God*, 16.

Interestingly, the nonsense activity of playfully rearranging the limits of the possible in some ways seems to have more in common with postmodern theology than with neighboring literary genres. There is not much that we would expect Thomas Gradgrind to have to say to the Mad Hatter, but there is equally little that Frodo Baggins and the March Hare have in common. Although both Carroll and Tolkien require from their reader an imaginative acceptance of the impossible, the nonsensical imagination seems to demand the *persistent* practice of accepting impossibilities in contrast to the initial acceptance required in order to enter a world such as Middle Earth, which, once inside, functions systematically and obeys its own rules in a consistent fashion—dragons have the property of flight, but it would be ludicrous to suggest that a dwarf might. Whereas Carroll's nonsense—where stones transform into cakes and babies morph into pigs—requires the reader to imagine "six impossible things before breakfast" and many more throughout the day. Hence, nonsense paradox entailing "both/and" collisions is logically problematic in the way that Gandalf's wizardry is not.

We have begun to explore the idea that the imaginative traversing of logical boundaries may have a theological significance and I want now to develop this by considering whether like nonsense literature, Christian theology includes paradox as an integral component, and, if so, in what sense religious paradox differs from the absurd contradictions created by nonsense writers.

CHRISTIANITY AND PARADOX

With reference to the title of his book, *Sense and Nonsense in Religion*, Sten Stenson explains, "the word 'nonsense' is meant to direct our attention to [. . .] the patent self-contradictions, the logical paradoxicality, of religious language."[27] What Stenson's proposition steers us towards is the indication that nonsense and theology share some commonality via paradox.[28] Such

27. Stenson, *Sense and Nonsense*, 22.

28. A similar claim has been recently put forward by Cameron Freeman in *Postmetaphysics*. Freeman discusses how we can speak theologically in the wake of Heidegger and Derrida. Freeman believes that "a language of radical paradox is quite possibly the only way we can speak of the mystery of God without missing the mark entirely and getting lost in dangerously 'one-sided' onto-theological categories that are easily open to deconstructive criticism" (108). Freeman grounds his belief in various parables and aphorisms of Christ and makes a compelling case that "the bi-polar reversals of meaning inform the deep structure of at least thirty of the parables that exist in the New Testament Gospels" (174). Given Freeman's postmodern agenda and his specific focus on paradox, it is hardly surprising that his conclusions speculate on the scandalous reception of Christ's radical reversals. He acknowledges, "this kind of

a proposal raises several questions, including: is paradox a real and central aspect of the Christian faith? Does paradox have the same meaning in literary nonsense and theology? In connection with Carrollian nonsense, paradox was classified as a breach of the law of non-contradiction and this definition accords with the main entry in the OED: "An apparently absurd or *self-contradictory statement*."

That Christianity contains such propositions ought not to be a contentious issue; the teachings of Jesus, the commentary of the fathers, the central creeds, as this chapter will demonstrate, contain a host of theological paradoxes. Yet, the word "paradox" is curiously absent from *The Cambridge Dictionary of Christian Theology*,[29] though the entry in *The Cambridge Dictionary of Christianity* declares that "For Christians, paradoxes abound; they are the very stuff of faith."[30] There seems to be a lack of clarity concerning the application of paradox to Christian theology today. As we will see, many consider it essential; others confine it to the obscure and mystical; and some would rather articulate faith without contravening this basic constraint of Western logic.

In his book *Christianity and Paradox*, Ronald Hepburn uses paradox to describe some central tenets of the Christian faith, such as the belief that God is both one and fully triune. He accepts that the doctrine of the Trinity appears as an impossible belief, but claims "paradoxical language is the *staple* of accounts of God's nature and is not confined to rhetorical extravaganzas."[31] Hepburn imagines the response of the unbeliever to the Christian profession of paradox:

> Talking with you is impossible. No matter what absurdity, inconsistency, incoherence I locate in your theology, you will

---

paradoxical language looks downright absurd, ridiculous, and even mad. The paradoxical stories of Jesus do not make things makes sense—they perplex, confound and unsettle us" (172). At the culmination of his treatise Freeman articulates precisely the starting point of this venture, and that is that "absolute truth looks like complete and utter non-sense from a purely rational perspective, as it undermines our pre-given assumptions about how the world works with a flagrant disregard for our established logical procedures" (254). The aims of this present work are in many ways parallel to those of Freeman and the project is likewise situated within the field of postmodern theology. It progresses from Freeman's observation that "absolute truth looks like complete and utter nonsense" and explores the value of this analogical association both for the believer and for the atheist.

29. Cambridge University Press: 2011. Contributors: Ian A. McFarland, David A. S. Fergusson, and Karen Kilby, Iain R. Torrance.

30. Volney P. Gay in Patte (ed.), *The Cambridge dictionary of Christianity* (Cambridge University Press, 2010).

31. Hepburn, *Christianity and Paradox*, 16.

(*verbally*, that is) transform it into a new exhibition of divine 'otherness.' You don't even recoil when I accuse you of using language without meaning; for, you say, 'God can use our non-sense as the vehicle of his revelation.' The argument, he feels, has become altogether unreal.[32]

There is certainly something unsettling, or at least curious, in the idea that Christianity might not seek to avoid the claim of "absurdity, inconsistency [and] incoherence."[33] Freud's proposal that belief in God provides "answers to the riddles that tempt the curiosity of man"[34] seems much more likely than Hepburn's assertion that "the theologian calmly *admits* [. . .] all these contradictions [. . .] and has no intention of abandoning his theology because of their presence." If, as Freud supposes, "man creates God in his image,"[35] it seems odd that he would create, or at least invest faith in, a doctrine full of glaring inconsistencies and impossible riddles.

Of course, it may be that this language of impossibility and absurdity is being misapplied. Perhaps, as Hepburn's unbeliever might protest, "paradox is too optimistic and too solemn a word for all this. It would be more honest to call it a language of *contradiction*."[36] This is indeed Hume's position. He suggests that Christianity *willingly* presents itself as paradoxical and rests securely in its semantic contradictions. Given the general desire in the eighteenth century to purge religion of superstition and to bring it in line with rational empiricism, it is not surprising that Hume disparages the Christian appeal to mystery:

> One may safely affirm that all popular theology [. . .] has a kind of appetite for absurdity and contradiction. If that theology went not beyond reason and common sense, her doctrines would appear too easy and familiar. Amazement must of necessity be raised: Mystery affected: Darkness and obscurity sought after: And a foundation of merit afforded to the devout votaries, who desire an opportunity of subduing their rebellious reason by the belief of the most unintelligible sophisms.[37]

32. Ibid., 17.

33. As Howard Kainz observes, "for most of the history of Western philosophy, paradoxes have been considered an embarrassment, to be avoided at all times, if you wish your argumentation to be considered properly rational." Yet Kainz also acknowledges that "[religion] for some reason, seemed to find no particular problem in dealing with apparent contradictions in paradoxes." Kainz, *Five Metaphysical Paradoxes*, 53.

34. Freud, *The Psychopathology of Everyday Life*, 26.

35. Ibid., 182.

36. Hepburn, *Christianity and Paradox*, 16.

37. Hume, *Natural History of Religion*, quoted by T. H. Huxley, *Hume*, 142.

Hume gives the impression here that the mystery and absurdity of theological doctrines is a rhetorical strategy employed to stimulate faith. Hume agrees that the paradoxes of theology go against Aristotelian logic; he maintains, however, that this is a *deliberate* contravention manufactured from empty premises.

In contrast to Hume's opinion, Henri de Lubac argues that far from believing absurdity and contradiction to be a desirable quality in religious teaching, many theologians exhibit an Enlightenment fear that religious belief may seem implausible if it involves maxims that defy rational or reasonable limits. As a result, de Lubac contends that vital paradoxes of faith have been significantly underemphasized. "We are too desirous of being set at ease," de Lubac writes, "and we do not consent to being taken out of our usual element. That is why we make a petty religion for ourselves and seek a petty salvation of our own petty proportions."[38] De Lubac views the avoidance of religious paradox as a weakened version of orthodox faith, a sentiment that is reiterated by Ben Quash and Michael Ward in their book on *Heresies*, in which they remind us that heresies often come about as a result of the attempt to circumvent paradox. Quash explains: "Heretics have often been shy of the full radicalness of orthodox Christianity, such that their alternatives have been almost rather common-sensical by comparison."[39] By associating heresies with a more common-sense interpretation of faith, Quash seems to reinforce the apparent connection between non-sense and orthodox faith.

At this point, it will be helpful to clarify the options canvassed so far. The prevalence of paradox in Christian doctrine can be explained in three ways. Firstly, as suggested by Freud, doctrinal "paradoxes" are not an impossible breach with rational thought since man has mentally created the God he desires. Paradox in this case is a rhetorical trope and should thus be viewed either poetically, if it is helpful to the individual, or dismissed as a deception, if it is unhelpful.[40] Secondly, based on Hume's account of Christianity, paradox may be a device used to deflect attention away from

38 De Lubac, *Paradoxes of Faith*, 15.

39. Ben Quash and Michael Ward (eds.), *Heresies and How to Avoid Them*, 7.

40. The logician Willard Quine believes paradoxes are never necessary and can always be explained away. In instances where logic seems to trap us in having to accept a paradox, Quine claims the correct thing to do is to dismiss one or more of the premises. For example, on Russell's insolvable barber paradox Quine writes: "the proper conclusion to draw is just that there is no such barber. [. . .] The paradox is simply a proof that no village can contain a man who shaves all and only those men in it who do not shave themselves." Quine, *The Ways of Paradox*, 3. Quine would apply this to theology and say that where there seems to be an irreconcilable collision one or other of the tensions must be dropped.

an empty premise to inspire a false sense of awe.[41] The third alternative, put forward by de Lubac, Hepburn, and Stenson, is that paradox is in fact an accurate description of a doctrine, which does not merely pertain to the order of language, but is rather an attempt to signify that which seems to be *of its nature* paradoxical. The main concern in this chapter is not to prove that what is deemed paradoxical is right, but to consider how accurately such a description reflects Christian doctrine.[42] The secondary, more controversial discussion is to do with the presentation of these paradoxes—whether they ought to be shrouded in solemn dignity or if it is appropriate to articulate them in conjunction with the nonsensical and use the ridiculous as a point of sacred initiation.

Before proceeding, however, a general caveat is necessary. The study of paradox within religion is inevitably approached anthropocentrically: we are only ever representing God to the human mind; not striving somehow attain to the divine essence. De Lubac is of the opinion that "paradox is the reverse of what, properly perceived, would be synthesis. But, proper view always eludes us."[43] This is an important point to bear in mind, for in thinking theologically, we never possess an ultimate or exhaustive perspective. What de Lubac seems to be saying is not that paradox is therefore a false conclusion—indeed; he maintains it is in our present state the most accurate way of expressing certain theological truths. Rather, de Lubac is referring to the fact that Christians conceive of reality as both partial and provisional. However, it is *within* this scope of partial understanding that Christians are prepared for and receive intimations of God's ultimate reality. The language of paradox therefore gestures towards this reality, but is inevitably inadequate to express it fully.

It is important to emphasize that this does not constitute an exemption from or a way around the language of illogicality and nonsense. By claiming that paradox is not an ultimate property of Christian dogma, many theologians seek to avoid the charges of irrationality. As I have already indicated, James Anderson's work on paradox concentrates on the *appearance* of contradiction enabling him to put forward his rational defense of theological

41. Matthew Bagger has also suggested that paradox can be seen as an enticing doctrinal quality insofar as it points to something beyond human comprehension. He writes: "to a thinker invested in bringing outsiders across the external boundary of the group, paradox will evoke awe and reverence." Bagger, *Uses of Paradox*, 10.

42. This trilogy of distinctions is not in reality so clear-cut. One might have legitimate grounds for asking how easy it is to draw the line between linguistic and ontological paradox. For example, if Christians are not expected to believe that a camel can really pass through the eye of a needle, it is arguably not immediately obvious that they should insist upon the seriousness of God's Triunity.

43. De Lubac, *Paradoxes of Faith*, 9.

paradox. "Paradoxical doctrines," he states, "do not involve real contradiction, that is, they do not posit logically impossible states of affairs. Rather, they are instances of merely apparent contradiction."[44] De Lubac's approach is different, though, because he focuses on the significance of the apparent contradiction and conducts his theology from what appears to be the case within our limited conceptions of the real. Anderson, by contrast, seeks to start immediately from the eschaton and thereby reassures himself and the reader that absurdity plays no part in theological paradox.

This desire to achieve logical credibility is not limited to Anderson's treatise. Two promising essays in a collection on Kierkegaard entitled "Christianity and Nonsense" and "Kierkegaard: 'Paradox' and Irrationalism" both seek to undo the charge that Kierkegaardian theology contains elements of the absurd and the nonsensical. Like Anderson, moments of unreason are rejected as insignificant on the basis that they are not ultimately unreasonable: "Kierkegaard's position is that even those claims which appear to unbelief as absurd or contradictory are not essentially, permanently, and incorrigibly so."[45] In contrast, there are certain theologians supporting de Lubac who want to acknowledge that the appearance of absurdity is itself of consequence. John Milbank, for example, recognizes the importance of de Lubac's central concern with paradox whilst also maintaining a belief in the ultimate harmony of God's kingdom. "Paradox," writes Milbank, rejecting Žižek's dialectic resolution, "affirms the full reality of the impossible and the contradictory."[46] Here, Milbank establishes the importance of observing the paradoxical dimension of Christian theology not because he believes the contradictory contains within itself any essential permanence, but rather, because paradox enables the possibility of theological reflection from our current fallen situation. In other words, the employment of paradox gives theology a language through which it can represent "impossible and contradictory" realities.

The desire to overstep the "full reality of the impossible" and focus only on the projected reality of ultimate resolution in many ways offers an impoverished account of Christian theology and can carry religious descriptions away from any recognizable view of reality. By contrast, the language of nonsense and paradox has the potential to address the "full reality" of life as it is conceived by Christianity—at once reconciled and yet still fallen. Faith always begins with the openness to a reality that is beyond

44. Anderson, *Paradox in Christian Theology*, 263.

45. Mckinnon, "Kierkegaard: 'Paradox' and Irrationalism," in Gill (ed.), *Essays on Kierkegaard*, 109.

46. Milbank, *The Monstrosity of Christ*, 198.

formal certainty, and to this extent, one would at some point expect there to be a crucial and problematic correspondence between language and reality, experience and truth. We are essentially asking whether we should conduct theology from a position of ultimate harmony or begin within the current state of fallen confusion. My proposal is that both are necessary and neither perspective can be negated without distortion. This in itself requires a type of paradoxical imagining as the proposition, "the world is and is not fallen" establishes a sort of theological paradox about paradox—that the "impossible and the contradictory" both is and is not a full reality. Perhaps an approach that incorporates the need at times to venture the other side of reason might in the end turn out to be a more rational path to the place of permanent reconciliation.

We are now in a position to respond to the question: what role, if any, does paradox assume in Christian dogma? At a fundamental level all theology is an exploration of the question "who is God?" Once some notion of divine existence has been accepted, the subsequent response tends to follow: "how can I relate to Him?" This second question can only be answered sufficiently by considering a third: "how does God relate to the world?" These three foundational questions will serve as our framework for examining various central tenets of orthodox Christianity to discover if they entail logical paradox. Given the titanic scope of this task and the practical limitations imposed, the response to these questions will incorporate sources from a range of periods and traditions in an attempt to demonstrate the pervasiveness of these paradoxes rooted in the Bible and sustained throughout patristic, medieval, and modern scholarship.

WHO IS GOD?

Trinity: plurality and unity

We begin, then, by asking, "Who is God"? And why might paradox be considered a necessary part of His nature? Before we respond, it should of course be pointed out that the phrasing of this question is inherently problematic since the concept of divine simplicity means it is incorrect to speak of God as made up of composite parts. When John pronounces, "God *is* love," he is not implying that God possesses love as a characteristic. The distinct absence of the predicative article in John's proclamation emphasizes how God's essential being is indistinguishable from the quality of love that He perfectly embodies. If it is shown that there is a paradoxical component to the divine nature then paradox, like love, runs deeper than mere association and should properly be considered coterminous with His very being.[47]

There does not appear to be anything paradoxical or even mildly controversial with the acceptance of John's answer to the question "who is God?" He tells us "God is love" and we have understood this within the context of divine simplicity and inferred that God is within Himself the supreme quintessence of this quality. The logical problem arises when we comprehend that God's love is independent of any created being and so He must in Himself participate in a co-eternal community of love and thus we arrive at the logical conundrum of the Trinity.

Richard of St. Victor (1112–1173) believed that if God is not triune, then neither is He the supreme embodiment of love. "Sharing of love," he explains, "cannot exist among any less than three persons."[48] Even though Richard admitted that the internal coherence of the Trinity goes beyond human comprehension, he nonetheless believed that upholding a paradoxical description of the Triune God was a matter of the utmost theological significance, chiefly in order to maintain the Johannine position that love is the nucleus of God's being. The doctrine of the Trinity is, from a purely rational perspective, one of the most overtly baffling beliefs of the Christian religion. The central problem is that the doctrine defies the logical principle that something numerically one cannot also be numerically three. The Athanasian Creed states: "the Father is God, the Son is God, and the Holy Spirit is God; and yet they are not three Gods, but one God."[49] The Creed seems to affirm the impossible that one God is contained in three separate hypostases, which are permanently interwoven and uniquely distinct: "neither confounding the persons nor dividing the substance."[50] However, is it really unavoidable for Christian faith that the believer subscribes to the rigid Athanasian description of the Trinity?

It is not immediately clear that strict adherence is necessary, particularly since there is no explicit reference to "the Trinity" within Scripture.[51]

47. Aquinas' famous discussion on esse/essentia can be found in chapter 4 of *De Ente et Essentia* in which he argues that God's essence is identical with his existence.

48. Richard of St. Victor, *Book Three of the Trinity*, 388.

49. Athanasian Creed (*c.* 500 A.D).

50. Ibid.

51. A certain amount of skepticism has arisen surrounding a definition of the Trinity as three distinct persons sharing one divine substance due to the discovery that an expressly Athanasian statement on the Trinity is a medieval insertion into the original biblical text. The Johannine comma, as it is called, states: "For there are three that bear record in heaven, the Father, the Word, and the Holy Ghost; and these are three in one" (1 John 5.7–9). Owing to the evidence that this phrase is not genuinely canonical, some regard the principle of "three in one" as potentially misleading.

As such, the paradoxical account of three persons united in one substance was deeply contested in the early church, chiefly by Sabellius (early third century) and Arius (*c.* 256–336). Sabellius offered a resolution to the conflict by describing the Father, Son, and Spirit as different appearances or manifestations of one deity. Sabellius sought to stress God's supreme singularity, and did so by denying his diversity. This departs from the Athanasian account because it denies the permanent embodiment of these expressions. The Creed, however, requires the belief that the Father, Son, and Spirit are eternal incarnations and not merely historical appearances.

An alternative divergence from the Athanasian Creed that also avoids a paradoxical understanding of the Trinity is the denial of divine *homoousios* (one substance) and the description of God as *homoiousios* (like substance). This is the position of Arianism, which holds that unity can only be achieved by making the Son and Spirit separate, inferior deities. Arianism seems on the one hand to make sense of certain biblical passages that testify to a hierarchy within the godhead, for example, Christ's admission: "the Father is greater than I."[52] But Arianism encounters a problem with conflicting statements such as Christ's testimony that "I and the Father are one."[53] A further attempt to dissolve the apparent logical contradiction of the Trinity is the account of *Tritheism*, which overemphasizes the distinction between the persons of the Trinity to the point of espousing a belief in three separate deities.

The particular appeal with Tritheism is that one can continue to promote the belief that "God is love" because love can be eternally and mutually existent between the three deities. Yet, according to the creed, the distinctions between the divine persons exist without division (though their unity is also without uniformity). Richard likewise accepts plurality within the divine nature, but unity is also championed as an equally integral aspect.[54] In what follows, the vital tensions of this paradox (unity and plurality) will be explored individually to establish whether the paradoxical character of the Trinity is a necessary, accidental or merely apparent feature of Christian doctrine.

---

52. John 14:28.

53. John 10:30.

54. "Now observe how incomprehensible is that coequality of greatness from every viewpoint and in every respect in that Trinity where unity does not lack plurality and plurality does not go beyond unity!" Richard, *Book Three of the Trinity*, 396.

Unity of substance

> *But the Godhead of the Father, of the Son, and of the Holy Spirit*
> *is all one, the glory equal, the majesty coeternal.*
>
> ATHANASIAN CREED

Richard describes the importance of expressing true unity of substance within the Trinity as "the overwhelming indivisibility of that oneness of God within which all things are banded together as one in the possession of a transcendent unity."[55] A "transcendent unity" in Richard's account affirms, in line with the Creed, that the persons of the Trinity are co-equal, co-eternal, and in essence identical. He writes, "Not only is what each person is completely the same; but each one is what each other is. And so, supreme simplicity is in each; true and supreme unity is in all together."[56] Richard's view of co-equality at the transcendental level consists in identicality. At a human level, co-equality equates to mutual similitude, but not necessarily identicality. Yet at the divine level if equality does not amount to sameness then, as Richard demonstrates, equality cannot be correctly applied, since their perfection requires a symmetry of pre-eminence.

A similar argument applies to the assertion of co-eternality: the triune attribute of eternity must be identical, as eternality has no degrees. As Richard affirms, "[t]here no one is greater than another, no one is less than another; there no one is before another; no one is after another."[57] Further, since Christianity holds that God is immutable, it is fundamental for Richard to emphasize that the divine persons exist co-eternally, as there is "no variation or shadow due to change"[58] in the triune God. There is nothing in the assertion of God's unity of substance that is by itself strikingly paradoxical, but we must now turn to the other side of the tension, the plurality of persons in the Trinity, whilst keeping in mind the necessity of his unity.

---

55. Richard, *The Twelve Patriarchs*, in *The Complete Works*, 129.
56. Richard, *Book Three of the Trinity*, 395.
57. Ibid., 394.
58. Jas 1:17.

Plurality of persons

> *For there is one person of the Father, another of the Son, and*
> *another of the Holy Spirit.*

ATHANASIAN CREED

Richard balances his account of absolute unity by also affirming in imperative terms the true plurality of God. He starts from the premise that God's
love is supremely perfect and supremely good and claims that charity is
a necessary part of goodness and therefore infers that God must be fully
charitable. Supreme charity for Richard is contingent upon the presence
of reciprocal and co-equal persons on whom to bestow charity, and from
whom to receive. Richard asserts that God's aseity is such that He cannot
depend on created beings to respond to divine charity, since this situates
the divine nature in potentiality, relying on created beings to articulate His
fullness. As a result, Richard contends, there must be a plurality of persons,
who are equal in majesty and eternally distinct in order to partake in infinite, supreme charity or love: "in Divinity it is impossible for two persons
not to be united to a third."[59]

Richard's account of the Trinity thus confirms the utter oneness of a
thing that is numerically plural. To accept both poles of this statement is
a logical paradox because the two premises held together contradict each
other. C. FitzSimons Allison phrases the paradox of the Trinity as a question
to which he can give no rational answer: "it is clear that the New Testament
teaches nothing of three gods, it is equally clear that there are significant
distinctions between Father, Jesus Christ, and the Holy Spirit. They are distinct, they are related, they are one. How can this be so?"[60] Despite the fact
that the coherence of the immanent Trinity surpasses human comprehension, Allison and Richard both agree with the Creed that the utter unity and
complete diversity of God is a necessary paradox.

Although, as we have noted, the particular word "Trinity" is not a
biblical expression, there are, however, numerous examples affirming both
unity and diversity within Scripture. When asked what is the most important commandment Christ answers: "Hear O Israel: The Lord our God, the
Lord is one."[61] This is held in tension with the designation of Christ himself

---

59. Richard, *Book Three of the Trinity*, 388.

60. Allison, *The Cruelty of Heresies*, 72.

61. Mark 12:29.

as "Lord" and "God."[62] In "The Great Commission" Christ testifies to the union and the diversity of the Trinity by instructing the apostles to "make disciples of the nations baptizing them in the name of the Father and of the Son and of the Holy Spirit."[63] What is significant here is that Christ refers to the "name" of the three persons as a singular appellation. These three distinctions are elsewhere shown to be eternally existent, as Christ claims that the Father loved him "before the foundation of the world"[64] and that there was (and is) a mutual indwelling and relationship between the Father and the Son prior to the existence of creation.[65] This suggests that Sabellianism and Arianism are not wholly satisfactory representations of Christian belief.

Karl Rahner writes, "the Dogma of the Trinity is an absolute mystery which we do not understand even after it has been revealed."[66] Richard suggests that although we cannot understand the mystery of the Trinity, we can know (through grace) that the Trinity is a mysterious unity of plurality. He believes that spiritual encounters enable humanity to sense the immanent Trinity and that Scripture facilitates participation in the economic Trinity. In his use of paradox, Richard is presenting what he sees as the best description of reality. He does not seem to be putting forward a logical paradox in order to confuse or mystify, but because to dispense with either God's unity or his plurality lessens the supremacy of His love.

To conclude: Richard represents the view of orthodox Christianity when he outlines the Trinity: "individuality in persons and unity in substance and equality in majesty."[67] The account of God's triunity expressed by Richard and the Athanasian Creed thus appears to be a precise and necessary description of God's essence, despite being paradoxical and in many ways unintelligible. Richard's account of the Trinity is in a basic sense then, unreasonable and nonsensical. However, to maintain that love is who God is and not merely an attribute contingent upon creation requires, as we have seen, the belief in a true diversity of persons within supreme singularity. Hence, for believers, the significance of the paradoxical status of the Trinity is that it allows Christians to describe God as the one, true, Supreme Being without diminishing the perfection of His love.

---

62. Thomas hails Jesus: "my Lord and my God" (John 20:28, see also 2 Pet 1:1; Rom 9:5; Titus 2:13; and John 10:30–33).

63. Matt 28:19.

64. "You loved me before the foundation of the world" (John 17:24).

65. Cf. John 17:5.

66. Rahner, "The Problem of the Concept of the Person," 51.

67. Richard, Book Three of the Trinity, 381.

Incarnation: divine and human

Christianity's answer to the question "who is God?" is principally located in the person of Christ. St. Paul declares him "the image of the invisible God";[68] the outward revelation of God's inner nature. John records Jesus' own claim: "whoever has seen me has seen the Father," which presents a direct union between the man Jesus and the transcendent Godhead. The writers of the Bible are clear that the manifestation of God in Christ is not partial or lacking in any way, but, rather, the complete and unadulterated essence of God. "In him the *whole fullness of God* dwells bodily." Significantly, as Thayer's lexicon points out, in this phrase Paul uses the word θεότης rather than θειότης signifying not merely divine qualities or attributes present in Christ, but the very essence and true nature of God. Accordingly, an essential way to investigate "who is God?" is to ask the question, "who is Jesus?"

A typical response to the question "who is Jesus?" is "the Son of God" and certainly this is a scripturally accurate affirmation containing within it the incomprehensible, beauteous, and mystical union of God himself preposterously made man. However, the trouble with this phrase is that this meaning is often not what is understood. The desire for cognitive ease has slowly dissolved the paradoxical tension so "the Son of God" has been subsumed into our everyday grammar and these words come to mean a simple description of Jesus' patriarchal lineage. Over-familiarization has eroded the outrageous meaning and has left us with the impression that there is nothing terribly illogical about God begetting a son; we have lost sight of the true scandal that in the incarnation God begat God.[69]

At base, the logical conflict involved in the doctrine of the incarnation pertains to the belief that Christ exists as a single hypostasis with two natures, which are united and yet remain distinct. The definition agreed on at Chalcedon states the following: "we all with one accord teach men to acknowledge one and the same Son, our Lord Jesus Christ, at once complete in Godhead and complete in manhood, truly God and truly man."[70] An inherent property of being human is not to be divine and the same would seem to be true of the reverse.[71] Framing the point as a matter of logic, Aristotle

---

68. Col 1:15.

69. The Nicene Creed (325 AD) preserves the logically problematic notion of God conceiving God. Here, Christ is described as "the Son of God, begotten of the Father, God of God, Light of Light, very God of very God, begotten, not made, being of one substance with the Father."

70. The Fourth Ecumenical Council held in Chalcedon in 451.

71. H. Lawrence Bond describes the union of two natures in Christ as "a union without mixing, compounding or comingling of the infinite and finite." He makes the

has informed us that "it is not possible that it should be simultaneously true to say that the same thing is a man and is not a man."[72] Yet this appears to be the affirmation of Chalcedon—Christ is properly a man insofar as he is fully human and he is by definition not a man because he is fully divine. The breach with the law of non-contradiction is explicit as the Chalcedonian definition provides a deliberate and adamant refusal to elevate one nature over another: "This is called the Absolute Paradox at which Reason can only stand appalled."[73]

How can we even begin a rational discussion of what seems such a rationally indefensible idea? Michael Goulder expresses the view that, "Paradoxes are a sign that we have to stop thinking anthropomorphically; and they are a tool for thinking theologically about the one who cannot be comprehended with clear-cut univocal terms."[74] It is clear that in discussing the incarnation we are trying to overcome some of the limits of univocal expression by contemplating one being who is "truly God and truly man." We need to find some manner of simultaneous identification, as it is the simultaneity of both God and man that seems to be central to any discussion of the incarnation.

In seeking a departure from "clear-cut univocal terms," perhaps an artistic depiction could prove helpful, since visual expression may have the potential to outwit the sequential tendencies of language by juxtaposing images in a single frame and thus preserving the call within Christian theology to have things "both ways." Jeremy Begbie has pointed out how music provides a useful analogy for the incarnation in the way that two notes can simultaneously occupy the same space and interpenetrate each other without losing or altering their identity: "we are reminded that we are not dealing with two realities vying for the same space, but with God interacting with the world intimately, without violating it or merging with it, liberating it to be more fully itself."[75] Similarly, an appeal to artistic interpretations of the incarnation might assist the attempt to find out whether what appears *prima facie* as a logical contradiction is actually as paradoxical as it seems.

It may not be immediately obvious that the ruling of Chalcedon represents the best possible description of the incarnation, and this has been evidenced by the various so-called heresies within the history of Christianity

important point that "coincidence does not make one thing into another." *Nicholas of Cusa*, 47.

72. Aristotle, *Metaphysics*, 1006.b.32, 10.

73. Campbell, "Lessing's Problem and Kierkegaard's Answer," in *Essays on Kierkegaard*, 77.

74. Goulder, *Incarnation and Myth*, 52.

75. Begbie, *Beholding the Glory*, 146.

that seek to avoid encountering paradox in the person of Christ. Nowhere is the desire to quash or circumvent paradox more evident than when considering the mystery of the incarnation. Arianism, for example, denies Christ's full divinity by claiming that God the Father created Christ his human son, who was not previously existent. We can see in Tristán de Escamilla's painting, *The Adoration of the Shepherds*,[76] that Christ has the potential to be mistaken for an Arian portrayal. In particular, the exposure of Christ's genitalia twinned with Mary's maternal attitude acts to emphasize his humanity. Additionally, there is a clear depiction of God the Father, with a banner proclaiming his majesty, but the light from heaven disperses by the time it reaches the child in the manger and we are left with a God in heaven and a baby on earth, but no definite link between them. This illustrates the underlying problem of Arianism, since Christ is not identified as a true member of the Trinity; he is neither co-eternal nor co-equal with the Father, which therefore shatters God's triunity.

The heresy of Docetism, conversely, holds that Christ was human in form, but his nature was solely divine. During the fourth century, Apollinarius of Laodicea (*c.* 310–*c.* 390) argued that Christ had neither a human mind nor soul. This became known as the heresy of Apollinarianism and was ruled as heterodox by the Council of Constantinople in 381. Geertgen tot Sint Jans' painting *The Nativity at Night*[77] could be considered as the presentation of a Docetic Christ, who lacks true identification with humanity. In this case, the Christ-child appears alone in the center detached from any physical affection. This gives him an unearthly appearance, which makes it difficult to recognize him as the Son of Man. Mary does not assume a maternal or nurturing pose (as we see with Tristán) but an attitude of worship. This makes the crib symbolic of an altar with the angels surrounding it adopting a similar pose. Notably, the front of the crib is left open inviting the viewer to approach the picture in a likewise reverent manner. Geertgen thus shows us a picture of God on earth who does not appear incognito as the Son. The solemnity of Mary, twinned with equally sombre angels, identifies Jesus as God's son but not Mary's. It is this lack of unity that is problematic in the Docetic heresy.

Nestorianism entails a different divisive heresy in the claim that Christ existed as two separate persons, not as a single unified hypostasis. The antithesis of Nestorianism is the heresy of Eutychianism, which mingles the two natures of Christ to the extent of claiming that Christ is a single subsistence

76. Luis Tristán de Escamilla, *The Adoration of the Shepherds* (1620), Fitzwilliam Museum, Cambridge.

77. Geertgen tot Sint Jans, *Nativity, at Night* (1484–90), National Gallery, London.

with one nature. Although the various deviations from Chalcedon outlined above are considered heterodox, they reveal that the paradoxical status of the incarnation is not easily accepted. Whilst conceding the Christian imperative to uphold two antitheses in harmony Cameron Freeman also accepts that "this kind of paradoxical language looks downright absurd, ridiculous, and even mad."[78] Thus when we are prepared to admit that the impossible combination proposed by Chalcedon frustrates the intellect and embarrasses the ego we can understand the appeal of heresy, and by contrast delineate the uncompromising bounds of orthodoxy.

At this stage, we might ask why Christianity insists that Christ be conceived of as an indivisible duality, or to phrase the question as Anselm does: *Cur Deus Homo*? Why God Man? The answer centers upon the doctrine of salvation and the belief that only a human could be the sacrificial substitute for the sin of humanity, and only God could be the perfect unblemished sacrifice to reconcile a fallen world. In the words of Anselm, the atonement for sin is something that "none but God can make and none but man ought to make, [thus] it is necessary for the God-man to make it."[79] By asserting that Christ is fully God and fully man, Christianity is able to state that Christ alone is distinctive in his enhypostatic existence, and as a sinless being is unique in his salvific capacity, and yet as man, he is able to take the place of everyman. Let us examine these two poles further to determine why Christian teaching seems to require such an oxymoronic conjunction.

Only God could be the perfect, sinless sacrifice for sin.

And being made perfect he became the source of eternal salvation to all who obey him.

Hebrews 5:9

The author of Hebrews locates the all-sufficiency of Christ's sacrifice in his divinity: "For Christ has entered [. . .] into heaven itself, now to appear in the presence of God on our behalf."[80] Here it is clear that Christ's offering as a sacrifice for the sin of man is of another order to the sacrifices made by the high priests in the earthly tabernacle; Christ presents himself on the divine altar as a divine sacrifice. Karl Barth stipulates that the world needed

78. Freeman, *Post-metaphysics*, 172–73.
79. Anselm, "Why God became man," in *The Major* Works, 223.
80. Heb 9:24.

to be redeemed by God, for God, and therefore agrees that only a divine sacrifice could be sufficient. Barth relatedly proposes that the one sent must also be the sender: one essence, in a triune mode. He writes: "His divine unity consists in the fact that in Himself He is both the one who is obeyed and another who obeys."[81] By maintaining the importance of "divine unity," Barth tells us that Christ is fully divine and in full unison with the divine essence.

Only man could be the substitutional sacrifice for everyman.

> *But when the fullness of time had come, God sent forth his Son, born of woman, born under the law, to redeem those who were under the law, so that we might receive adoption as sons.*
>
> GALATIANS 4:4-5

The acceptance that Jesus Christ is fully divine begs an important question concerning how divinity can "stand in" for humanity. Logic would appear to dictate that if it is man who has fallen then it must be man who atones. The author who describes Christ as "the exact imprint"[82] of divine nature also stipulates, "he had to be made like his brothers in every respect, so that he might [. . .] make propitiation for the sins of the people."[83] Propitiation here designates a satisfactory sacrifice, effecting atonement on behalf of the one(s) for whom the sacrifice was made. On this point, Paul is clear: "For as by the one man's disobedience the many were made sinners, so by the one man's obedience the many will be made righteous."[84] In order for Christ's propitiation to be redemptive for humanity, his mode as man must not simply be an appearance, but a full participation in the essence of "man-ness." The apostles are told in the book of Acts "this Jesus, who was taken up from you into heaven, will come in the same way as you saw him go into heaven."[85] In other words, Christians believe that Christ will retain his humanity even after his ascension. Hence, insofar as Christ is man, his human mode is the manifestation of his soteriological mission presently, historically, and perpetually.

81. Barth, *Church Dogmatics 4.1*, 201.
82. Heb 1:3.
83. Heb 2:17.
84. Rom 5:19.
85. Acts 1:11.

The supreme mediator

> *For there is one God, and there is one mediator between God and men, the man Christ Jesus.*

1 TIMOTHY 2:5

Something of the careful balancing of the above two poles can be seen in Guido Reni's painting, *The Adoration of the Shepherds*.[86] Reni depicts light spilling from heaven, which illuminates and enhances earth. This portrayal seems to merge the divinity of Geertgen's painting with the humanity of Tristán's. On the one hand, Reni's shepherds are gathered around the child, cradled by his mother. In this sense, the observer can relate to Christ as the Son of Man. Yet, at the same time, the child is illumined by celestial light from above. The stable is otherwise dark (unlike Trisatán's stable where the divine light is almost superfluous to the brightness of the painting), which gives the luminescent child a sense of the otherworldly. Reni thus effectively communicates Christ's divine presence *and* his human status by depicting the tension between his manhood and his divinity in a single frame.

R. T. Herbert preserves the paradoxical status of the incarnation in his reflection upon the logical unintelligibility of the doctrine with reference to Kierkegaard's employment of the term "God-man." He concludes, "whether it was written inadvertently in confusion or intentionally in moments of great clarity is here a question that need not concern us [. . .] the idea is absurd; it does involve contradiction; it is a breach with all thinking; it is unintelligible."[87] The "breach with all thinking" is the proclamation that Christ has "assumed a human being into the unity of his person, so that the two natures, namely, the divine and the human, are one person."[88] These two natures, according to the Chalcedonian definition are fully united and remain fully distinct, a single subsistence existent both in time and not in time, dying whilst never ceasing.

So we are left once again with a proposition that appears to carry us "beyond and above the light of the law and reason": one plus one equals one (and two). From a secular perspective, it would seem that humans cannot engage meaningfully with such an absurd concept. Yet, Christianity claims not to promote a fantasy of hypostatic insanity but instead regards the dual natures of Christ as a necessity for entering into a salvific relationship with

86. Guido Reni, *The Adoration of the Shepherds* (c. 1640), National Gallery, London.
87. Herbert, *Paradox and Identity in Theology*, 83.
88. Anselm, "On the Incarnation of the Word," in *The Major Works*, 252.

God. The paradoxical formulation of the doctrine of the incarnation seems to be the most precise and perhaps even the only way of holding onto all aspects of this complex reality. The Chalcedonian definition is therefore not a matter of mere rhetoric, but a meaningful and indispensable articulation of orthodox Christian teaching, *by virtue* and not in spite of its non-compliance with the law of non-contradiction.

And so it would seem that the Christian cannot opt out of this transgression of the possible; there is no rational alternative that can be sought. This is why religious contemplation can be thought of as a type of unknowing, requiring the deconstruction of knowledge as the basic premises of Western logic fall short of conceiving the paralogic of Christ. If we insist on the unqualified application of the law of non-contradiction, we cannot at the same time meet the requirements of orthodoxy. For believers, a satisfactory response to the question, "who is God?" is directly answered in the person of Jesus, though this will not of course appease the skeptic or the heretic who, like Philip, may fail to grasp the mystical unity of Christ's dual nature.[89] Therefore, the imagination must be invoked and rationality subdued in order to behold Immanuel—God in our midst, God incarnate.

HOW CAN I RELATE TO GOD?

Knowledge: veiled and disclosed

The second foundational question asked by theologians, which follows naturally from the establishment of a supreme being, concerns our ability to know and relate to the divine. The triune emphasis on God as love indicates a relational impulse at the core of God's character and the incarnation traverses the gulf between divinity and humanity as God reveals himself in human form. Together, these two tenets of faith indicate it is both likely and possible that man can have a relationship with God. At base, any connection we make with a person, or even an object, assumes that we possess a certain amount of knowledge of that to which we are relating. We could not, for example, claim to have a relationship with a "qwoozleig" because we know nothing about this neologism. "God," however is not a neologism and His character is depicted in a variety of sources so there seems no problem *per se* with relating to the divine. Of course, we would not

---

89 "Philip said to him, 'Lord, show us the Father, and it is enough for us.' Jesus said to him, 'Have I been with you so long, and you still do not know me, Philip? Whoever has seen me has seen the Father. How can you say, "Show us the Father?" Do you not believe that I am in the Father and the Father is in me?'" (John 14:8–10).

presume to possess exhaustive knowledge of God, but we can know Him in certain ways comprehensible to us, the attributes He has chosen to make known, whilst accepting that other characteristics belong to a supremely transcendent nature.

This appears to accord with St. Paul's letter to the Corinthians, in which he tells them: "for now we see in a mirror dimly, but then face to face. Now I know in part; then I shall know fully."[90] It seems therefore that there is no need to apply the term paradox in this situation, as it is clear that the current condition of human knowledge of the divine is limited to some extent. This conclusion does not breach the law of non-contradiction since it accepts that God is in part immanently knowable and in part uniquely transcendent. In a similar way I know certain things about a friend without possessing an entire comprehension of that person and the same seems to be true of our relationship with God.

However, Paul complicates his own statement in the very same letter by describing a supreme unity between the believer and God's inmost Spirit. He writes:

> these things God has revealed to us through the Spirit. For the Spirit searches everything even the depths of God. For who knows a person's thoughts except the spirit of that person, which is in him? So also no one comprehends the thoughts of God except the spirit of God. Now we have received not the spirit of the word, but the Spirit who is from God, that we might understand the things freely given us by God. And we impart this in words not taught by human wisdom but taught by the Spirit [. . .] we have the mind of Christ.[91]

Here, Paul presents knowledge of God as a union with the "mind of Christ" and the Spirit of God, which is God himself. Paul believes Christians inherit this Spirit of true comprehension, albeit subject to the limitations of the finite mind, which presents us with a very different reality to the previous description of seeing through the mirror dimly. What can we make of this? One possibility is that Paul is mistaken in one or both of the accounts. Another option though is that taken together they point towards a reality, which individually they are inadequate to express. This, of course, is the logic of paradox. Paul seems to be holding in tension two opposing ideas, neither of which Christian teaching appears willing to relinquish: God *both* reveals himself in His essence *and* remains transcendent, even within His immanent self-disclosure. Is this, however, a paradox?

90. 1 Cor 13:12.

91. 1 Cor 2:10–13, 16.

These twin aspects emerge later as a split between Western and Eastern traditions, of which Aquinas and Palamas may be taken as respective representatives (although both traditions reveal their own paradoxical core at the center of the question of God's knowability). Thus, Aquinas teaches that although human knowledge of God is limited, through grace humanity is raised to an intellectual vision of *the divine essence itself*, whereas Palamas conceives of supreme unknowability as an exclusive property of divinity. As we shall see below, Palamas believes that we can participate in and know God through his *energies* (the outward expression of his internal essence), whilst upholding an impenetrable barrier between God's infinite essence and human finite comprehension.

Let us consider the differences in more detail in order to ascertain how the accounts differ, why there is a paradoxical tension in uniting them, and if this act of unification is a necessary one. At this stage, the concern is solely with Christianity's presentation of how God is known by humanity, I do not seek to promote one perspective above the other, merely to explore whether maintaining the language of paradox is unavoidable if we are to attempt an orthodox response to the question of human knowledge of God.

Aquinas: graced intellect

Whoever has seen me has seen the Father

JOHN 14:9

"It must be absolutely granted," states Aquinas, "that the blessed see the essence of God."[92] In order to understand Aquinas' position, we must begin, as he does, from Augustine's premise that "God is truly and absolutely simple."[93] Aquinas develops the doctrine of simplicity to emphasize that God's properties are identical with who He is. So, for example, God does not merely *have* love, but He *is* love. As a consequence of this belief, Aquinas observes, "His nature does not differ from His 'suppositum'; nor His essence from His existence [. . . ,] therefore, it is clear that God is nowise composite, but is altogether simple."[94] The corollary of this proposal is that we cannot think of God in part, as God is not composed of parts. In God, all attributes are united because He is simple. This implies that to posit God at all

---

92. Aquinas, *Summa Theologica*, 1, q.12. a.1., ans.

93. Augustine, *De Trinitate*, iv, 6,7.

94. Aquinas, *Summa*, 1, q. 3 a. 7.

is to posit God entirely, and as man has a composite nature and discursive reason, it would seem that it is impossible for him to comprehend infinite simplicity.

The problem as presented by Aquinas harkens back to our discussion of John's proclamation "God *is* love"; if God cannot be known in His essence, He cannot be known *at all* because His essence *is* His existence. Aquinas thus acknowledges "it is impossible for any created intellect to see the essence of God by its own natural power,"[95] though he proceeds to suggest that "to see the essence of God is possible to the created intellect by grace."[96]

According to the Thomist emphasis, then, it is accurate to state that a human can know God's essential nature if God grants an individual the gift of graced intelligibility. An important aspect of Aquinas' description is that unintelligibility in relation to the divine is to do with the inborn fallen capacity of human intellect, rather than any inscrutability within God's nature. Fundamentally, Aquinas insists, "Since everything is knowable according as it is actual, God, who is pure act without any admixture of potentiality, is in Himself supremely knowable."[97]

Palamas: essential inaccessibility

No one has ever seen God
JOHN 1:18

An alternative theory of the knowledge of God proposed by Palamas distinguishes between God's energies and His essence and he believes it is possible to establish certain positive predicates about God's essential being whilst insisting that these predicates stem from God's energies and *not* the divine essence itself. "The Holy Fathers," he writes, "affirm unanimously that it is impossible to find a name to manifest the nature of the uncreated Trinity, but that the names belong to the energies."[98] Palamas, like Aquinas, is cautious to retain God's integral unity by explaining that "God complete is

---

95. Ibid., 1, q. 12, a. 4, ans.

96. Ibid., a. 4, sed contra.

97. Ibid., a. 1, ans. The Thomist position is of course not quite so clear-cut; he retains at some ultimate level the principle of absolute transcendence or the *via eminentiae*. However, for the sake of demonstrating the Eastern/Western divide I have emphasized Aquinas' commentary on the supreme knowability of God.

98. Palamas, *The Triads*, 97.

present in each of the divine energies,"[99] but unlike Aquinas, he insists that unknowability is an indissoluble property of divine nature. This creates a somewhat paradoxical expression: "God is entirely present in each of the divine energies [. . .] although it is clear that He transcends all of them."[100]

Palamas seems to be insisting that God's energies both manifest and preserve His unknowable essence. He tells us that God is both beyond His creation *and* intimately accessible through it. Palamas' theory of knowledge of the divine combines concealment with disclosure, insisting that God's essence is unknowable, but is nonetheless directly experienced through His energies. Like Aquinas, Palamas believes the experience of God is related to an individual's state of grace.

At this stage, to summarize, we have seen how Aquinas stipulates that if God is known, He is known in His essential simplicity, whilst maintaining that humanity lacks the noetic faculty to comprehend God (hence the necessary elevation of the intellect through grace). Palamas, on the other hand, states that God can give Himself to be known in some sense via his energies, whilst remaining eminently transcendent. Put simply and formulated according to the principal of non-contradiction, Aquinas states, "we think of God and yet we cannot think of God," and Palamas proposes, "we can think of God and yet God cannot be thought of." The first is an epistemological problem concerned with how humans relate to God (since through the grace of God in revelation, humanity is able to comprehend the incomprehensible). The second is concerned with the category of revelation, according to which Palamas maintains God is both within His self-disclosure and yet remains distinct from it. We may identify the underlying continuity of these views with reference to a third perspective.

Denys: beyond unknowing

Both Aquinas and Palamas are concerned with the question of knowability—how can we comprehend an ineffable God? Denys approaches the question by asking the reverse—how can we not comprehend God? He writes, "[t]here is nothing in the world without a share in the Beautiful and the Good."[101] Denys celebrates the paradoxical dynamism of knowledge of God. He writes: "it says of the One who is present in all things and who may be discovered from all things that he is ungraspable and inscrutable."[102] This

99. Ibid., 95.

100. Ibid., 95–6.

101. Pseudo-Dionysius "The Divine Names," 77. Cf. Rom 1:19–20.

102. Ibid., 105, based on Rom 11:33.

claim is based on a latter part of the same Pauline epistle in which its author professes: "Oh, the depth of the riches and wisdom and knowledge of God! How unsearchable are his judgments and how inscrutable his ways!"[103]

In identifying God as a being "who may be discovered from all things" and who yet remains "inscrutable," Denys affirms, like Aquinas, the division between God's simple being and human discursive understanding while maintaining a Palamite emphasis of cataphatic self-disclosure through cosmic expressions. This is why Denys praises God in the tongue of paradox proclaiming him the source of all, as every name and yet above any name and as the nameless one.[104] This communicates that from a Christian perspective it is proper, and indeed praiseworthy, to uphold the paradox that God cannot be known and cannot not be known.

Nicholas of Cusa: approaching the unapproachable through learned ignorance

Denys' appeal to paradox is not in the manner of one who, having exhausted every other option is forced to turn to paradox as an inadequate last resort. On the contrary, as Bagger observes, "he [Denys] argues that the individual can paradoxically achieve more adequate 'mystical' knowledge of God through 'unknowing.'"[105] Here we find the surprising suggestion that paradox is not only the most suitable way to conceive of God, but despite the cognitive frustration it entails, paradox is also the mode of thought offering greatest clarity and insight. Drawing upon Denys' mystical theology, Nicholas of Cusa sets out his own theory of relating to God starting from the perplexing concept that wisdom is gained through "learned ignorance." "One will be the more learned," he writes, "the more one knows that one is ignorant."[106]

In order to make sense of Cusa's mystagogical theory of "learned ignorance," he—like Aquinas, Palamas, and Denys before him—begins by stating that God is wholly unapproachable. In *De Visione Dei,* he writes: "no one can approach you because you are unapproachable [. . .] what could be more absurd than to ask that you give yourself to me, you who are all in all?"[107] By appreciating God's supreme unknowability Cusa infers that human reasoning must be abandoned as a means of reaching enlightenment.

---

103. Rom 11:33.

104. Pseudo-Dionysius, *The Divine Names,* 54.

105. Bagger, *Uses of Paradox,* 33.

106. Cusa, *De Doctrina Ignorantia,* in *Nicholas of Cusa,* 1.1.4.

107. Cusa, *De Visione Dei,* 7.25.

He invokes "the wall of paradise" as a metaphor for the dwelling place of God, which is also representative of the coincidence of opposites. We are told, "the wall's gate is guarded by the highest spirit of reason, and unless it is overpowered, the way in will not lie open."[108] Hence, Cusa affirms that our vision of God cannot be grasped by rational thought. He draws a distinction between *ratio* (discursive reason) and *intellectus* (a direct vision) and emphasizes that knowledge of God can only be experienced via *intellectus*. This is why for Cusa the divine is known only through unknowing since we must overcome our discursive reasoning and unweave our rational mind to become fully ignorant in order that we might begin to learn. Only then, believes Cusa, "we may incomprehensibly contemplate Christ above all reason and intelligence."[109]

Cusa's paradoxical language concerning the coincidence of knowing and non-knowing can appear complicated and problematic. Yet, Cusa believes the experience of divine insight is "a *simplicity* where contradictories coincide."[110] Perhaps above all, what Cusa's writing suggests is that there is something mystical about paradox, something that can only be grasped and not reasoned. Moreover, this mystical approach to knowledge at a fundamental level threatens the metaphysical heritage of the West. Freeman remarks, "the language of paradox is post-metaphysical in that it requires none of the traditional metaphysical postulates of the Western philosophical tradition."[111] The basic concept of *post*-metaphysics by definition calls for the dissolution of the onto-theological framework, and so a paradoxical account of faith, situating itself outside this tradition, immunizes itself against rational repudiation. Thus, in the wake of God's death, the charge of irrationality has itself become absurd.

In summary, the response to the question "how can I relate to God?" began by identifying the logical problem present in a Christian account of knowledge of God and it is this: God gives Himself to be known and yet He remains simultaneously unknown. We described how the gap between created things and their Creator both is and is not absolute; it is traversed both "positively" according to Aquinas and "negatively" by Palamas. Important to both is the unique combination of presence and eminence which reveals a God who is "not only beyond all affirmations but all negations too."[112] Cusa's mystical account of incomprehensible contemplation gestures

---

108. Ibid., 9, 37.

109. Cusa, *De Doctrina Ignorantia*, 3.11.245.

110. Ibid., "Epistola" 3.263 (my emphasis).

111. Freeman , *Post-metaphysics*, 6.

112. Pseudo-Dionysius, *Mystical Theology*, 104.

to a non-rational form of knowing in the paradoxical recognition that true understanding can only emerge out of a state of ignorance.

Thus, we are left in an orthodox theological space—whether that orthodoxy is defined from an Eastern or Western point of view—and yet it is also a space that troubles the law of non-contradiction, for, as Denys has suggested, "God is beyond understanding and reason," and simultaneously "beyond every denial."[113] It seems in this instance that Christianity accepts the contravention of the law of non-contradiction as the most accurate way of describing reality in order to allow for "the paradoxical coincidence of God's transcendence and immanence."[114] The theologians discussed in this section seem to praise mystery and paradox as the commendable attempt to speak of God and the joyous inevitability of falling short of supreme clarity, as if the partial is itself a proper expression of divine majesty. A paradoxical account of knowledge of God—which advertises a conceptual inadequacy in pointing towards a complex reality—therefore seems to be both more workable and a more accurate reflection of that which is the case (in spite of its contradictions) than a purely "rational" resolution.

The human will: bound and free

If it is the case that we can, in the sense outlined above, possess knowledge of God and so relate to Him, the question arises, to what extent am I free to pursue or to refuse this relationship? And here we find ourselves wrestling with another conundrum. The conflict surrounding the Christian description of the will revolves around the insistence that entering into a salvific relationship rests upon humanity's autonomous choice to follow God, but this is twinned with the simultaneous teaching that this "choice" is fully reliant on God's grace. On the one hand, the Bible indicates that justification is "through faith [. . .] for all who believe,"[115] while on the other hand it makes clear that salvation is achieved solely "by grace [which] is not your own doing; it is the gift of God."[116] A logical problem arises from the conflicting descriptions of the status of the will prior to salvation: humanity is both captive by sin[117] and dead in our transgressions,[118] but we are somehow

---

113. Ibid., 141.
114. Bagger, *Uses of Paradox*, 32.
115. Rom 3:22.
116. Eph 2:8.
117. Rom 7:6.
118. Eph 2:1.

required actively to repent and turn away[119] from the deadness and imprisonment that is our own antecedent nature.

In considering whether the foregoing conflict is in fact a paradox—rather than a contradiction arising from the deficiency of language—I shall appeal to a range of poetical works, alongside theoretical explanations, that attempt an articulation of the struggle between autonomy and grace, and autonomy and sin. This is once again because art is perhaps better equipped to signify "impossible" combinations than propositional discourse, since it is free to speak ambiguously and polysemously. Poetry may therefore signify a state that seems both inconsistent and true without needing to justify rationally how or why this is the case.

As in previous sections, in order to test the validity of my contention—that central tenets of Christian doctrine involve real and not merely apparent paradox—I shall begin by considering the *sed contra*—in this case, the possibility that there is no paradoxical dimension to the Christian conception of our desire for God as argued by, for example, open theists. Open theism is a recent challenge to the traditional understanding of divine prescience as it insists that since the future is unfixed; it is therefore logically unknowable by God.[120] It is effectively a position of incompatibilism, maintaining that the only way human autonomy can be genuine is if God's knowledge of the future is limited.[121] Hence, according to proponents of open theism, there is no logical paradox between human willing and divine grace, since God has no knowledge of the contingent future and the choices people will make.

One of the principal concerns of open theism is to uphold the absolute freedom of human choice, and, as William Hasker articulates there are two ways to preserve autonomy. Before Hasker settles on the annulment of divine prescience he accepts that an alternative response would be to countenance the paradoxical status of the antinomy, embracing both free will and foreknowledge. However, Hasker quickly suppresses the legitimacy of this possibility, saying that for him logical contradiction is a sufficient reason

---

119. Acts 3:19.

120. Although challenges to God's omniscience have been present throughout the history of Christianity, the term "open theism" stems from Richard Rice's book, *The Openness of God: The Relationship of Divine Foreknowledge and Human Free Will* published in 1980. The ideas promoted continue to cause significant debate, particularly in evangelical circles, and much has been published on this controversy, including William Hasker, *God, Time and Knowledge* (1998). William Lane Craig and Millard Erikson among many others have argued fervently against the advocacy of open theism as compatible with biblical Christianity.

121. "We hold that comprehensive divine foreknowledge is incompatible with libertarian free will for creatures." Hasker, *Providence, Evil and the Openness of God*, 97.

for rejecting a theological position.[122] In contrast to open theism, Augustine upholds the traditional duality stipulating that on the one hand every event that occurs does so according to divine will, and on the other hand God's foreknowledge does not force the future to happen.[123] Rather, his foreknowledge perfectly reflects and initiates the causal order in which human wills operate freely. Yet there is still a sense in which God's involvement in the world initiates the created order and also brings about all second-order, or intra-creational causes. Hence, Augustine appears to be claiming that divine causation and human causation paradoxically coincide; God can—incomprehensibly—cause human free actions and yet allow humans to remain entirely volitional.

Augustine argued against seeking a "solution" to this contradiction by refusing to enter into what he believed was Cicero's false dichotomy: "He [Cicero] constrains the religious soul to this dilemma, forcing it to choose between two propositions: either there is some scope for our will, or there is foreknowledge. He thinks that both cannot be true; to affirm one is to deny the other. If we choose foreknowledge, free will is annihilated; if we choose free will, prescience is abolished."[124] Anselm supported Augustine's embrace of the co-existence of both poles and described the human will as "both slave and free."[125] He explains: "because it cannot return from sin, it is a slave; because it cannot be robbed of rectitude it is free."[126] We can now discern the poles that constitute the paradox of the human will: on the one hand, our freedom to turn to God and the grace which compels us; and on the other, our freedom to turn away from God and the sin that binds us. The central questions to be asked are: "to what extent are humans responsible for their own salvation?" and, "is sin ever a choice?"

Turning to God

Man shall not quite be lost, but sav'd who will,
Yet not of will in him, but grace in me.

MILTON, *PARADISE LOST*, BK III

122. Ibid., 152.

123. "The fact that God foreknew that a man would sin does not make a man sin. [. . .] A man does not sin unless he wills to sin; and if he had willed not to sin, then God would have foreseen that refusal." Augustine, *City of God*, 195.

124. Ibid., 191.

125. Anselm, "On Free Will" in *The Major Works*, 189.

126. Ibid.

As Milton's God announces, a tension exists between the fallen nature of humanity and the Christian account of salvation, which considers human freewill as imperative in order to turn from the sinful nature to receive God's grace. The quotation tells us that only he who wills shall be saved, but emphasizes the necessity and perhaps the primacy of God's grace. It is the moment of turning that seems to be paradoxical, since relationship with God is an apparently autonomous decision, yet it is only desired and further, only made possible, through God's prevenient grace. Anselm describes the logical problem of the Christian account of salvation: "no one preserves this received uprightness without willing it. But no one can will it without having it. And no one can have it at all accept by grace."[127] "The question arises," Anselm acknowledges, "from the fact that the Bible speaks at times as if that grace alone seems to avail for salvation and free choice not at all, but at other times as though our salvation entirely depends on free choice."[128]

Repentance (μετανοέω) means to change one's mind, to turn actively away from, and this, it would seem, requires a re-orientation of the will. Repent is an active verb suggesting that the individual is not being acted upon from without, but is internally motivated: "Repent therefore, and turn again, that your sins may be blotted out."[129] Here Peter's address demands action on behalf of the listeners. Paul's letter to the Romans likewise insists that righteousness comes "through faith in Jesus Christ for all who believe."[130] As with Milton's God, Paul recognizes that man is "sav'd who will," thus making it clear that man is responsible for his own salvific relationship.

Whilst there is clarity in the plain assertion that *metanoia* is contingent on the will of the individual, we cannot ignore the second half of Milton's couplet: "Yet not of will in him, but grace in me." This begs the question—is the Christian concept of grace incompatible with free will? "For by grace you have been saved," Paul writes to the Ephesians, "And this is *not your own doing*; it is the *gift* of God."[131] This would seem to suggest that God's role in our communion with him is sovereign and that man is fully reliant on his grace. The idea of salvation as a gift is a recurrent description in the Bible and carries the implicit connotation that the will of man is the latent recipient of divine graciousness, rather than an active, enabling force. The real force or the catalyst of salvific action is Christ, who acts on behalf of mankind. Paul tells the Romans, "all have sinned and fall short of the glory

---

127. St. Anselm, "De Concordia" in *The Major Works*, 456.

128. Ibid., 452.

129. Acts 3:19.

130. Acts 3:22.

131. Eph 2:9 (my emphasis).

of God, and are justified by his grace *as a gift*, through the redemption that is in Christ Jesus."[132] In this quotation, we can identify God as the instigator and gift-giver, Christ as the catalyst, and man as the recipient. Again, there is internal coherence within this description if we leave aside the earlier evidence that Christianity preaches the significance of personal choice.

Yet, to add a further complication, we need to take account of Paul's observation that "all have sinned" and as a result depend on God's gift of grace to save man from himself. R. A. Markus, commenting on Augustinian theology, describes the post-lapsarian condition as "a *massa damnationis* from which no one can escape save by the divine gift of grace that cannot be requested."[133] Markus appears to imply that human free will is not free outside of relationship with God. The notion that sin might work against human freedom creates an additional conundrum: do we sin volitionally or are we determined by our fallen impulses?

Turning away from God

Oh wearisome condition of Humanity!
Borne under one Law, to another bound:
Vainely begot, and yet forbidden vanity,
Created sicke, commanded to be sound.

LORD BROOKE, "CHORUS SACERDOTUM"

Brooke's lament at the seemingly impossible situation of humanity articulates the confusion over the role of human will in turning away from God, or in "choosing" to sin. He describes the fall as being born under the law of sin, of being bound to its disposition by inheritance, an idea that is given particular emphasis by using the poetic form. The rhyme scheme Brooke employs acts to impress his theological concern upon the reader; the link between "humanity" and its innate condition of "vanity" is uniquely brought to the surface in this poem as the rhyme and meter enhance the relationship between the two words. Augustine writes on a similar theme: "even when we do see what is right and will to do it, we cannot do it because of the unruliness of our mortal inheritance,"[134] thus indicating that *cupiditas* operates apart from the will and corrupts the decision to strive for what

132. Rom 3:23.
133. Armstrong, *Cambridge History*, 484.
134. Augustine, *On Free Choice of the Will*, 106.

is pure. However, this same unruliness, according to Anselm, is itself the product of radical human freedom. "The human race," he writes, "fell into this helplessness precisely because it freely abandoned the state of justice."[135] Hence, there seems to be a contradiction developing: through our free will, we sin, and through sin we forfeit our free will.

In certain parts of the Bible, one can find definite evidence to support the contention that man is not enslaved by sin, and his free will enables him to turn away from iniquity. Paul, for example, warns the Galatians, "do not use your freedom as an opportunity for the flesh,"[136] which suggests that sin is a choice. Augustine likewise proposes that man's fallen nature and his subsequent inordinate desire testifies that the will is indeed free. He writes: "Only its own will and free choice can make the mind a companion of cupidity."[137] Augustine lists lust, greed, and anger as examples of inordinate desires; man acts out of cupidity when he surrenders to these impulses. One could suggest that these are external determining factors, corrupting the rational mind from outside. Augustine counters this attack on human autonomy though, arguing, "nothing can make the mind a slave to inordinate desire except its own will,"[138] endorsing the belief that man has a real choice to seek what is good or to embrace his cupidity. How, then, do we respond to the following passage?

> And you were dead in the trespasses and sins in which you once walked, following the course of this world, following the prince of the power of the air, the spirit that is now at work in the sons of disobedience—among whom we all once lived in the passions of our flesh, carrying out the desires of the body and the mind, and were by nature children of wrath, like the rest of mankind. But God, being rich in mercy, because of the great love with which he loved us, even when we were dead in our trespasses, made us alive together with Christ—by grace you have been saved.[139]

The problem seems to be that there is no motivation prior to the receipt of grace for humans to turn towards God and away from the course of the world. If it is the case that outside of salvation man is in submission to

---

135. Anselm, "De Concordia," 462.

136. Gal 5:13.

137. Augustine, *On Free Choice of the Will*, 17.

138. Ibid., 71.

139. Eph 2:1–5.

a "yoke of slavery"[140] and held "captive"[141] by "the law of sin and death,"[142] how is it that he is free to choose to contradict his own "sicke" nature and yearn for a relationship with God? Again, we find an unlikely dual emphasis that, on the one hand, a human has the opportunity to choose to follow God,[143] and that, on the other hand, a human is chosen by God to be His follower.[144] A man is somehow required to choose to follow God's path when he is already on another course, a choice that God has predestined but from which man can turn away.

It is not enough simply to conclude that free choice often coexists and co-operates with grace. Nor is soteriology purely linear in the sense that man, using first his will must desire God, who only then pours out his grace. Instead, it seems necessary for Christianity to affirm that *both* free will *and* grace co-exist within the nature of man, and although there is an element of contrary logic in the suggestion that fallen man, with inordinate intent would desire grace, before knowing grace, this contradiction seems indispensable. Anselm remains emphatic that "grace always aids one's innate free choice."[145] Here, Anselm understands grace as both the path to and the destination of relationship with God.

John Donne's "Holy Sonnet" contains strong language of contradiction and rapture, conveying the sensation that true freedom is born of a sort of divine "bondage": "Take me to you, imprison mee, for I / Except you'enthrall mee, never shall be free, / Nor ever chast, except you ravish mee."[146] The Bible testifies to this paradoxical sentiment. Paul, for example, speaks of being "set free from sin, [to] become slaves of righteousness,"[147] and declares he is "going to Jerusalem, constrained by the Spirit."[148] This use of the verb "constrained"—(*deō*) meaning "to bind, tie or constrain"—is similar in its overtones to Donne's experience of rapture, a baffling freedom in chains through God's grace that is both resistible and ineluctable. It would seem, then, that the Christian understanding of human free will as at once both

140. Gal 5:1.

141. Rom 7: 6.

142. Rom 8:2.

143. Deut 30:19 "I have set before you life and death, blessing and curse, therefore choose life, that you and your offspring may live."

144. Eph 1:4–5, "he chose us in him before the foundation of the world, that we should be holy and blameless before him. In love he predestined us for adoption through Jesus Christ, according to the purpose of his will."

145. Anselm, "De Concordia," 455.

146. Donne, "Holy Sonnet" in *The Metaphysical Poets*, 84.

147. Rom 6:18.

148. Acts 20:22–23.

bound and free is indeed a paradox, in which humans freely seek what their fallen nature prevents.

To summarize our discussion, we have witnessed two paradoxes that emerge in a faithful examination of Christian teachings on the human relationship with God. Firstly, we noted how the Bible insists that sin is always a choice, whilst also acknowledging the ineluctable pull of *cupiditas*. Secondly, we observed the tension that exists between God's overwhelming, irresistible grace and the importance attached to seeking a relationship as a free and personal choice. Given the central significance of both sin and salvation in Christian doctrine, we are dealing with vital tensions for the believer, not merely meaningless contradictions that could be solved if we were to relinquish one side of the paradox. To override the contradictory status, one must either downplay the reality of sin or negate the sovereign force of grace, neither option of which Christianity appears to endorse. There seems to be no alternative which satisfies both classical logic and orthodox Christianity, thus once more, by virtue of its deviance from the law of non-contradiction, the Christian understanding of how we choose to turn towards or away from divine communion is most accurately described in paradoxical terms.

HOW DOES GOD RELATE TO THE WORLD?

Space: everywhere and nowhere

In classical theism, a relationship with God is not exclusively humanity's venture. As we have seen God reciprocates, and in a sense also initiates, human relationships. In the Bible, God establishes covenantal unions with individuals, families, and nations and reiterates these promises throughout: "I will be your God and you will be my people. And I will walk among you and will be your God, and you shall be my people."[149] Whether literal or metaphorical, God's presence in our world is articulated by all religious traditions, and a close proximity between God and creatures is palpable throughout Scripture. It is natural, therefore, for the theologian to inquire into the nature of God's extension in space, since there seems to be several logically incompatible aspects.

Firstly, there is the belief that God is the extrinsic author of space, who remains external to the dimension while also dwelling within it. Secondly, that the same God, who abides nowhere and everywhere, entered

---

149. Lev 16:12. This is a recurring epithet in the Bible, which is repeated, slightly rephrased, on thirty-three separate occasions.

and embodied human space in the specific incarnate form of Christ. And thirdly, the belief that one can choose to enter into God's presence while maintaining His inescapable omnipresence. As in our previous examples, the breach with the law of non-contradiction seems explicit and "incorrigibly so." The claim is less rationally problematic if the Bible is viewed entirely poetically, the event of the cross symbolically, and the Holy Spirit as a purely imaginative aid. However, the case for paradox surfaces if one insists, as many Christian traditions do, on God's actual physical presence, be it in the Eucharist, the person of Christ or the heart of an individual. The primary question that these apparently paradoxical statements about divine space provoke fixes on the location of God: where is he?[150]

The Bible speaks at times of God's spatial transcendence—"The LORD is exalted for he dwells on high"[151]—and at other times of His immanent relationship with creation, "Behold, the dwelling place of God is with man."[152] If either one of these aspects is under-emphasized it becomes possible to dispense with the paradoxical character of divine space. If, however, the duality is upheld, then Christianity would seem to be claiming that God as Christ appeared in human space, whilst as creator God exists in no space, and simultaneously, as Spirit he inhabits in every space. The paradox of divine spaces thus appears to be threefold, and for the sake of clarity, I will deal with each instance individually.

God is outside space and inside space

God as the Creator is described in Genesis as producing "an expanse" from an absence of form, and causing earth to emerge and situate itself from out of the void. From this, we understand that God is the cause of all space and as such, He is prior to space; that is to say, He has existence independent of the dimension, and exceeds even heaven, insofar as it is conceived of as spatial. When speaking of the Christian God, we therefore understand this to be a God whom "heaven and the highest heaven cannot contain,"[153] who is "Most High" and "does not dwell in houses made by hands."[154]

---

150. Nicholas of Cusa addresses the issue of God's spatial extension and characteristically evokes paradox as the best means of communicating God's presence. He writes that "its [the universe's] circumference and centre is God, who is everywhere and nowhere" *De Doctrina Ignorantia*, 2.12.162.

151. Isa 33:5.

152. Rev 21:3.

153. 2 Chr 6:18.

154. Acts 7:47–48.

On the other hand, if we consider God as Creator in relation to His creation, it would seem that His involvement is necessarily intimate and imminent. In a panentheistic sense, God is "excessively" spatial insofar as every grain of creation is completely full of godliness, even though His presence exceeds it. Catherine Pickstock explains that "although God is not in a place for He is infinite, He is not non-spatial, for He situates sites themselves. And therefore He is the eminent (or pre-eminent) space of preoccupation which gives space its job in advance of itself."[155] Pickstock indicates that is proper to speak of God's spatial identity in his continual situation of space and the ineluctable imprint of the Creator upon his creation.

Perhaps, then, we are speaking of a God who is supra-spatial, who through the act of creation has embedded Himself in every space and yet, as the Scriptures assert, is not contained within any particular space. This conception is complicated further if we bear in mind that His involvement in created space is not only as the abstract force behind creation and as the invisible occupant of all space, but also as the personal God who enters into covenants with His creation. God, the Bible seems to affirm, dwells nowhere, everywhere, and uniquely with humanity: "Behold, the dwelling place of God is with man. He will dwell with them, and they will be his people, and God himself will be with them as their God."[156] We witness in this verse God's promise to situate Himself in a personal way within the creation, which He both transcends and immaterially dwells within.

God who is everywhere and nowhere is incarnate in the specific person of Christ

Within Christian theology, God's promise to dwell with man has the additional paradoxical dimension of dwelling *as* man: "For in him the whole fullness of deity dwells bodily." Here, and as we saw earlier, the New Testament makes clear that the incarnation does not simply involve a part of the transcendent divine Spirit becoming temporarily involved in humanity, but rather the "whole fullness of deity" eternally incarnate. Augustine describes the paradox thus: "He didn't depart from heaven, when he came down to us from there; nor did he depart from us, when he ascended into heaven again. I mean, he was still there while he was here."[157] The logical problem of Christological space seems to have emerged as a matter of the modality of presence. Christianity succumbs to Arianism if it denies the spatial

155. Pickstock, *After Writing*, 229.

156. Rev 21:3.

157. Augustine, *Sermons*, III 7:263, 219.

existence of the divine nature in the person of Christ, but at the same time, Christians continue to worship God in his transcendent Spirit-mode.

Something of this logical contradiction is staged in Southwell's poem "New Heaven, New Warre": "Come kiss the maunger [*sic*] where he lies / This is your bliss above the skies."[158] "This is your bliss," writes Southwell, emphasizing that the Christ child is no mere representation, but divine bliss itself. Southwell's poetic description involves the surreal stretching of the deitic "this" to encompass an infinity at once elsewhere, "above the clouds" *and* present in the manger. It is a vivid and precise dramatization of the paradox, which refuses to play down either the divinity of the incarnate Christ or the immanent transcendence of the Creator, who as Augustine reminds us was "there whilst he was here."

It is possible to enter into the presence of an omnipresent God

In addition to divine space understood as both a specific incarnation and as a transcendent beyond, Christians also believe that God has omnipresence in the world. This means there is no space that is outside God. The psalmist describes the inescapability of God's omnipresence:

> Where shall I go from your Spirit?
>
> Or where shall I flee from your presence?
>
> If I ascend to heaven, you are there!
>
> If I make my bed in Sheol, you are there![159]

In these lines, the believer describes God's omnipresence as sovereign no matter the location of the individual (in both a physical and a spiritual sense). This would indicate that there are no degrees of God's nearness and that there is no qualitative distinction in his spatial extension. This in turn appears to suggest that God is equally present in the saint as in the sinner. Nevertheless, Paul's prayer for the Ephesians is that they "may be filled with all the fullness of God,"[160] thus suggesting that it is indeed possible to experience different gradations of God's presence. Paul reminds the Ephesians they "were *separated* from Christ, *alienated* from the commonwealth of Israel and *strangers* to the covenants of promise, having no hope and *without God* in the world." He explains how "in Christ" those "who once

---

158. Southwell, "New Heaven, New Warre," in *The Metaphysical Poets*, 40.

159. Ps 139:7–8.

160. Eph 3:19.

were *far off* have been *brought near*."[161] The varying range between man and God dominate his language. It may of course be the case that Paul is simply describing a spiritual distance using the metaphorical language of physical distance. However, could it also be that there is some metaphysical correlate between the dimensions of spirit and space? This begs the further question, is the spiritual realm in any sense spatial?

Certainly, orthodox Christianity distances itself from Gnosticism by insisting that the physical body is a dwelling place for the Spirit of God.[162] Hence, when talking about human spiritual nearness, there is some warrant to suggest that this entails physical involvement. Hopkins depicts something of the spiritual occupation of physical space in his poem, "As Kingfishers Catch Fire": "For Christ plays in ten thousand places, / Lovely in limbs, and lovely in eyes not his."[163] Once more, we find an emphasis on the physical presence of God's Spirit. Hopkins' depiction of Christ "playing" in human limbs connotes movement and vitality; there is a sense of both Puck *and* Ariel in Hopkins' Christ, a sort of elemental essence, who is at once both an "airy spirit"[164] and a "merry wanderer."[165] A close reading of Hopkins' poem might also notice the absent or elided copula in the phrase "lovely in limbs, and lovely in eyes not his." "Lovely," as an adjective, implies a missing "he is" and in the omission of the copulative verb, the lines stage a passing over from "plays" to an inferred but unsignified "is." One of the effects of this literary device is that it subtly figures a mode of presence "without being." This reading complicates what perhaps at first glance seems like Christ acting as a puppeteer, giving the illusion of life in otherwise motionless limbs. For, by eliding the predicative verb, Hopkins invests Christ with a more subtle presence in the lives of individuals, participating in and sharing their experience, whilst in some sense simultaneously remaining beyond them, rather than dominating or controlling their motion.

However we interpret the nuances of Hopkins' imagery, the poem ultimately illustrates the biblical teaching that God is crucially involved in particular space and dwells *with* man and *in* man. Yet, this is only one aspect of the Christian description of divine space for, as we have seen, the multifarious portrayals in the Bible suggest that it is possible to "come into

---

161. Eph 2:12–13 (my emphasis).

162. "Your body is a temple of the Holy Spirit within you" (1 Cor 6:19).

163. Hopkins, "As Kingfishers Catch Fire," in *The Poems*, 90.

164. Shakespeare's description of "Ariel," in the Dramatis Personae of *The Tempest*.

165. Shakespeare, *A Midsummer Night's Dream*, Act 2 Sc 1.

[the] presence"[166] of a god who "fill[s] heaven and earth."[167] The Scriptures tell us we can be separated from God and yet we cannot escape Him; that He dwells fully beyond heaven and completely within humanity; and that as pure spirit He sustains us physically.

As with the preceding instances, I am not making the case that God's extension in the universe is an ultimate paradox. Rather, I am saying that from an anthropocentric perspective the Christian depiction of divine space inevitably has this appearance. Catherine Pickstock identifies "apparently oxymoronic combinations" as "a definitive feature of liturgical space."[168] She describes the goal of the liturgical journey as "simultaneously attained and postponed, before and after, within and without, 'to hand' and distant."[169] Pickstock does not present this as a logical problem that needs to be solved, but rather as the "radiant and excessive structure of divine space," which she believes "defamiliarize[s] mundane topologies."[170] The word "defamiliarize" is vital here, as it suggests that when considering how our conception of space corresponds to aspects of divinity, it is necessary to accept that human perspective and human understanding is limited, and not to assume that our customary perspective is the ultimate or exhaustive viewpoint.

Paradox, as we have seen, is a necessary description of divine space if we are to speak of the multi-faceted spatial depictions of God without sidelining or overemphasizing certain aspects. Perhaps Christianity, more so than any other religion, cannot avoid encountering tensions when considering God's manifestation in the universe because of the affirmation that the same God who is transcendent spirit has become God incarnate. Trevor Hart forcefully affirms that central to the Christian message is that "God has 'taken flesh' and given himself to be known in faith."[171] That is to say, God, as "Immanuel" has given Himself to be known in space and in corpus. When Christ ascends to the heavenly realm he assures his disciples "I am always with you, to the end of the age,"[172] whilst affirming that at the same time he is seated at the right hand of the Father.

Drawing this section to a close, we have identified three main areas of spatial complexity and discussed in greater depth why Christianity insists on retaining positions that seem to contradict each other. The Bible testifies

166. Ps 95:2.

167. Jer 23:24.

168. Pickstock, *After Writing*, 229.

169. Ibid.

170. Ibid.

171. Hart, *Through the Arts*, 3.

172. Matt 28:20.

to God's presence both in the world *and* outside the world, both in Christ *and* in man. These tensions importantly allow Christians to speak of God's transcendence *and* His immanence and therefore make possible the bilateral relationship between humanity and divinity. Hence, when Christians describe entering God's presence the expression is more than just figurative, the incarnation testifies to a physical God, one who dwells fully in the human body of Christ, one who enters into, and animates his creation whilst not being intrinsically spatial or limited to any co-ordinate.

Pickstock's account of the liturgy's figuring of a perspective outside our quotidian conception of space indicates the limitations of the human vantage point and this has prompted us to suggest that our sense of spatial possibility is a provisional, this-worldly perspective. That is not to say it is wrong, merely that it is necessary to acknowledge a difference between God's ultimate vantage point and our limited one. To return to de Lubac we might conclude that this dichotomy follows inevitably from the belief that "proper view always eludes us." To assume, as logic dictates, that the regulative principles of space governing our experience must apply absolutely and in all instances would lead to the restriction of God's omnipresent Spirit and the sacrifice of several of God's integral manifest modes. Christians must therefore be prepared to suggest that our common-sense comprehension of spatial properties does not provide an exhaustive perspective, and that in some instances paradoxical both/and expressions come closer to an accurate to representation of divine reality.

The kingdom: already and not yet

Following our discussion that God is in some sense spatially manifest in creation, we might conjecture that there is a similarly complicated temporal aspect to God's involvement. Scripture asserts that as omnipotent Creator God's sovereignty is clearly identified in the world "now" however, the full establishment of His reign is described as being "yet to come." This puzzle of God's kingship also involves the conviction that Christians themselves encounter a temporal dislocation in communion with God as they too experience the tension of existing in the "already" and the "not yet." Kierkegaard expresses this unified duality in his assertion that "man is [. . .] a synthesis of the temporal and the eternal."[173]

It might be possible to avoid logical difficulties if we describe the parallel existence of two separate time frames, one in which the kingdom of God is established "now" and one in which it is "yet to come." This is

---

173. Kierkegaard, *Concept of Anxiety*, 85.

not so much a paradoxical temporality, rather a co-existent duality. C. S. Lewis expresses such an idea analogically in his Narnia chronicles. Lucy observes: "However long we seemed to have lived in Narnia, when we got back through the wardrobe it seemed to have taken no time at all [...;] once you're out of Narnia, you have no idea how Narnian time is passing."[174] This depicts a reality where there are two distinct temporal dimensions that exist in parallel, sometimes the children participate in one, sometimes the other. However, this analogy is not quite accurate because the children can only be in one or the other at any given time. If we heed Kierkegaard's description of man as a *"synthesis* of the temporal and the eternal," it would seem that the Christian participates in *both* time frames simultaneously, experiencing the not-yet within the already.

In a similar manner, we could speculate on a duality of kingdoms and suggest that the kingdom of God exists in its own eternal realm, but is "not yet" manifest on earth. The theological problem encountered with a sole emphasis on the otherworldly nature of the kingdom, is that it confines the eternal kingdom to a perpetual "not yet." This construal enters into the same linguistic trap articulated by White Queen in *Through the Looking-Glass* when she offers Alice "'jam every other day.' 'It *must* come sometimes "jam to-day,"' Alice objected. 'No, it ca'n't,' said the Queen. 'It's jam every *other* day: to-day isn't any *other* day, you know.'"[175] Roger Holmes both affirms and opposes the Queen's staunch denial that jam can ever arrive. He explains, "by its nature tomorrow must come, also by its very definition it can never come. The Queen promises Alice jam, but tells her in the same words that she can never have it! Here is one of the famous paradoxes connected with time."[176] "Can we ever have jam in the todayness of tomorrow?" Holmes asks, and answers both yes and no. Similarly, the paradox phrased in theological terms asks: "Can we ever have the kingdom of God in the not-yetness of today?" Likewise, the answer appears to be both affirmative and negative; hence, we are dealing with a unity of two distinct time frames, situated both in the world and not in the world. Let us now take each component of the paradox separately in order to see if either aspect can be dispensed with or de-emphasized.

174. Lewis, *The Silver Chair*, 330.

175. Carroll, *LG*, 150.

176. Holmes "The Philosopher's Alice in Wonderland," in *Aspects of Alice*, 215.

The kingdom of God is now

The Bible appears to speak patently of the arrival and actual presence of the kingdom of heaven manifest presently on earth. Jesus describes God's kingdom as not only "near"[177] but also "at hand"[178] and as already "come upon"[179] those whom he has healed. Christians claim that the supreme reign of the kingdom of God is experienced now, even *before* the event of the parousia. The belief that Christians already share in the awaited vision is not dressed up in the language of Gnosticism but seen as a real immanent manifestation.[180] "We therefore have to understand," urges Moltmann, "the liberating activity of God as the immanence of the eschatological kingdom of God, and the coming of the kingdom as the transcendence of the present lordship of God."[181] One of the most significant verses in support of this describes the situation of the kingdom as having already arrived, unseen, "in the midst" of man: "Being asked by the Pharisees when the kingdom of God would come, he answered them "The kingdom of God is not coming with signs to be observed, nor will they say, 'Look, here it is!' or 'There!' for behold, the kingdom of God is in the midst of you."[182]

The kingdom of God is not yet

Whilst it is has been shown that the Bible speaks at times as if the kingdom of heaven is already constituted on earth, there seems to be equal stress given to the contrary claim that the consummation of the kingdom is still a future event, and that it is an eschatological glory, not yet visible in its fullness. "*Then comes the end*," Paul writes, "when he delivers the kingdom to God the Father after destroying every rule, every authority and power."[183] Reinforcing this, Christians may point to the continuance of poverty, illness, death, and war as evidence that the kingdom of God is not yet established, since the Bible promises the end of all these sufferings. Perhaps

177. "Heal the sick and say 'the kingdom of God has come near to you'" (Luke 10:9).

178. "The time is here, the kingdom of God is at hand" (Mark 1:15).

179. "But if it is by the Spirit of God that I cast out demons, then the kingdom of God has come upon you" (Matt 12:28).

180. "The christophanies were not interpreted as mystical translations into a world beyond. They were viewed as radiance thrown ahead of itself, the radiance of God's coming glory on the first day of the new world's creation. And these christophanies are daylight visions, not phantasms of the night." Moltmann, *The Way of Jesus Christ*, 219.

181. Ibid., 98.

182. Luke 17:20–21.

183 1 Cor 15:24; See also 2 Pet 1:10–11 and Matt 7:21.

most significantly, Christ instructs his followers in the Lord's Prayer, which includes the phrase: "your kingdom come, your will be done, on earth at it is in heaven."[184] Here, we see again a demarcation between how things will be and how things currently are, a schism it seems, between the kingdom of heaven and the kingdom of earth, demonstrating that the richness and vitality of God's kingdom has yet to come.

The teachings concerning the shape of the kingdom of God also have paradoxical character, for they reverse or invert commonplace assumptions concerning human ideas of precedence.[185] For example, Christ's caution: "Whoever finds his life will lose it, and whoever loses his life for my sake will find it."[186] In reference to the salvation of humanity, this is the suggestion that the losing of life is not a temporal instant but a perpetual sinking into eternity and rising again into the midst of linear time. The conflation of time and eternity is intrinsically Christological in the sense that "time is the form chosen by Christ (and thus adequate) for manifesting the true eternity."[187] Therefore, if the kingdom of God is experienced as "already and not yet," so too is the belief in salvation: man is already saved, but the fullness of his salvation awaits the eschaton. Man, it seems, is saved from this world, in order to take his place in that same world, just as God's kingdom is "not of this world,"[188] and at the same time "in the midst"[189] of it.

This paradox is summarized in the declaration that the heavenly kingdom has thus arrived in full and yet remains veiled, and Christians in a state of constant rejoicing and simultaneous anticipation. The kingdom yet to come is frequently anticipated as arriving from without, and whilst this is in some sense an accurate depiction, it has also emerged that this ultimate vision will come from within, as a centrifugal force, in a world created and sustained by God, but fallen in every respect. Moltmann writes: "The Gospel does not merely bring the kingdom of God to the poor; it also discovers the kingdom of the poor which is God's kingdom."[190] From this perspective, the kingdom of heaven illumines what is already on earth, which further emphasizes the paradoxical character of the "already" and "not-yet" world.

---

184. Matt 6:10.

185. Cf. Luke 14:11; Rom 6:18; 1 Cor 3:18.

186. Matt 10:39.

187. Balthasar, *La Theologie de l'Histoire*, quoted in Hepburn, *Christianity and Paradox*, 76.

188. John 18:36.

189. Luke 17:21.

190. Moltmann, *Way of Jesus Christ*, 100.

The conclusion of this section can be summarized by Moltmann's description of "this last of days" as "also the dawn of the new creation,"[191] a dawn that rises on the old creation, illuminating the old and dispelling darkness so that the city of man is transformed into the kingdom of God both from within and without. As we have seen, Christians claim a current access to these future spiritual gifts, further testifying that the church preaches the "already" in what is still a "not yet" world. To speak of God's kingdom in non-contradictory terms seems to involve covering up or skirting around a multiplicity of biblical passages, which are in tension with one another. Aristotelian logic tells us that either the kingdom has come, or it has not—it cannot both be present and absent as this paradox maintains. Yet, as we have seen, Christians believe that through Christ they gain access to a recovered paradise whilst recognizing that at the same time they live in a fallen world and as such are under the many limitations to that beatific vision. Therefore a faithful articulation of God's relationship to the world involves a departure from common-sense temporality and an acceptance of a paradoxical both/and timeframe whereby one can hold the "already" together with the "not yet."

CONCLUSION: THE WAIT FOR SYNTHESIS

What has emerged from the foregoing discussion is the idea that paradox is indispensable and central to a faithful account of Christian doctrine. In each case examined, it was shown that the paradox could not be reduced to a mere poetic description, or linguistic accident, but rather surfaced as a necessary attempt to hold two contrary ideas together in order to avoid heterodoxy. Freeman concludes likewise: "such a language of radical paradox is quite possibly the only way we can speak of the mystery of God without missing the mark entirely."[192] We are now in a position to address the unanswered questions from the chapter's introduction concerning the distinction between paradoxes used in nonsense literature and the moments of conflicting logic in religious doctrine.

Matthew Bagger defines a paradox as: "a claim that apparently entails a self-contradiction to which one feels at least some inclination to assent because it is supported by at least one form of epistemic authority that one recognizes."[193] The appeal to epistemic authority is akin to the methodology

191. Ibid., 327.

192. Freeman, *Post-metaphysics*, 108.

193. Bagger, *Uses of Paradox*, 3. Bagger acknowledges that "reason, of course, is one form of epistemic authority, but testimony, tradition, the verdicts of specialists or

used in this chapter as we established each paradox by examining important sources of authority within the Christian faith: the Bible, the Creeds, patristic texts, and eminent theologians. In contrast, the paradoxes of literary nonsense do not seem to share the same epistemic endorsement. Bagger describes paradoxes found in fiction as merely "rhetorical" in contrast to those in theology that he deems in some sense "literal."[194]

It might seem obvious that a further fundamental demarcation between paradox in literature and paradox in theology is that theological paradoxes are self-emergent and are therefore both necessary and involuntary, whereas absurd contradictions within literary nonsense are created deliberately by the author. Despite the multifarious protestations of heresy, orthodoxy continues to preach that points of logical conflict in doctrine belong not only to the description but also to the thing described—to both the sign and the signified. Paradoxical language is therefore applied by the theologian to that which is of its nature paradoxical—he has no alternative; the nonsense author, by contrast, elects his absurd discourse.

Yet, is the distinction really so clear-cut? As we saw in the introduction, Deleuze and Lecercle point to a correlation between the absurd linguistic play within nonsense and paradoxical encounters in everyday language and logic. Lecercle refers to both instances of paradox when he writes: "One is caught in the hesitancy of paradox, unable to escape from the perpetual exchange between sense and nonsense."[195] Likewise, the paradox that "I speak words" yet "words speak me" finds a comic incarnation in Carroll's stories because we recognize it as being an ironic aspect of our own speech. Marijke Boucherie situates her account of nonsense literature within the history of hermeneutics and reminds us that the nonsense of Carroll, Lear and Dickens appeared "at the same time as nineteenth-century poets come to terms with the painful realization that meaning does not naturally flow over into language."[196] Here is the suggestion that Carroll's literary nonsense, peppered with absurd puns and paradoxes, actually makes an insightful observation about the way in which communication works and is in this sense as unavoidable as doctrinal paradox.

---

masters, revelation and divination also have the power to render claims credible." 4.

194. "In whimsical or literary moods we may appreciate a rhetorical paradox, but we usually take great pains to avoid a literal paradox [. . . ;] however, one of the most noteworthy features of religious discourse is that it seems exempt from this tendency to shun paradox." Ibid., ix.

195. Lecercle, *Philosophy Through the Looking-Glass*, 108.

196. Boucherie "Nonsense and Other Senses," in Tarantino (ed.), *Nonsense and Other Senses*, 266.

Hence, we cannot entirely divorce religious paradox from literary paradox on the grounds that one is literal and the other rhetorical. Nor can we mark the divide by stating that paradoxes of faith have epistemological credence whereas those found in nonsense are based on pure whimsy. Instead, there seems to be a correspondent appeal to paradox in both theology and nonsense on the grounds that certain ideas and modes of cognition go beyond the limits of linear speech and are best (if not only) expressed through the paradoxical, a conclusion reached also by Howard Kainz:

> The paradoxical conclusion I arrive at is this: *Paradox itself, in literature, religion, and even in philosophy may be the clearest, and even the simplest, way to express concepts which would have diminished force, and even diminished validity, if expressed in normal assertoric speech modes*. In other words, complexities and oppositions in reality and human life are perhaps best captured by paradoxical language.[197]

Reflecting on our findings, we may thus legitimately endorse Stenson's claim that "paradox characterizes the language of religion,"[198] and affirm that the law of non-contradiction does not always hold in theological territory. This leaves us with several options. Firstly, we could conclude that Aristotelian logic is true in all instances, and believe therefore that Christianity is false since it transgresses important logical maxims.[199] Secondly, we might determine that the laws of logic are wrong and ought to be overturned in the face of the existence of central theological paradoxes. As a third alternative, we could propose that both the law of non-contradiction and Christianity are true and suggest that paradoxes demonstrate not that Aristotelian logic or Christian teachings are wrong, but that human understanding is partial and limited.

This third possibility would be accepted by de Lubac who describes paradox as "the search or wait for synthesis," this, he believes, is "the provisional expression of a view which remains incomplete, but whose orientation is towards fullness."[200] As we mentioned previously, the emphasis on future completion suggests that religious paradox is an attempt to express faithfully the inexpressible, accepting that the "dark glass" of perception is

---

197. Kainz, *Five Metaphysical Paradoxes*, 58.

198. Stenson, *Sense and Nonsense*, 39.

199. This is the conclusion reached by Ermanno Bencivenga. He attempts to overcome the religious appeal to paradox by suggesting that the "absurdity invoked by [paradoxical] charges [. . .] are not so much contradictory as just plain stupid." *Logic and Other Nonsense*, 51–52.

200. De Lubac, *Paradoxes of Faith*, 9.

sufficient for now, because of the promise of a future unveiled relationship. Paradox can thus be seen as a celebration of what is presently known and a testimony that there is more to come.

Such a conclusion might in some ways seem unsatisfactory given the human impulse for immediacy and certainty; nevertheless, it seems accurately to reflect Christianity's account of man's current condition. Paul describes our situation as a "groaning" after synthesis.[201] He explains that although we "groan inwardly" we must "wait eagerly" for the hope that is promised. This characterizes the paradoxical nature of Christian reality in which we and the whole creation are groaning after a synthesis that has in one sense been made though is still yet to come. Therefore, the affirmation of paradox in Christianity is a sign of trust in the continual revelation of God's plan for mankind. Humility, then, a central virtue of Christianity, also features as a consequence of accepting the centrality of religious paradox within faith.[202]

An overarching concern in this chapter has been to discredit the assumption that the Christian ought to cover up or modify implausible elements of faith on the basis that logical credibility is the only measure of rectitude. By viewing paradox as the most accurate way to express truths that remain partly veiled, we do not have to negate the validity of logic, in fact, if we hold the law of non-contradiction in tension with Christian paradoxes, this disconnect becomes its own signpost testifying that "the synthesis of the world has not been made." And so it would seem natural (perhaps even logical) that in describing divine reality we inevitably transgress the boundary of rational conceivability and so maybe we should expect theological sense to present itself as logical nonsense this side of the synthesis. The language of paradox is thus the most fitting way we can understand on earth certain harmonies of the kingdom of heaven, which for now we see darkly and must therefore await an eschatological light.

---

201. Rom 8:22–23.

202. We might also speculate that this point of humility is an important departure from nonsense paradox, since Carroll's absurdisms do not tend to engender a feeling of awe, reverence or humility in the same way the acknowledgment of a religious paradox might.

CHAPTER 2

The Anarchic ⎯⎯⎯⎯⎯⎯

NONSENSE AND ANARCHY

THE PRECEDING CHAPTER ON paradox revealed a particular tendency within literary nonsense to defy the law of non-contradiction by uniting opposites and transgressing firm principles of logical. This act of transgression gestures towards a strong element of conflict present within the nonsensical. Jeffrey Stern describes Carroll's frequent recourse to opposition and contradiction as a "rebellious framework." Stern gestures to the barefaced conflict of "nonsense against sense, the dream against the mundane, Wonderland against Victorian England, and so on."[1] Stern's proposal that the basic framework of the *Alice* books is structured by rebellion invites us to consider the prevalence of this theme. The fact that both stories end with Alice's revolt against the prevailing power supports the theory that there is a significant sense of rebellion or anarchy present in the narrative structure of both stories.[2]

How can we characterize this theme of conflict and defiance? Donald Gray observes that there is "now an orthodox interest of twentieth-century

---

1. Stern, "Lewis Carroll the Surrealist," 133.

2. *Alice in Wonderland* ends with Alice overturning the jury stands and knocking down the playing card court: "'Hold your tongue!' said the Queen, turning purple. 'I won't!' said Alice [. . . ,] 'You're nothing but a pack of cards!'" *AW*, 97. In *Through the Looking-Glass* she demolishes the royal banquet crying: "'I can't stand this any longer!' she cried, as she jumped up and seized the tablecloth with both hands: one good pull, and plates, dishes, guests, and candles came crashing down together in a heap on the floor." *LG*, 204.

readers in the subversive and anarchic qualities of [Carroll's] writing."[3] Similarly, Donald Rackin's extensive study of the *Alice* novels has led him to promote the anarchic as a central concept, commenting on the "literal anarchy of Alice's adventures and the metaphysical and moral anarchy they encapsulate."[4] At face value, the word "anarchy" seems to capture something of nonsensical conflict and rebellion,[5] but is this a precise and accurate usage?

The word "anarchy" derives from the Greek *an* "without" and *arcia* meaning "leader" or "ruler." Peter Marshall in *A History of Anarchism* defines the modern usage of the term in accordance with the original Greek: "to describe the condition of a people living without any constituted authority."[6] The idea that authority is un-constituted seems to convey accurately how power works in Alice's worlds. It is not that she encounters an absence of authority figures,[7] but rather that she finds those in the possession of power frequently have their authority undercut, mocked or deconstructed.[8] It would seem, then, that Carroll's nonsense worlds are anarchic in a literal

3. Carroll, *AW*, viii.

4. Donald Rackin "Blessed Rage," in Grey (ed.), *Alice in Wonderland*, Norton Critical Edition, 403.

5. There is also an interesting argument to be made for the presence of anarchy in nonsense by means of its blind following of logic, rather than its undercutting. Both Lecercle and Schwab comment on this peculiar subversion of sense by means of its extensive promotion. Schwab puts it thus: "Nonsense, one could say, beats the system with its own means by imploding it from within. Rather than resulting from a rebellion against law and order, dissolution and anarchy are produced by an overly rigid insistence on rules." Schwab, "Nonsense and Metacommunication," 175. Lecercle makes a similar observation: "Nonsense breaks rules not by forgetting about them, but by following them to the letter, in a deliberately blind fashion." *Philosophy of Nonsense*, 48. This is significant, not only as it once again affirms the theme of rebellion, but also because it champions the anarchic potential within nonsense even when confronted with the opposing view that literary nonsense can hardly be subversive when it relies so heavily on the laws of logic.

6. Marshall, *History of Anarchism*, 3.

7. In fact, the reverse seems to be the case; Cohen acknowledges that "Wonderland is, in fact, overpopulated with downright tyrants, heartless figures of authority. Besides the Queen of Hearts, we have the Caterpillar, the Hatter, the Duchess, the Red Queen, and even Humpty Dumpty—all vying for first prize." Cohen, *Lewis Carroll*, 335.

8. For example, in *Through the Looking-Glass*, the reader is encouraged by Tenniel's illustration to ridicule the tiny, indignant White King, and also by Alice's exclamation: "Oh! *Please* don't make such faces, my dear! [. . .] You make me laugh so that I can hardly hold you!" Even at the first entrance of the Queen of Hearts Alice is unfazed by the royal procession stating: "why, they're only a pack of cards, after all. I needn't be afraid of them!" Carroll, *AW*, 63.

sense, in that they consistently disestablish the constituted power of those in authority.

Yet it is not only in relation to the characters and narrative that the *Alice* stories involve anarchy, but there also seems to be a case for suggesting that the reader experiences a type of imaginative anarchy in the willed suspension of conventional logic and habits of thought. Robert Polhemus believes that a governing principle of Carroll's fantasy worlds involves "considering things from the very opposite of the conventional point of view."[9] This diversion from convention is further emphasized by Cohen when he addresses the question of what, if anything, the *Alice* books mean and concludes: "To understand what they mean, we have to realize that Wonderland and the world behind the looking-glass are mysterious places where characters do not live by conventional rules and that meaning does not play a conventional role. Even the laws of nature, the law of gravity for instance, do not work as they should."[10] The reader, like Alice, has to imagine how to pass a cake round first and cut it up afterwards.

The point here is simply that fundamental to the reading of the stories is the reader's capacity to think in terms that contradict or unsettle the governing principles of the familiar world. The reader must walk with Alice in the opposite direction to her destination in order to arrive there. Unlike many other fantasies where there is a single instance of suspension of everyday logic, Carroll's stories require the reader to enter into an enchanted world, whose narrative authority is recurrently disrupted. With a sudden jolt, Alice is transported from a shop to a rowing boat. Once this activity is established "the oars, and the boat, and the river, had vanished all in a moment and she was back again in the little dark shop."[11] We can find no constituted norms that govern her adventures; a pig could turn into a baby, but then again it might not. Rackin believes that Alice pines for "some familiar signposts of intelligible order,"[12] but this is denied her. There is "no *telos*, no final goal or ultimate 'meaning' [. . . ,] their games are essentially ruleless, circular, and without end—games undoubtedly for 'mad people.'"[13] This radical degree of instability supports the description of the stories as having an anarchic character in the sense that her encounters are without

9. Polhemus "Play, Nonsense, and Games," in *Alice in Wonderland*, Norton Critical Edition, 370.

10. Cohen, *Lewis Carroll*, 143.

11. Lewis Carroll, *AW*, 157–58.

12. Rackin, "Blessed Rage," 399.

13. Ibid., 400.

any permanent or discernible authority and the reader too, like Alice, must try to adjust to a world without any "intelligible order."

At this point we find that nonsense literature has challenged fundamental empirical assumptions such as "I can trust my senses" or "I can verify what is real." In Tigges' anthology of nonsense, Lisa Ede makes a similar case for an anarchic interpretation of nonsense literature on the basis that "because the nonsense world is a play world, it exists apart from society [. . .] yet, it sometimes even questions the 'reality' of the 'real' world itself."[14] The anarchy involved in questioning the reality of the real world seems to resemble certain aspects of Christian belief which dispute established claims about the nature of reality, such as: death is the end of life or objects of a certain density sink in water. Indeed, Robert Polhemus has suggested that "Lewis Carroll's words and images are to the formulation of a comic faith what Jesus's parables are to Christian doctrine: they create a fiction so radical that it can bring its audience to look with fresh wonder at the structure and meaning of experience."[15] In this chapter, I want to explore whether Christian teaching does in fact unsettle constitutional norms and provoke its followers to question the nature of the real as it appears to us. Before doing so, however, we first need to consider in detail whether anarchy is in any sense an apposite theological descriptor, for this language of riot and rebellion whilst suited to Wonderland might seem to some to be the very antithesis of Christian faith.

CHRISTIANITY AND ANARCHY

There is undoubtedly a sense of incongruity elicited by the conjunction of the words "Christianity" and "anarchism." The familiar anarchist slogan encapsulates this discord: "Neither God nor Master."[16] The apparent inconsonance derives from the assumption that Christianity is about observing rules and anarchism is about breaking them. The traditional depiction of God as an authoritarian father figure is anathema to many anarchists. Equally, anarchism is often seen as disorderly and aggressive, which is removed from a Christian view of compassionate citizenship and the hierarchical order of heaven.

14. Ede, "An Introduction to the Nonsense Literature of Edward Lear and Lewis Carroll," in Tigges (ed.), *Explorations in the Field of Nonsense*, 60.

15. Polhemus "Play, Nonsense, and Games," 365.

16. This phrase was coined by the socialist Auguste Blanqui in 1880, when he published a journal entitled: "Neither God nor Master." It became an anarchist slogan when it was later used by Mikael Bakunin.

Whilst this sense of incongruity is obviously not without foundation, there is nevertheless a variety of thinkers for whom the union of Christianity with anarchism is both fitting and significant. The Christian anarchist Jacques Ellul explains: "The more I understood seriously the Biblical message in its entirety [. . .] the more I came to see how impossible it is to give simple obedience to the state and how there is in the Bible the orientation to a certain anarchism."[17] Peter Marshall, likewise, points out that "Christian anarchism is not an attempt to synthesize two systems of thought but rather an attempt to realize the message of the Gospels."[18] My aim in this chapter is to explore whether there is any biblical support for suggesting that Christianity exhibits the type of anarchy identified in Carroll's nonsense—an unsettling of common-place assumptions about the nature of the real. A similar sense of disturbing commonplace assumptions can be found in the writing of the Russian Christian anarchist Nicholas Berdyaev (1874–1948). In this chapter, I attempt to neither prove nor oppose Berdyaev's theology; instead, my aim is to find out whether Berdyaev's model of anarchism accords with orthodox Christian teaching.

THE TWO REALMS

My kingdom is not of this realm

JOHN 18:36

The most obvious and fundamental principle upon which Berdyaev's anarchism is founded is his militant claim: "Until the end of time, there will always be two kingdoms [. . .] a struggle of the Spirit against Caesar."[19] This gives the impression of a perpetual opposition and attempts no reconciliation between the kingdom of God and the kingdom of man. In an analogous manner, Carroll presents us with two competing ontologies: sense and nonsense. Throughout both stories, Alice tries to uphold the authority of her world's norms and condemns the absurd grounds on which Wonderland appears to be run. In turn, the creatures Alice meets react to her with a

17. Ellul, *Anarchy and Christianity*, 3.

18. Marshall, *History of Anarchism*, 85. Garrett Green similarly contends: "even if the Christian chooses to support a revolutionary policy, he must realize that his support comes from his Christian commitment rather than a commitment to revolution." Green, *A Kingdom Not of This World*, 28.

19. Berdyaev, *Realm of Spirit*, 108. Berdyaev uses "Caesar" to represent the various authorities that conflict with God's kingdom and "Spirit" to designate God's rule.

similar response, suggesting that her assumptions about the mechanics of the universe are absurd or silly.[20] Nonsense humor is frequently located at this point of conflict between the two grammars since the unfamiliar seems preposterous to both parties. In the work of Berdyaev, there is constant reference to a two-realm antagonism and although the conflict does not ostensibly generate humor, this tension is seen as a space of creativity and revelation. As we will see subsequently, by articulating a clear dualism this affords Christianity a means by which to transcend the world and thereby assume the role of prophet and judge. A similar claim has been made about the potential for nonsense texts to stand outside and so criticize or comment on the real world, a contention that I will address later in the chapter.

For Berdyaev, the outcome of the clash is already established even as the struggle goes on. He recognizes the invisible authority of Spirit and the powerlessness of Caesar, and claims that Christianity situates itself in the anarchic limbo between Caesar's defeat and Christ's return. This conception of anarchy has a direct connection to the final paradox addressed in the previous chapter—the now and not-yet reality of the kingdom of God—in which it was stated that the authorities of death, sin, and of secular government have been overcome by Christ, even though the constitution of his divine authority is still held in abeyance; which is to say, the rule of the kingdom of God has not yet arrived in the fullness of its anticipated supremacy. We can see how this relates to the definition of anarchism as "the condition of living without constituted authority," since Christianity challenges the legitimacy of Caesar's reign, whilst acknowledging Caesar's continued presence in human history.

A possible objection, which could collapse Berdyaev's carefully maintained dialectic, is the suggestion that there should be a *resolution* between the two realms, rather than an *overcoming*. Perhaps the Christian can adopt a less dramatic position by holding that governmental authority ought not to be obeyed blindly, but can be reformed through a democratic morality influenced by Christian sentiments. As Vernard Eller suggests, "The Christian is to live above the law, and when the law would require him to do something contrary to the will of God he is to defy *that particular law*."[21] This position could imply that secular government is not in aggressive opposition to the Spirit, but that authority must be to God first. If this view can be upheld as orthodox Christian teaching, it would counter Berdyaev's

---

20. Alice explains to the Queen in Looking-Glass land: "'In *our* country [. . .] there's only one day at a time' to which the Red Queen scornfully retorts: 'That's a poor thin way of doing things.'" Carroll, *LG*, 195.

21. Eller, *Kierkegaard and Radical Discipleship*, 216.

more radical stance that political rule is not only misguided but "has poison within itself."[22]

The case for Berdyaev's Christian anarchism, and the reason that Christians may react against Eller's suggestion, hinges on the identification of Christ as an anarchist and not as a political activist. Jesus' prayer for his disciples seems to support Berdyaev's belief that Christ and his followers are separated from political activism by maintaining that the authority of Caesar's reign has already been overcome.[23] In John's Gospel, Jesus says his disciples "are not of the world, just as I am not of the world [. . .] as you sent me into the world, so I have sent them into the world."[24] Although Christ entered into the world, he did not belong to it in the way that a political activist must. For instance, he remained silent when asked to defend himself in the political trial in front of Pilate. In doing this, argues Ellul, Jesus effectively extracts himself from submitting to the grammar of political judgment.[25] This explanation suggests that Christ's silence is the only possible response from a non-political perspective. Ellul's interpretation, therefore, seems to complement Berdyaev's two-realm theory in his proclamation that "there never was and there never can be such things as a Christian state, a Christian economy."[26]

Jonathan Bartley in his book *Faith and Politics after Christendom: The Church as a Movement for Anarchy*, makes the relevant point that "secular government is 'secular' not in the sense that it is irreligious but in the sense that its role is confined to this age (in Latin, *saeculum*) that is passing away. It does not and cannot in any way represent the promise of the new age that comes in with Christ."[27] This supports Berdyaev's stance that Christianity establishes genuinely new and revolutionary principles of gov-

---

22. Berdyaev, *Realm of Spirit*, 85.

23. "Overcome" does seem to be the scriptural term to use, for example in 1 John 5:4–5 it states: "For everyone who has been born of God overcomes the world. And this is the victory that has overcome the world—our faith. Who is it that overcomes the world except the one who believes that Jesus Christ is the Son of God."

24. John 17:16–18.

25. Ellul writes: "It seems that Jesus did not regard these authorities as in any way just and that it was thus completely useless to defend himself." Ellul, *Anarchy and Christianity*, 68. See also Matt 26:62–63.

26. Berdyaev, *The Destiny of Man*, 133. Likewise, it would seem, there can never be such things as an anarchist state or economy. As Linda Damico explains: "the anarchists caution that the State must not be used to destroy the State. No attempt must be made to legislate the State out of existence nor to affect its demise through the use of its own organizational and structural machinery." Damico, *The Anarchist Dimension of Liberation Theology*, 75.

27. Bartley, *Faith and Politics After Christendom*," 10.

ernment, which are not contained within the grammar of a secular system. "The higher spiritual world," he writes, "ought never to be thought of on the analogy of the State, that is of power and authority."[28] The realm of Christ is moreover consistent with a biblical account of leadership, which deflects personal achievement and insists instead upon the sovereignty of God's will thereby identifying forgiveness and sacrifice as central rather than power or status. To this extent, secular government does not appear to fit comfortably into a theocratic system. Even so, one might suggest that Berdyaev and Bartley's rigid separation between divine and secular territory seems to raise the secular economy to the status of dialectic rival. Perhaps a *more* anarchic opposition to the realm of Caesar would stress the "alreadyness" of the conquest of the Spirit.

In this light, the response of the Christian to the realm of Caesar might be more accurately considered as a sort of compassionate detachment rather than the aggressive opposition articulated by Berdyaev and Bartley, which seems to assume a timelessness of "the state." Yet, whilst Berdyaev might appear to go too far in establishing the dichotomy of Spirit and Caesar, he at least exposes the radical element of the gospel message—the Christ presented in the Bible calls for a whole new way of living—a call that is often clouded by the integration of church into state.

The word "anarchy" in connection to Christianity could help to communicate to non-believers the radical, revolutionary aspect of New Testament teaching that is often hidden beneath stereotypes of Christians as law-abiding and rule-orientated. At the same time, associating anarchy with Christianity might direct Christians to see the authority of secular government as provisional. There is certainly an attitude of "non-attachment" to worldly endeavor that we can locate in Scripture. Christ preaches: "do not be anxious, saying, 'What shall we eat?' or 'What shall we drink?' or 'What shall we wear?' For the pagans seek after all these things, and your heavenly Father knows that you need them all. But seek first the kingdom of God and his righteousness, and all these things will be added to you."[29] Here the idea of non-attachment is manifest in the contrast between the attitude of the Christian and the pagan to physical concerns.

Christ's teaching has an anarchic implication because it seeks to detach the believer from a this-worldly fixation, which is the chief concern of governments. I am of course not suggesting that Christ is indifferent to physical needs—indeed, a major portion of his miracles are bodily healings, and the feeding of the five thousand is obviously a response to the this-worldly

28. Berdyaev, *Truth and Revelation*, 150.
29. Matt 6:31–33.

anxiety of what to eat. What I am proposing is that Christ preaches a freedom from the *preoccupation* with the physical and an elevation of this-worldly concerns. The freedom from the anxiety of worldly existence is, according to Berdyaev, emphatically rooted in the realm of Spirit and not in Caesar. Whilst this does maintain the supreme distinction between living with the belief in the unseen reign of Spirit and living under the apparent rule of Caesar, the distinction does not need to give way to aggressive antagonism, but the description "anarchist" could be helpful as an indicator that for the Christian a wholly new way of thinking politically is called for.

Highlighting the need for an anarchic stance against the regime of secular government, Berdyaev identifies Caesar as the symbol of human authority and the lust for power. "Render unto Caesar," he argues, "does not mean a religious definition of Caesar and his realm; it does not imply evaluation at all. This is merely distinguishing between two different spheres which cannot be combined one with the other."[30] Berdyaev claims that this reveals Christ's non-political identity: "Give to Caesar what is Caesar's" he says, and then, arguably in a completely new grammar preaches: "Give to God what is God's." Berdyaev believes that in this exchange Christ exposes the impermanence of Caesar's kingdom and enters into an "as if" relationship to worldly powers, which reiterates the anarchic formula whereby the Spirit rules *as if* in being, and Caesar is in being *as if* ruling.[31]

A similar rendering of the impermanence of Caesar's governance occurs in Christ's explanation to Pilate: "My kingdom is not of this world. If my kingdom were of this world, then my servants would be fighting so that I would not be handed over to the Jews; but as it is, my kingdom is not of this realm."[32] There seems to be an anarchic connotation in the undercutting of the political sphere and the disciples' allegiance to an unconstituted authority. Christ not only proclaims the reality of another, higher kingdom, but also his sovereignty over it. Similarly, in the name of Christ, Paul articulates the power of God's sovereignty *in absentia*. He challenges the Corinthians writing: "For though absent in body, I am present in spirit; and *as if* present I have already pronounced judgment."[33] Paul's use of "as if" contradicts the secular preoccupation with a tangible display of power and claims instead that spiritual presence, though invisible, has authority. This supports Berdyaev's proposal that even prior to the parousia, allegiance must be to

---

30. Berdyaev, *Freedom and the Spirit*, 69–70.

31. Berdyaev refers to the state's "false pretensions to sovereignty," describing its "relative and transient functional significance." Berdyaev, *Truth and Revelation*, 150.

32. John 18:36–37.

33. 1 Cor 5:3. My emphasis.

God alone and that modern Christians, like the Corinthians, ought to act *as if* God's authority were tangible. We might therefore understand the "as if" as operative in a dual directive—the world of Caesar as if it is not and the kingdom of God as if it is.

It is consequently necessary for Berdyaev to highlight the division between the two realms in order to convey a sense of the radical difference and shattering newness that is ushered in with God's kingdom. Berdyaev believes that the rule of the Spirit "concerns something much greater than a new society. What is involved is a new cosmos."[34] Only a type of apophatic anarchism can come close to describing the difference between the reign of Caesar and the sovereignty of the Spirit. In a similar way, the association of Christianity with nonsense might help to communicate something of the radically alternative mentality required for a genuine acceptance of the paradoxes of Christianity. To assert that Christ was raised from the dead more than just disagrees with modern empiricism, for many it is a statement on par with the Mad Hatter's insane utterances and thereby fundamentally demarcates religious faith from secular thought. An entirely new way of thinking is called for. "The coming of a new aeon," writes Berdyaev "presupposes a change in the human mind."[35] Ultimately, what Berdyaev teaches is that there is no way of modifying the realm of Caesar to establish or resemble the realm of Spirit and his paradigm of oppositional realms identifies effectively the irreconcilability between divine and secular rule. In order to demonstrate this, I will look at three significant exemplary cases: the incarnation, the church, and the disciple. In each of these, something of the anarchic sense of opposition is manifest. They all announce that there is an alternative reality that challenges the authority of the secular world.

The Incarnation

The previous chapter on paradox affirmed that Christianity upholds the complete divinity of the fully human Christ. We are now in a position to explore the incarnation as an anarchic embodiment of the tension between the two realms. John Caputo distinguishes two logics rather than two realms when he describes a similar fundamental duality between God's kingdom and the world's. More precisely, he discriminates between "the logic of the mundane constituted economies and the logic of the event." He explains: "I see in Jesus of Nazareth an exemplary embodiment of the logic or paralogic of the gift, who told paradoxical parables about and who was himself

34. Berdyaev, *Truth and Revelation*, 149.
35. Ibid., 151.

a parable of the kingdom of God, which he opposed to the economy of the 'world.'"[36] In this quotation, Caputo locates within the person of Christ a force that overturns the world's logic. It is a point of conflict in which a paradoxical logic triumphs over "the logic of the mundane" and to this end, it would seem that Christ's incarnation can be viewed symbolically as the herald of an anarchic age.

It should be noted that the reason Berdyaev considers the event of God becoming man anarchic is not because of any internal struggle between the divine and human natures within the hypostatic union, but rather because it announces the defeat of Caesar, sin, and death. Christians might legitimately term this anarchic because such a claim displaces the governing authority but is not recognized by those in power. Christ affirms, "I have overcome the world," and yet still warns his disciples, "in the world you will have tribulation."[37]

It is once again necessary to highlight the paradoxical aspect of this statement. From a heavenly perspective, the realm of Caesar is already defeated; however, from the point of view of human history, soteriology has a linear appearance. This would suggest that if anarchy is an apposite descriptor at all, it refers to the *current* epoch. It is in his incarnate form that Christ announces the powerlessness of secular government whilst proclaiming the not-yetness of the heavenly kingdom. Christ's earthly existence contradicts and shatters the expectations of the world's standard; the King of kings is born in a manger, the long-awaited Messiah enters Jerusalem on a colt. The incarnation inverts the common conception of power and wealth. By dwelling with man and as man, Christ represents an anarchic disturbance not only in his words but also in his person. Karl Barth encapsulates this idea in his statement that Christ "overcomes the flesh in becoming flesh."[38] Barth understands Christ's enfleshment as his victory and his person as his mission.

In this regard, it could be suggested that Barth shares a Berdyaevean emphasis in his view that the incarnation both brings about redemption and opens the way for man to participate in its salvific effect. This participation is made possible insofar as in entering humanity God has taken on the very essence of manhood. For Berdyaev, this is an important theme, as he sees Christ's birth ultimately as the birth of all, and indeed as the perpetual birth of man in Christ and Christ in man. In *Freedom and the Spirit*, he states: "through the Son we return to the bosom of the Father. With Him a new

36. Caputo, *After the Death of God*, 82.

37. John 16:33.

38. Barth, *Church Dogmatics* 4:1, 251.

race of human beings begins, the race of Christ, born and regenerated in the Spirit. Christ is in man and man is in Christ."[39] Depicted in this light, the incarnation is not only an announcement of what is to come but also acts as the analogical bond of reconciliation between man and God, which disturbs and overcomes the sovereignty of sin.

Significantly, this kenotic suspension enables Christ's analogous embodiment of humanity's situation. Kenosis is a letting go of divinity that corresponds to man's condition in the "not-yet" manifestation of divine sovereignty. In giving himself to be known, Christ "preposterously" announces the future state of his own eternal rule[40] whilst simultaneously opposing the authority of Caesar, thus bringing about a state without constituted authority; the condition of *anarcia*. We noted in the previous chapter that the kenosis is radically localized and temporalized, elevating the significance Christians attach to the status of the church as Christ's resurrected body. The New Testament proclaims the guarantee of the unfailing presence of the Spirit to the church and in this sense, the anarchic epoch is not simply about awaiting salvation, but concerns an active carrying-out of future promise. It is to this ecclesial manifestation that we now turn.

The Church

In ultimate terms, Berdyaev sees in the moment of incarnation the unification of the invisible with the visible. "Incarnation," he writes, "is symbolization; the visible Church is the symbolization of the Church invisible, the earthly hierarchy of the heavenly."[41] Berdyaev is articulating the belief that Christ is the image of the invisible God and at once the ascended and invisible ruler of the visible church. Hence, church for Berdyaev is holy territory—it is demarcated off from Caesar's reign in a manner evocative of the Celtic monastic tradition. In Celtic times, the territory of the *monasteria* was physically separated by the *vallum* (a ditch surrounding the monastery), which Ian Bradley explains "delineated an area that was to be regarded as sacred and in which the values of the Kingdom of God rather than the world of humankind would prevail."[42] Berdyaev's account of the clash between the two realms captures something of this ancient sense of holy separateness. He writes that there is "an eternal conflict between Christ the God-Man, and

---

39. Berdyaev, *Freedom and the Spirit*, 198.

40. Here I am using "preposterous" to mean that which in a certain sense can be both read backwards and precedes itself.

41. Berdyaev, *Freedom and the Spirit*, 335.

42. Bradley, *Colonies of Heaven*, 18–19.

Caesar the man-god," and then suggests that this entails that "Christianity cannot be reconciled to the sovereignty of any kind of earthly authority."[43]

Ultimately, what is evident here is that the rule of Spirit contains within it the non-rule of Caesar and the church occupies this in-between space, announcing and preparing the way for the full arrival of that which is, but which is also yet to come. Christ ordains this lacuna by establishing the church, which through the sacraments demonstrate the already within the not-yet, providing visible signs of invisible authority. This liberates the church to practice "weakness" and charity as the revelation of the counter-cultural strength of the anarchic order of the Spirit. In Christ, there is both a rejection of the authority of visible powers and a participatory celebration in the unseen conquest. By accepting the eternal significance of the incarnation, the church is not beset with eschatological angst, but is liberated to experience in the present the salvific assurance of the future.

The Disciple

We have now described two vital manifestations of Berdyaev's two-realm theory. We discussed the incarnation as the herald of the Spirit triumphant and considered the church as the visible and present instantiation of the invisible, future reign. The third dimension demarcating the realm of Spirit from the realm of Caesar is the witness of the disciple.

We have already acknowledged that from a heavenly perspective the "conflict" between the two realms is not a struggle in the sense that the sovereignty is undecided. Yet, Berdyaev wants at the same time to emphasize that Christ's sovereign relinquishing of the perspective of the Father gives him a radical identification with humanity, which creates an example that his followers can emulate.[44] Through Christ, the individual is connected to the eschatological kingdom and participates in this alternate reality. Whilst on earth Christ leaves his disciples with the gift of peace: "my peace I give to you. Not as the world gives do I give to you. Let not your hearts be troubled, neither let them be afraid." This phrase demonstrates how Christ invites his disciples to partake in the eschatological security of the triumph of the Spirit, which he acknowledges is neither given nor received according to the rules of this world.

It is important to understand that the concept of discipleship is not solely a matter of metaphysical awareness of Christ's sovereignty, but it also

43. Berdyaev, *Realm of Spirit*, 72.

44. Though at the same time, Berdyaev upholds that Christ's involvement in the Trinity is still radically different from ours.

seems to entail a disruptive political dimension. In Luke's Gospel, Christ professes that his followers "will be brought before kings and governors because of my name," but emphasizes that, "not a hair [. . .] will perish."[45] This indicates that the communication of Christ's message will aggravate those in authority, suggesting that the disciple's task is subversive of conventional powers. One of the reasons why Berdyaev's association of Christianity with anarchism seems to work is because its extremity is consistent with Christ's teaching of radical division between the disciples and the world. John 15:19 states: "If you were of the world, the world would love its own; but because you are not of the world, but I chose you out of the world, because of this the world hates you."[46]

The estrangement between Christ's followers and the rest of the world is further emphasized in Christ's command to be holy. "Just as he who called you is holy, so be holy in all you do; for it is written 'Be holy, because I am holy.'"[47] The initial command in Leviticus uses the Hebrew word for holy (*kadosh*) which also means "separateness." Accordingly, the obligation for the Christian is to be set apart from the ideals, values and methods of the world's politics. It is a command to anarchism, where anarchism is identified as an elected separateness deriving from faith in an unseen power. Christ explains to his disciples that he will cease to be visible in the world but will retain his rulership over it: "I am going to the Father and you will see me no longer [. . . .] I have conquered the world."[48] Belief in this statement suggests that it might be helpful to define the Christian imagination as anarchic in the sense that being a disciple of Christ requires the mental agility to "overaccept"[49] earthly signs that oppose the reality of Christ's eternal

45. Luke 21:12, 18.

46. John 15:19.

47. 1 Pet 1:15–16.

48. John 16:10,33.

49. I am using the term "overaccept" following Samuel Wells, who develops a theory of overacceptance as a way to respond to opposition to Christian theology. "Overaccepting," he writes "is accepting in the light of a larger story." Wells explains that one can "block" a challenge to Christ's message simply by discounting it, or one can accept such a proposition and therefore give in to the demands of atheism. However, the third alternative is the concept that it is possible to accept the skeptic's comment but explain that they have not understood the whole picture. For example, a consistent dispute with Christianity is the belief that it is impossible to rise from the dead. To block this would be simply to state "no it isn't"; to accept it is to oblige the skeptic and reform one's own view; but to overaccept is to agree that it is indeed a logical and scientific impossibility but to explain that there is another grammar in which rising from the dead makes perfect sense. Wells, *Improvisation*, 131.

conquest. In doing so, Berdyaev believes the Christian participates in the unseen reality of the not-yet kingdom.

THEOLOGICAL ESTRANGEMENT

Put to death all that is earthly in you.

Colossians 3:5

We began this chapter by discussing how a basic prerequisite for engaging with nonsense literature is the willingness to unsettle quotidian norms. Like Berdyaev's account of the two rival kingdoms, Carroll's Wonderland also encompasses two conflicting realms. We observed how this tension has provoked nonsense critics and theologians alike to utilize the word "anarchism" in order to describe how their respective dualities fuel an antagonistic conflict. In nonsense literature, we witnessed the rebellion against the world of conventional logic and described how Alice's introduction to nonsense principles causes her to question the reliability of her preconceived norms.[50] For Lecercle this is a political demonstration, opposed to regulative systems of authority. "Reading *Alice* is a political act," he writes, "[. . .] as a statement of linguistic liberation."[51]

Having looked at the idea that Christ's triumph disturbs and unsettles the governing principles of the physical world, we can now explore how the believer disassociates himself from the visible kingdom of Caesar in order to submit to the invisible rule of the Spirit. Or, in the words of Coleridge, how we can "awake[n] the mind's attention from the lethargy of custom and direc[t] it to the loveliness and the wonders of the world before us."[52] To apply anarchy in a Christian context, therefore, we must first look at the theory and practice of revelatory disturbance.

---

50. It is worth mentioning that in both stories the playful, anarchic realm of nonsense is itself undermined by the sporadic return of sense at the close of the books, where it is revealed it was only a dream after all, puncturing the imaginative vision with an allusion to realm outside. This could be described as a double disturbance or reflexive rebellion whereby the reader must first defy everyday logic by engaging in a nonsense world and then turn this topsy-turvy world on its head by resurfacing in the world of sense.

51. Lecercle, "Nonsense and Politics" in *Nonsense and Other Senses*, 371.

52. Coleridge, *Biographia Literaria*, 314.

The theory of revelatory disturbance

The American contemporary of Berdyaev, William James, writing at the end of the nineteenth century claimed: "the greatest revolution of our generation is the discovery that human beings, by changing the inner attitude of their minds can change the outer aspects of their lives."[53] The idea that the imagination has outward transformative power is a sentiment articulated in the Bible,[54] and recognized by Berdyaev.[55] In the succeeding section, I will be considering the constructive aspect of this transformation, but before that, we need to address its disturbance, which for Berdyaev begins with the imaginative deconstruction of its constituted authority.

Like Christ in the "far country," he instructs his followers to assume the role of stranger and not seek rest or satisfaction in the realm of Caesar.[56] This conviction looks a lot like anarchism from the perspective of the state, since it actively denounces conformity to the conventional powers. Whilst it will be important to recognize the practical implications of seeking the role of stranger within a secular polis, I want to argue that it is in the imagination that the mental stimulus for such action takes root. The imagination is commonly understood within nonsense literature as the portal by which an individual can enter or access alternative worlds. However, one might argue that the act of imagining different worlds has the effect of detaching the individual from the familiar and inviting a critical assessment of everyday existence. Following the biblical outline of faith, the primary step to imagining an alternative reality is creatively to abstract oneself from the seen reality. Since the function of the imagination as a means of conscious alienation from society is a prominent element in the theory and work of Bertolt Brecht, it may be instructive to consider his concept of *Verfremdungseffekt*.[57]

53. James, quoted in *Clinical Addiction Psychiatry*, eds., David Brizer and Ricardo Castaneda, 58.

54. Christ's miracles often require the individual to attune their mind to the possibility of being healed in order for this to become a reality. For example Luke 18:42 states: "And Jesus said to him, 'Recover your sight; your faith has made you well.'"

55. "Creative fancy is capable of producing real and vital consequences." Berdyaev, *The Beginning and the End*, 117.

56. Cf. Luke 9:58.

57. This is translated as having the effect of "distancing" or "alienating." It is very interesting for our thesis that Schwab in "Nonsense and Metacommunication" also uses the same German word to describe the reader's experience of distorted logic. She describes it as "[the] sense of a productive *Verfremdung* and a practical disturbance of communication." Ibid., 168.

This might seem a deeply incongruous approach given Brecht's deep-rooted dislike and mistrust of all religious systems, particularly Christianity, which he viewed as a corrupt and oppressive force. Yet, if we focus on the anarchic component of the Christian imagination, we find a surprising overlap between Brechtian sociopolitical satire and Berdyaev's Christian anarchism. Much of Brecht's writing, like Berdyaev's was extremely subversive in his own political climate. For example, during the premier of his play *The Rise and Fall of the City Mahogany* in 1930, Nazis in the audience rioted in protest. By 1929, Brecht had already embraced Communism and was significantly influenced by Marx. From this period, Brecht not only satirized capitalist ideas and public figures, but also encouraged his audience to sympathise with his Marxist ideology. Douglas Kellner explains, "He wanted his spectators [. . .] to participate in an active process of critical thought that would provide insights into the workings of society, and to see the need for and to implement radical social change."[58] This same sentiment could be applied to Berdyaev's writing, which overtly promoted both Marxism and anarchism.[59]

Among other devices, Brecht's "epic theatre" used montage and tableaux to depict social injustice. These contributed to his primary theatrical interest of creating the *Verfremdungseffekt*. Kellner explains that "this was intended to 'estrange' or 'distance' the spectator and thus prevent empathy and identification with the situation and the characters and allow the adoption of a critical attitude toward the actions in the play."[60] Brecht was resolute that in order to achieve this degree of analytical political observation, an imaginative detachment was required. The audience was supposed to be critically aware and not entranced, since Brecht wanted to remind them that they were watching a piece of theatre. This he achieved in many ways, such as keeping the auditorium lit, having the actors direct their speech to the audience and employing the "play within a play" technique.

We can begin to sense some similarities with an anarchic account of Christianity, which, likewise, desires to exhibit the world as a counter-reality and to provoke its "audience" to engage critically in the unfolding of the global drama and approach it from a detached perspective. According to Alison Milbank, "we need estranging techniques if we are to shock people into engagement with reality, so that they may appreciate the religious sense

58. Kellner, "Brecht's Marxist Aesthetic," in Weber and Heinen (eds.), *Bertolt Brecht: Political Theory and Literary Practice*, 32.

59. In September 1922 Berdyaev was exiled from Russia on the "Philosopher's ship" since the Bolshevik authorities were concerned that Berdyaev's writing and lecturing was leading to unrest and rebellion.

60. Kellner, "Brecht's Marxist Aesthetic," 32.

and we can begin to explain the Christian faith at all."[61] Given its connotations of riot and rebellion, the word "anarchy" is perhaps the "shock" required to rouse individuals from "the lethargy of custom" and to stimulate a desire to question given norms.

Hence, in spite of their wholly secular aesthetic origins, certain aspects of Brecht's theatrical technique may be helpful for explaining the scriptural notion of alienation, such as the command in Romans 12:2: "Do not be conformed to the present age but be transformed by the renewal of your mind." The anarcho-theistic imagination considered in accordance with Romans corresponds to Brechtian practices in the sense that the Christian stands apart from the present age and believes in the power of mental transformation to re-envisage the world. This contention is mirrored in Walter Benjamin's explanation that "the response to epic theatre should be: 'Things can happen this way, but they can also happen a quite different way.'"[62] From this perspective Benjamin unintentionally seems to unite the utopic vision of Christian eschatology with Brechtian social satire. Benjamin brings to the surface the basic premise that Brechtian theatre encompasses its own two-world dialectic, where involvement in one leads to the disturbance of the other.

There has been some relevant investigation into the link between religious eschatology and Brechtian satire. For example, Keith Dickson in *Towards Utopia: A Study of Brecht* argues that "the utopian is a satirist in disguise." He continues: "His [Brecht's] ideal commonwealth is an implicit criticism of his own society, the shortcomings of which can be measured against the standards of an imaginary world."[63] This interpretation of Brechtian theatre as both critical and utopic parallels the aspect of revelatory disturbance in Berdyaev's anarchism. The belief in an imaginary world requires a cognitive alienation comparable to the biblical advocacy of non-attachment: "[let] those who deal with the world [live] as though they had no dealings with it. For the present form of this world is passing away."[64] Such a sentiment further emphasizes both Berdyaev and Brecht's belief that there is an alternative reality that requires a mental estrangement from what is immediately observable. It is upon this lack of satisfaction with the apparent reality that Berdyaev founds the anarchism of the Christian imagination: "the world does not begin and end with this condition, which

---

61. Alison Milbank, "Apologetics and the Imagination," in Davison, (ed.), *Imaginative Apologetics*, 38.

62. Quoted by Kellner in "Brecht's Marxist Aesthetic," 32.

63. Dickson, *Towards Utopia*, 2.

64. 1 Cor 7:31.

is actually our fallen state: another condition of the world is possible and it requires another type of knowing."[65] Such a state of dissatisfaction is the principal goal of disturbance since experiencing the inadequacy of the secular approach can provide the impetus for seeking a spiritual alternative.

Of course, the analogy between Brecht's *Verfremdungseffekt* and Christian detachment is not entirely apposite. Firstly, as Dickson notes, Brecht's sensationalist undercurrent is in tension with many aspects of orthodox Christianity.[66] Secondly, Brecht is solely concerned with the criticism and disturbance of the world, as, unlike Berdyaev, he does not believe in the "alreadiness" of his socialist ideal. Dickson addresses this theme, commenting, "writers almost invariably find the contradictions of the present world a much more rewarding subject than a future world in which the gulf between actuality and the ideal has been bridged. Brecht is no exception."[67] The focus on negation *above* transfiguration reduces the revolutionary potential of Brecht's work, making his contextual political satire more of a modern romantic utopia. Efim Etkind, a great supporter of Brechtian technique, accepts nevertheless that Brecht's vision has lost some of its revolutionary force: "the greatest misfortune that could have befallen Brecht was to become a classic. Unfortunately, this has happened. Brecht has truly become a classic."[68]

Brecht's intention to turn theatre into propaganda, allowed him to satirize powerfully his own political climate, but in so doing, prevented his plays from being continually revolutionary. An important difference between satire and anarchism seems to be that in general anarchism signifies an ideology of perpetual transformation and opposition to *all* forms of constituted authority, whereas satire seems to be more targeted towards particular individuals or groups (although satire can of course have relevance beyond its particulars and anarchy can be directed to specific circumstances or states). The association of Christianity and anarchism thus identifies the Gospel narratives with eternal revolution, suggesting that the Gospels, unlike Brecht's theatre, can never be set aside as a classic in Etkind's sense. However, demonstrating a degree of verisimilitude between Berdyaev and Brecht has been helpful to understand the theory of disturbance as the imaginative deconstruction of the principles of the realm of Caesar

---

65. Berdyaev, *Freedom and the Spirit*, 31.

66. Dickson explains "the other-world-liness of so much traditional Christian thought was anathema to the sensualist in Brecht, who in one of his first poems extolled tobacco and brandy as sacraments." Dickson, *Towards Utopia*, 133.

67. Ibid., 3.

68. Etkind, "Brecht and the Soviet Theatre," in *Bertolt Brecht*, 81.

The Practice of Revelatory Disturbance

Disturbing law and lawfulness

We are now in a position to address the ramifications of the theory of revelatory disturbance and discuss how this helps us to understand Berdyaev's association of anarchism with Christianity. Perhaps the foremost consequence of devaluing the principalities of this world is the legalistic implication of non-belonging, and so we will begin by looking at Berdyaev's belief that faith in Christ effects a certain detachment from the law of Caesar. This will lead us into social and judicial territories, which together form the second major area in which the unsettling of secular norms results in an anarchic deconstruction of constituted authorities.

Christianity has always had a complex relationship with the concept of law (both the Mosaic law and the law of the state). As one would expect from an anarchic writer like Berdyaev the contrast between freedom and law is a major concern throughout his work. However, as it has hopefully been made clear, law, hierarchy, and order are not necessarily at odds with an anarchic reading of Christianity, but the terms require precise and careful definition. The philosopher Giorgio Agamben offers some insightful commentary on the Christian attitude to law, which will help elucidate and consolidate Berdyaev's position. Agamben's messianic narrative involves a revocation and redefinition of the authority of law, and it is within Agamben's notion of "messianic time" that we can locate Berdyaev's concept of freedom and use this to articulate the experience of living between the two competing ontologies of Spirit and Caesar.

We have described anarchism as an era or an epoch traversing the period between Christ's defeat of Caesar and the full sovereignty of his reign. Agamben's representation of messianic time likewise takes its cue from the paradox of the now and the not yet.[69] Briefly, messianic time corresponds to the anarchic era insofar as both are concerned with action in the moment of suspension. Agamben describes messianic time as "the time *that* we ourselves are, and for this very reason, is the only real time, the only time we have."[70] For Berdyaev this era between times is the only time in which we can make a free decision, it is the space of immediate freedom that has been carved out of the kingdom of man and re-oriented to the kingdom of God.

69. In *The Time that Remains*, Agamben writes: "The messianic event has already happened, salvation has already been achieved according to believers. But, nevertheless, in order to truly be fulfilled, this implies an additional time." Agamben, *The Time that Remains*, 69.

70. Ibid., 68.

Similarly, Agamben defines messianic time as "that part of secular time which undergoes an entirely transformative contraction."[71] This transformation from secular temporality reveals the stifling limitations of legalism and opens up the possibility of freedom and autonomy.

Agamben wants to understand how in the process of transformation a Christian can integrate the law and yet remain apart from it. Although this is not the same as Berdyaev's anarchism, it nevertheless reveals a certain correspondent attitude to law as both writers comment on the insufficiency of the law whilst conceding the necessity of its presence. Agamben writes, "the messianic is not the destruction but the deactivation of the law, rendering the law inexecutable,"[72] and here we can see that like Berdyaev the *fact* of the law is upheld, but the *power* of the law is deactivated: Caesar is in *being* but his *authority* has been unsettled.

Perhaps at this stage it will be helpful to clarify what we mean by "law" in a Christian context. In Paul's epistle to the Romans, the meaning of the word "law" is subject to some debate. In general, his references indicate that he is referring to the Mosaic law and contrasting salvation through grace with justification by adherence to religious rules. However, Paul also extends the meaning of *nomos* to cover a wider application of law in terms of the governance of sin and death. He writes: "I find it to be a law that when I want to do right, evil lies close at hand. For I delight in the law of God, in my inner being, but I see in my members another law waging war against the law of my mind and making me captive to the law of sin."[73] The Berdyaevean discrimination between Spirit and Caesar seems to be apparent in the division between "the law of God" and "the law of sin." Berdyaev himself refers at times to the "law of Christ"[74] and the "law of Caesar."[75]

Using Paul's more general application of the concept of law, it becomes evident that there must be dissatisfaction with the "law of sin" prior to encountering messianic freedom.[76] Yet, as Paul indicates elsewhere, life in the Spirit is also acquiescence to a law of a different kind: "For the law of the Spirit of life has set you free in Christ Jesus from the law of sin and death."[77] The juxtaposition of freedom through law brings us back to the territory

71. Ibid., 64.

72. Ibid., 98.

73. Rom 7:21–23.

74. Berdyaev, *The Russian Idea*, 211.

75. Berdyaev, *Realm of Spirit*, 65.

76. Paul's contrast between law and salvation is particularly emphatic in Rom 10:4 where he states "Christ is the end of the law, that everyone who has faith may be justified."

77. Rom 8:2.

of paradox where autonomy and authority "impossibly" co-mingle. If we understand God as the source of freedom, the religious imagination can be seen as a voluntary submission to the wellspring of all freedom.

The identification of Christianity with anarchism becomes particularly important here, since such a conjunction could help to prevent the Christian understanding of submission to freedom from being mistaken for a secular version of Kantian autonomy. Peter Marshall claims that anarchism accepts Kant's view of autonomy as self-imposed rules, which have been freely taken on by the individual.[78] Yet, Paul's epistle to the Romans teaches that outside of relationship with Christ there are no free choices as man is bound by his inordinate desire.[79] Agamben would likewise argue that the secular world has an unawareness of messianic time, which prevents participation in the moment of freedom from the law. A radical revolution is required to make one aware of messianic time, as Paul indicates: "by dying to what once bound us, we have been released from the law so that we serve in the new way of the Spirit."[80] Here we can recognize the moment of disturbance as a necessary precursor to following Christ. The act of "dying to" or "putting to death" worldly values is perhaps the ultimate expression of theological estrangement, which Paul presents as a mandatory initiation in order to enter into the freedom of the Spirit.

In *Destiny of Man*, we can find a similar pattern demanding the total dismantling of the principle of law prior to receiving Christ's message: "the Gospel overcomes and abolishes the ethic of law and replaces it by another, the higher and noble ethic of love and freedom. Christianity opens the way to the Kingdom of God, where there is no longer any law."[81] That is not to say that the kingdom of God is without order, but that "law" is not needed where the Spirit has supreme reign. This is based on the understanding that it is not the law that prevents the individual from sinning, but the power of Christ's resurrection imparted through the Spirit.

An interesting interpretation of the Christian attitude to law can be found in Evagrius of Pontus' discussion on *apatheia* written at the end of the fourth century. *Apatheia* (translated as "impassability") is, according to Evagrius, the status reached when one is able to combat sinful passions. He writes, "The one who is perfect does not practice abstinence and the

78. Marshall, *History of Anarchism*, 38.

79. For example Rom 7:15, 20 indicates that sin usurps freedom "For I do not understand my own actions. For I do not do what I want, but I do the very thing I hate. [. . .] Now if I do what I do not want, it is no longer I who do it, but sin that dwells within me."

80. Rom 7:5–6.

81. Quoted in Lowrie (ed. and trans.), *Christian Existentialism*, 195–96.

one who is impassible does not practice perseverance, since perseverance is for the person subject to the passions and abstinence for the person who is troubled."[82] This state of *apatheia*, which is in keeping with the idea of a detached attitude to the physical world, provides a parallel with Paul's teaching: "if you are led by the Spirit you are not under the law."[83] This freedom from the law once again reflects the conditions of *anarchia*, whereby the law retains a superficial ontology, but its potency has been comprehensively destabilized.

Disturbing the social and judicial

The deconstruction of the concept of law witnessed in the New Testament is not only pitched against religious *halakha* but also extends into the territory of sociopolitical laws concerning class systems and the division of power. It might therefore not come as a surprise that in areas of dramatic social and political injustice, Christians have led some of the major rebellions against the state, and in modern times, this attitude has led to the foundation of Liberation Theology. Leonardo Boff, a central figure of the movement currently working in Brazil, echoes Paul's words to the Galatians in his own ministry. For Boff, it is a manifest truth that "to enter the kingdom it is not sufficient to do what the law ordains." He explains: "the present order of things cannot save people from their fundamental alienation. It is order in the midst of disorder. A change of life is required, a complete turnabout of the old situation."[84]

Boff considers this "turnabout" to be the non-conformity to earthly authorities, brought about by an imaginative disturbance of secular rule. In reference to the sentiments revealed in the Sermon on the Mount, Boff is emphatic this demonstrates that "Christ did not come to bring a more radical and severe law, nor did he preach a more perfect pharisaism. He preached a gospel, which signifies good news: It is not the law that saves but love."[85] According to both Boff and Berdyaev, the supreme anarchic dimension to the Sermon on the Mount is its disestablishment of commonplace

---

82. Evagrius of Pontus *c.* 345–99 had a significant influence on virtually all Byzantine monastic teaching and he is still widely used today within the Catholic model. Evagrius of Pontus, "Praktikos," 109.

83. Gal 5:18.

84. Boff, *Jesus Christ Liberator*, 73. For further information on the relationship between anarchism and liberation theology see Damico, *Anarchist Dimension of Liberation Theology*, She concludes that "Liberation theology's new society, in whatever language it is presents, is anarchist in essence," 199.

85. Boff, *Jesus Christ Liberator*, 73.

norms, which Boff believes, "checkmates all fetishistic and inhuman subordination to a system, be it social or religious."[86]

The anarchic process of disturbing the social sphere, interestingly, corresponds to the type of political nihilism practiced by the Russian nihilists in the 1860s, in which there was an ideological revolution that sought to break down and expose elitism embedded in Russian society.[87] The historian Riasanovsky explains: "The earnest young men and women [nihilists] of the 1860s wanted to cut through every polite veneer, to get rid of all conventional sham, to get to the bottom of things."[88] This, in some sense, echoes the agenda of theologians such as Boff and Berdyaev, but more fundamentally, it shares in the basic sentiment of the Gospels that God's grace cannot be bought, earned or won by social status.

One could perhaps recognize a nihilistic dimension to the Christian teaching of righteousness through faith. In Paul's letter to the Romans he echoes the despondent words of the Psalmist: "None is righteous, no, not one [. . .;] all have turned aside; together they have become worthless; no one does good, not even one."[89] This moment of all-encompassing negation of human righteousness is in one sense an echo of the nihilistic belief that all human pretension to honor and virtue is baseless. Of course, within Christianity this anarcho-nihilistic sentiment is offered alongside the jubilatory proclamation that through Christ we can attain righteousness and worth. However, the sense of jubilation is only so rich and so joyous because of the contemplation of the desperate situation of man's inability to redeem himself. So, although an anarcho-nihilistic stance is not at all an accurate depiction of Christian belief, the association with nihilism, like anarchism, nevertheless communicates the ineffectual nature of all worldly systems of righteousness, echoing Paul's claim: "all have sinned and fall short of the glory of God."[90] Hence, the abandonment of faith in humanity's system of valuation shared by the anarchist and nihilist is perhaps closer to the message of salvation than the attempt to justify oneself through obeying a set of rules or conformity to a model of social acceptability.

A further reason Berdyaev gives for seeking to undermine the validity of secular justice is that it ignores the divine authorship of its moral standard. He believes that one of the central problems of secular government

86. Ibid., 71.

87. Berdyaev himself never sympathized with the nihilists and within his texts there is little interaction with their ideas.

88. Riasanovsky, *History of Russia*, 381.

89. Rom 3:10, 12.

90. Rom 3:23–24.

consists in its failure to recognize that "good" has a divine ontology and that this denial reveals the ultimate rebellion against the authority of the kingdom of God. According to Berdyaev, "the concepts of good and evil incarnate in customs, depend on society, on the social whole, but good and evil themselves do not; on the contrary, society depends upon good and evil, upon their ontology."[91] Berdyaev reacts against the secular attempt to section off ontology from legality as he sees it as resistance to the permeation of the Spirit in the realm of Caesar and as a form of authoritarianism subjecting people to judgment whilst failing to account for the ontology of their measurement of justice. Berdyaev's message remains relevant in the current secular world where governments implement moral standards without recognition of a spiritual foundation. The application of Christian anarchism in this context seeks to disturb the secular system in order to reveal the theological basis of moral discourse. Berdyaev believes that aspects of the Spirit are shackled within Caesar's reign, and teaches that a radical stripping away of its secular trappings is required.

A final, practical ramification of associating Christianity with an anarchic disturbance is the ability to communicate dissatisfaction with the basic concept of secular government. Peter Marshall reminds us: "anarchists believe not only that power corrupts, and power corrupts absolutely, but that power destroys both the executioner and victim of power."[92] From the perspective of Christianity, the victim of political power is not only the man who is wronged by bureaucracy, but also the man who feels a sense of moral satisfaction in his lawful abiding. It is easy for the law-keeping atheist to harbor an apathetic approach to divine salvation, having experienced an impression of justification and righteousness through the law. The Christian endorsement of secular morality can additionally generate the common misconception that Christianity is about redemption through works and observing rules. Berdyaev's concatenation of anarchy with Christianity prevents the spread of this fallacy and promotes an imaginative undoing of the values, practices and goals of the kingdom of Caesar.

Accordingly, it seems appropriate for the Christian to use Berdyaev's dramatic language to respond to the command to overcome the world in light of the conviction of things to come. Working from the conclusions reached regarding the distinction between the two realms and the effect of living in the freedom of messianic time, it follows that orthodox Christian thought is in line with Berdyaev's conviction that the coming of God's kingdom terminates the authority of the kingdom of man. The book of

91. Berdyaev, *Destiny of Man*, 24.

92. Marshall, *History of Anarchy*, 45.

Revelation declares "the former things have passed away,"[93] until this is fully constituted Christians seem called imaginatively to transcend the authority of sin, death, and secular government in order to fulfill the command: "Put to death all that is earthly in you."[94]

CONSTRUCTIVE DISTURBANCE

Behold the kingdom of God is in the midst of you

LUKE 17:21

When we think of political anarchy, we tend to imagine an ideology that breaks, defies, or deconstructs, and would not normally perhaps conceive of a restorative or reconstructive dimension to anarchy. While it is clear that the type of sociopolitical disturbance discussed above is indeed a vital anarchic component, Berdyaev advances the idea that Christian anarchy also transforms and restores the world it has deconstructed. "The new aeon," he observes, "does not simply belong to the other world, to the other side of the grave, it is not something entirely different. It is also our world enlightened and transfigured and which has become creatively free."[95] Although this might appear to be an unlikely aspect of anarchy, Marshall has indicated that anarchy is not simply the moment of defiance, but the ongoing "condition of a people living." Anarchy *does* break, but for Berdyaev it is in order to rebuild; it *is* defiant, but so that it can reclaim; it intentionally unsettles, but always with the desire to transform.

This process of disturbing in order to recreate has something in common with Tolkien's description of fairy-tales, which he believes follows the pattern of "escape, recovery and consolation."[96] In her essay, "Apologetics and the Imagination: Making Strange" Alison Milbank discusses the first two aspects of Tolkien's three-fold definition, explaining: "Escape speaks to our desire to burst the limits of our ordinary experience. [. . .] The second function, recovery, returns us to our own world but seen in a new way."[97] This pattern of disturbing the ordinary in order to accomplish its creative re-vision, as we will see, is a close echo of Berdyaev's account of Christian

93. Rev 21:4.
94. Col 3:5.
95. Berdyaev, *Truth and Revelation*, 153.
96. Tolkien, "On Fairy-Stories," 128.
97. Alison Milbank, "Apologetics and the Imagination," 39.

anarchy, which, having "burst the limits" of the conventional, then seeks to restore and reveal the holy within the everyday.

Tolkien's model—in particular the aspect of recovery—can also help to convey the effect of the end of the *Alice* stories upon the reader's imagination. We have discussed how the *Alice* narratives both culminate in revolt. Without wanting to undercut this violent climax it would be misleading to leave the discussion there, since in neither book is the end of Alice's adventures the close of the story. The aim of recovery, Tolkien concludes, is to free the mundane "from the drab blur of triteness or familiarity."[98] In a similar way, Carroll closes both stories by appealing to dream and memory, which, as before, disturbs the world of sense, but this time in order to awaken an appreciation of the marvelous within the commonplace, rather than simply overturning or undermining its governing principles. We might allude to Coleridge's description of Wordsworth's poetry as representative of literature's transformative potential, and endeavor to find out if Carroll's nonsense has the same ability: "to give the charm of novelty to things of every day, and to excite a feeling analogous to the supernatural."[99]

In the first book, Alice wakes from the dream-world and relays the dream to her sister. This affects the sister's experience of the real world, which becomes oddly enchanted by Alice's tale. Carroll tells us the sister "began dreaming after a fashion [. . . ,] the whole place around her became alive with the strange creatures of her little sister's dream."[100] There is confusion here between dream and reality—her senses appear bewitched as she experiences aspects of Alice's adventures for herself in a semi-conscious state where fantasy and dream crossover into the commonplace. Still, the idea of transformation in the first novel is somewhat limited, for although the sister "half believed herself in Wonderland" she anticipates that when she opens her eyes "all would change to dull reality—the grass would be only rustling in the wind [. . . ,] the rattling teacups would change to tinkling sheep-bells."[101] Nevertheless, despite the return to the mundane, Alice's nonsense tale has brought, albeit fleetingly, a "charm of novelty to things of every day."

By the close of *Through the Looking-Glass*, however, the transformation of the commonplace has been intensified and Carroll never fixedly establishes the demarcation between the dream world and reality. The book ends with a poem that not only reflects on a distant fantasy but draws the past into his present. Carroll acknowledges on the one hand that his reality

---

98. Tolkien, "On Fairy-Stories," 129.

99. Coleridge, *Biographia Literaria*, 314.

100. Carroll, *AW*, 98.

101. Ibid.

has returned to the everyday: "Long had paled that sunny sky/Autumn frosts have slain July." Yet he also indicates, on the other hand, that a sense of the wondrous lingers or returns:

> *A boat beneath a sunny sky,*
>
> *Lingering onward dreamily*
>
> *In an evening of July*

Carroll implies that his fantasy has been disturbed and disrupted both by the waking of his character in the story and the adult awakening of the child, Alice Liddell. And yet *something* has lingered, July has both been slain and still remains. Carroll accepts that in a temporal sense we are "Ever drifting down the stream" although his focus is on the experience of "Lingering in the golden gleam." Hence, the concluding poem is not simply nostalgia or pessimism as some scholars have indicated.[102] Rather, there is a more complex interpenetration of disturbance and transformation. Part of the complexity is the haunting experience of memory, for at the end of the story we find no certainty but both a presence and an absence, an anarchic paradox holding together commonplace reality with its simultaneous wondrous re-imagining.

Another way of expressing the lingering sensation of half-recollecting an impression of the marvelous would be to describe it as a sort of "homesickness." Alison Milbank notes how the objective of certain fantasy writers is "to awaken in the reader this feeling of homesickness for the truth."[103] Carroll's nonsense stories do not end with a feeling of "homesickness for the truth," but they do invoke a sense of homesickness for the fantastic, a sort of yearning after the wondrous, "whose echoes live in memories yet."[104] It could be argued that the feeling of longing here is merely Carroll's own wistfulness for "'happy summer days' gone by,"[105] though he does seem to "excite a feeling analogous to the supernatural" by transporting the reader back to their own childhood when the world was strange and mystical. Perhaps this is just a homesickness for the youth we can never recapture; however, the recollection and re-enactment of childhood's sense of the fantastic can also be seen as an endeavor that endows the reader with the ability to conceive of an alternative version of reality—one of the foremost aims of Berdyaev's theology.

---

102. See Knoepflmacher, *Ventures Into Childland* , 157.

103. Alison Milbank, "Apologetics and the Imagination," 33. Milbank is referring specifically to the Romantic project of Novalis.

104. Prefatory poem to *LG*, 103.

105. Ibid.

The creation of the new: transforming the individual

The transformation of the commonplace in many ways intensifies anarchic subversion, since it involves a double rebellion—a subversion of the original subversion. To put this another way, anarchy, might not simply be an act which breaks down, but a revolution that also rebuilds and re-creates. We will explore this contention by considering the transformation of the self and the re-creation of the world as the counterpart to anarchic disturbance. Within the Christian narrative, rebirth and new life follow naturally from the putting to death of the laws of Caesar. St. Paul explains: "Now we are released from the law, having died to that which held us captive, so that we serve in the new way of the Spirit and not in the old way."[106] Berdyaev's understanding of spiritual revolution closely echoes this statement. We have seen anarchy's destructive capacity; we turn now to its creative endeavor.

Berdyaev's concept of creativity has its roots in the *Imago Dei*. Since God is a creator and we are made in his image, Berdyaev believes humanity's purpose is to create, and like God, to create *ex nihilo*.[107] Berdyaev describes the nature of creativeness as "the making of something new that had not existed before."[108] A dominant theme in *The Realm of Spirit and the Realm of Caesar* is the creation of the new man, which I will discuss as the transformation of self. The connection to anarchy is still central in the process of transformation, since the creation of the new for Berdyaev is the ultimate goal of spiritual revolution.

The principle of newness according to Berdyaev is what distinguishes spiritual revolution from secular revolt. He proposes that Christianity alone is revolutionary and that secular revolutions are revolutionary in a much weaker sense or not at all, since he believes that God alone is able to effect change at a fundamental level:

> It must be said of political revolutions, even the most radical of them change man comparatively little. We hear much of the great difference between the bourgeois and the communist man, but the victorious communist, once he has got into power, may

106. Rom 7:6.

107. He explains: "the creative act of a man cannot be completely determined by the material which is given by the world; in it there is newness that is not determined by the outside world. This is the element of freedom that comes into any real creative act. This is the mystery of creativity. In this sense, creativity is creation from nothing." Berdyaev, *Self-cognition*, 213.

108. Quoted by Nucho in *Berdyaev's Philosophy*, 99. It is worth noting, however, that some theologians might object to the unqualified analogy between divine and human creation. Tolkien, for example, would refuse the use of creation for man, since he believes man always creates *ex materia*—from what is already given.

be inwardly and spiritually, to the very marrow of his bones, a
bourgeois. [. . .] Only a new birth, the birth of the spiritual man,
[. . .] may be the real appearance of a new man.[109]

Leonardo Boff, though writing in a different century and continent,
makes a very similar argument. He considers "newness" to be a definitional
characteristic of revolution that differentiates the reformer from the revolutionary. "Reformers," Boff writes, "want to better their social and religious
world. Reformers do not seek to create something absolutely new. [. . .]
Revolutionaries, in contrast to reformers, do not merely want to improve
the situation. They envisage the introduction of something new, the changing of the social and religious game rules."[110]

Consequently, for both thinkers, authentic revolution is not contained
within the sociopolitical sphere, as here they see no potential to bring about
the quality of genuine newness. "A political revolt," Berdyaev writes, "is a
reaction against the old without creating something new."[111] It is effectively
disturbance without transformation. Garrett Green presses this point in his
examination of Berdyaev and implies that Christianity is unable to accept
contemporary political revolution because it is not revolutionary enough.
This explains why for Berdyaev the social and political components of anarchism are propelled by, and only fully realized in, the Christian imagination. In addition to (and as a result of) the creation of the new, Berdyaev
identifies the emergence of personality as another central aspect of spiritual
revolution. Paul preaches that the new man in Christ is one who has cast off
his "old self" and received through grace a new and truer self,[112] or to use
Berdyaev's terminology, he has gained, for the first time, real personality.

For both Paul and Berdyaev the creation of the new man has an eternal
dimension, and insofar as the kingdom of man is bound to the finite, the
emergence of personality heralds the presence of an infinite power. "Personality," Berdyaev declares, "is a break-through, a break with this world."[113] As
ever, the tension between the two realms is evident and we have seen how
this rift engenders a spiritual deconstruction of Caesar's terms. Now it is becoming clear that the destruction of the old self gives way to its re-creation.

109. Berdyaev, *Realm of Spirit*, 162. The concept of the "new man" is prevalent
throughout the New Testament, exemplified in Paul's teaching: "if anyone is in Christ
he is a new creation" (2 Cor 5:17).

110. Boff, *Jesus Christ Liberator*, 239–40.

111. Berdyaev, *The Realm of Spirit*, 166.

112. "You have put off the old self with its practices and have put on the new self,
which is being renewed in knowledge after the image of its creator" (Col 2:9–10).

113. Berdyaev, *Solitude and Society* (1934), quoted in Lowrie (ed. and trans.), *Christian Existentialism*, 72.

This is the same language Paul uses to communicate the radical transformation of the self in conversion: "If anyone is in Christ, he is a new creation. The old has passed away; behold, the new has come."[114]

A final important aspect of the creation of the new concerns the transformation of the will, whereby the freedom of the will imparted by the Spirit combats an individual's predilection to sin. Like personality, Berdyaev defines freedom as an eruption within the delimitations of the realm of Caesar. "Freedom breaks into this world," he writes, "Freedom comes from another world: it contradicts and overthrows the law of this world."[115] It is clear from this that Berdyaev sees freedom as destructive, but there is also room for suggesting that freedom is reconstructive as it restores the creative potential of the *Imago Dei* within the individual. The interjection of freedom to the kingdom of man demonstrates that God is able to enter into and radically reorient the will of individuals. In the scope of Berdyaev's writing, freedom is one of the most pervasive themes. Berdyaev synthesizes freedom with truth. He pairs it with personality and links it to the creative imagination; freedom is the foundation of both personality and newness. Within Berdyaev's anarchism, the transformation of the will also involves the baptism of the imagination, a phrase associated with C. S. Lewis.[116] Michael Ward explains how when Lewis read George MacDonald's *Phantastes*, it awoke "Lewis's imaginative capacity for understanding 'holiness.'" It led to the

> sanctification of all common everyday things, not by throwing them out in order to make room for some transcendent but alien reality, still less by replacing them with an irrational, fantastic never-never land, but by changing their *meaning* from the inside, transforming them, illuminating them with a different light.[117]

Ward summarizes here the essential point of the analogy between Christianity and nonsense literature. We are not arguing that after reading the *Alice* novels we should try to integrate nonsense aesthetics into our picture of reality. Rather, we are suggesting that they may help us to recast "common everyday things" in the light of something supernatural or wondrous.

---

114. 2 Cor 5:17.

115. Berdyaev, *Realm of Spirit*, 105.

116. In *Surprised by Joy*, C. S. Lewis describes how his imagination was "baptized" by reading MacDonald's *Phantastes*. By this he suggests that on some aesthetic level he was drawn to the Christian atmosphere of MacDonald's works paving the way for his conscious intellectual mind to later follow. In Lewis' case the baptism of the imagination was a revolutionary moment in Lewis' spiritual journey.

117. Ward, "The Good Serves the Better," in Davison (ed.), *Imaginative Apologetics*, 63.

Alison Milbank has suggested that creative imagining has an implic-
itly theological function, and she makes the important statement that it is
not only when our imagination is directed towards the religious that it has
a theological role, but considers that there is something in all imaginative
creativity that connects the participant to the divine. She writes: "God works
in us through the imagination: it is his instrument. When we consciously
imagine, in the sense of making art or poetry, we engage in a similar, if
lesser, act of re-creation, seeking meaning and unity in what we experience,
dissolving only to re-create."[118] The pursuit of reading nonsense on one
level causes us to imagine in terms that revise the conditions of the familiar
world; so a rabbit hole turns into the portal to a magical world, the common
horse fly transforms into "a rocking-horse fly."

To return to Berdyaev's understanding of the imagination, he believes
that the transformation from living under the conditions of Caesar to those
of the Spirit is enabled by the power of the imagination to alter the perception of the real in order to discover the spiritual reality of the kingdom of
God. Berdyaev explains: "the unseen world is not a reality forced upon us
or compelling us; it derives from freedom of the spirit. And what the free
spirit creates, is the most real."[119] Once the individual has been made free
in Christ, his imagination is reborn, enabling him to see for the first time
the reality that God's invisible reign is already established on earth. The belief that there *is* an attainable and ideal alternate world, which has *already*
usurped the reign of Caesar appears as anarchism to the secular mind. The
believer's mental transformation of the world of appearances imaginatively
suspends the vision of reality and establishes the anarchic moment wherein
the supreme reign is not visibly constituted, in a world where the ruling
power is not actually ruling.

The restoration of the old: re-creating the world

We have discussed transformation as a force of imaginative freedom that
inspires individuals to seek an alternative mode of engaging with the world.
Whilst it is both fitting and orthodox to speak of a race of new men, if we
end our process of transformation at the level of individual restoration this
could potentially lead to two misrepresentations of Christian anarchy: one
could conceive of a spiritual race imaginatively elevated above the secular
realm; or alternatively it might lead to the idea that Christians see themselves
as the only remaining survivors amid the ashes of Caesar. Instead, the Bible

118. Milbank, "Apologetics and the Imagination," 35.
119. Berdyaev, *Realm of Spirit*, 101.

affirms that the kingdom of God is *already* transforming and re-creating the kingdom of man from within the historical: "The kingdom of God is not coming with signs to be observed, nor will they say 'Look here it is!' or 'There!' for behold the kingdom of God is in the midst of you."[120] Thus, what we are looking for in Berdyaev's account of Christianity is evidence that anarchic disturbance gives way to a vivid restorative transformation of the physical and historical. We are aiming to discover if Berdyaev's Christian anarchism agrees with Boff's conviction that, "The Kingdom of God is not to be in another world but is the old world transformed into a new one."[121]

Berdyaev's theology is sometimes criticized as gnostic and heterodox owing to his sympathy with hermeticism and mysticism. The American theologian Carnegie Calian raises a characteristic Presbyterian concern with respect to Berdyaev's theology: "there is within Berdyaev's thoughts a distinct dualism which is not found in the biblical view of the world and which is not without its dangers. This view is the outspoken gnostic-dualistic devaluation of this world."[122] Critics have suggested that Berdyaev's emphasis on revolution as a spiritual takeover leaves us with a gnosticized church and a cosmologized Caesar. This could imply that Berdyaev's anarchism is not really anarchic enough, as he does not allow for a true restoration of the historical. An orthodox interpretation of "spiritual revolution" requires a revitalization of the world from within *and* without. Giving equal emphasis to the historical is an important demonstration of God's ultimate sovereignty as it reveals God's ability to redeem history in a way, which both preserves historical reality and transfigures it to become the perfect reflection of transcendental truth.

There are indeed certain grounds for suggesting that Berdyaev perhaps downplays the internal redemption of the realm of Caesar,[123] but this feature is still nonetheless present in his theology and to overlook it entirely as Calian does is unfair. Although Berdyaev defines himself as a Christian theosophist in the introduction to *Freedom and the Spirit*, in the same paragraph he emphasizes: "my purpose is not to introduce heresy of any kind."[124] Berdyaev describes truth as "the kindling of a light within being,"[125] which posits an eschatological revitalization of the world. He insists that

120. Luke 17:20–21.

121. Boff, *Jesus Christ Liberator*, 53.

122. Calian, *Eschatology in Berdyaev*, 124.

123. Bedyaev often appears to place greater emphasis on the deconstructive force of Christianity, such as his claim in *Destiny of Man*, 132, that "The Gospel frightens the world and seems to be destructive."

124. Berdyaev, *Freedom and the Spirit*, xix.

125. Berdyaev, *Truth and Revelation*, 26.

even for the unbeliever "there is the experience of the meaning of history, hidden behind its meaninglessness."[126] This concept of the hidden nature of spiritual truth contributes to its status as anarchic by emphasizing that the change has not yet come into visible fullness, but is nevertheless operative in all spheres of life, including the social and historical. This unseen defeat and unobserved restoration can be considered as a creative form of negative positing, which obliterates and simultaneously recreates the realm of Caesar under the sovereignty of Spirit.

For Berdyaev, then, it would be more accurate to state that the revolutionary component of Christianity is not only exhibited in its destructive capacity, but also in its restorative power.[127] He identifies the devastating effects of the victory of Christ as the glorious transformation of the individual, social and cosmic: "the Kingdom of God is the transfiguration of the world, the transfiguration of the individual man, but social and cosmic transfiguration as well."[128] This demonstrates that Berdyaev's spiritual revolution is not as gnostic as it first appears. Berdyaev *is* concerned about the redemption of the historical, and although he sees the gospel as a destructive force, destruction as we have seen is part of the process of transfiguration.

Both the destruction of Caesar and the construction of Spirit coalesce in "the creative transfiguration of reality."[129] This is the dynamic, paradoxical assertion that at the point of the abolition of Caesar its transfiguration is taking place. Boff makes a similar assertion: "the Kingdom of God is a total, global and structural transfiguration and revolution of the reality of human beings; it is the cosmos purified of all evils and full of the reality of God."[130] Boff implies that Christianity is truly revolutionary because it is *this* world that will be, and is being, transformed. In other words, whilst the kingdom of man is being destroyed and impeded, it is also being enlightened and reborn. This is the paradoxical conclusion of the principle that "the kingdom is already present and fermenting within the old world."[131]

---

126. Ibid., 78.

127. Berdyaev left Russia in 1922 unwillingly, committed to his belief in the redemption of the socio-political. He writes in his autobiography: "I never wanted to leave Russia and become an émigré, for I had faith in the possibility of the spiritual regeneration and liberation of Communist Russia from within." Berdyaev, *Dream and Reality*, 236.

128. Berdyaev, *The Russian Idea* (1946), quoted in Lowrie (ed. and trans.), *Christian Existentialism*, 216.

129. Berdyaev, *Truth and Revelation*, 15.

130. Boff, *Jesus Christ Liberator*, 53.

131. Ibid., 54.

The transformation of the world thus involves man's imaginative participation in Christ's victory.

The church has an integral role in the transformation of the reality and as we discussed in the section on the two realms, the church is both present in the "old world" and maintains a degree of holy separateness. The transparent language of anarchy helps to make the Christian understanding of allegiance clear. In reference to the status and role of the church within the realm of Caesar, Berdyaev writes: "the Church is not manifested and revealed in all the fullness of its being and does not realize all the possibilities contained within itself. Its complete actualization and Incarnation will mean the transfiguration of the cosmos, the coming of a new world, the setting up of the Kingdom of God."[132] This quotation demonstrates Berdyaev's commitment to transformation and not merely disturbance by suggesting that the presence of the church in the world has a transfigurative power.

The eschatological authority of the "inwards church"[133] is one example of the Christian attachment to what is not yet, which indicates that the constitution of God's kingdom is eschatological and inward. Yet, Christianity also teaches that it is equally important to emphasize how the eschaton is already present and manifest (albeit imperfectly) in the church, the body of Christ. By upholding the already/not-yet paradox, the anticipation of the inwards church is also conceived of as a present encounter experienced now as a different sort of ruling. Therefore, we can see how Berdyaev's description of the "inwards church" is not entirely divorced from its outward expression, though his emphasis is on an eschatological now, restoring the past and present by anticipating a future reality. The paradoxical status of the church thus entails the revelatory disturbance of our conventional conception of time and linearity as well as a radical alteration of our concept of power. This creates a direct challenge to the logic of the secular realm, demonstrating that the perverse rationality of Wonderland might offer valuable insight into the Christian attitude of living in the now and the not-yet.

132. Berdyaev, *Freedom and the Spirit*, 334.

133. Berdyaev makes the distinction between the "inward church" (the mystical and invisible elements) and the "outward church" (the teachings, the history and the eschatology).

CONCLUSION: "EMBODIED TWILIGHT"[134]

In both Christianity and nonsense, we have witnessed a lifting of "the film of familiarity"[135] through an imaginative process of the disturbance and transformation of the commonplace. Our discussion of the anarchic dimension to the *Alice* books concluded by demonstrating a similar transformative disruption—whilst the dream-world is subverted by the intrusion of reality, remnants of the fantastic linger on and enchant the real-world. Carroll closes his book by asking: "Life, what is it but a dream?" prompting the reader to question the distinction between perception and imagination.

This is also an important theme emergent in Berdyaev's work; it is particularly central in his philosophical autobiography, *Dream and Reality*. Berdyaev holds a Neoplatonic belief that dream describes the objective realm of Caesar, while true reality concerns the kingdom of God. The imagination is therefore critical in facilitating the transformation of the world of appearances and a re-envisioning of the secular realm under a divine rule, which is both present and eschatological. Christianity, as we have seen, does not teach that the kingdom of God is unrelated to this world, but neither does it claim that it has arrived in full. The era of anarchy is not final; it is a temporary measure describing the current "now and not yet" condition of the world where we await the fullness of God's revelation. To return to our conclusion from the chapter on paradox, one could see how describing Christianity as anarchic is a further realization of de Lubac's pronouncement that "the synthesis of the world has not been made."

The anarchic aspect of the Christian imagination thus seems to be in-keeping with the paradoxical dimension as it involves a blend of incompatible pairs; rebellion and submission; human freedom and divine law; integral engagement and absolute detachment. Berdyaev insists on articulating the tension of man's existence, describing the human condition as "at the border-line between two worlds."[136] This interplay between sacred and secular, Spirit and Caesar, could be described as a "twilight" or in-between realm in which the final consummation of the kingdom of God is both betokened and yet to be realized. The Christian must not lose sight of the vision of God, or abandon the broken world. He is twixt-light or tween-light; "a being belonging to two worlds";[137] in the world but not of the world; preaching a message which destroys and re-builds. From our analysis of

134. Carroll, *Sylvie and Bruno Concluded*, 560.
135. Coleridge, *Biographia Literaria*, 314.
136. Berdyaev, *Dream and Reality*, 56–57.
137. Berdyaev, *Destiny of Man*, 36.

Berdyaev's theology, it has become apparent that the mental straddling of the two kingdoms requires an imagination of contrary states: a perpetual noetic twilight.[138]

Accordingly, Christianity finds itself in the anarchic era of transition between "Christianity this side of the end, to eschatological Christianity, which foreshadows the end of this spell-bound world of ours."[139] Berdyaev insists, "this is not a period of fear, inertia and frustration, but one of daring and creative endeavour."[140] The imagination therefore performs a vital role in advancing the kingdom of God through a corrective disordering or an anarchic re-envisaging of the world in the light of the resurrection claim. Likewise, we have seen how literary nonsense "unsettles mental habits formed by rhetorical conventions and thus induces the pleasures of both a temporary relief from the boundaries of internalized rules and an increased flexibility of mind."[141] Again, the imagination is employed to elicit the un-settling of mental habits and then to play and create in the new space of cognitive freedom.

Life under the sovereignty of Spirit brings with it a necessary estrange-ment from the familiar, which is a pattern that as we have seen occurs in nonsense literature where the appearance of things is often misleading.[142] Human creative capacity to envisage the world contrary to how it seems "requires," as Berdyaev writes, "another type of knowing."[143] This "type of knowing," I want to suggest, is more akin to nonsense narratives than modern rationality, since both Christianity and literary nonsense demand a cognitive reversal of the conventional perspective. Nonsense signals that the given-ness of reality as it appears to us *can* be questioned. Christian-ity believes that because there is a post-lapsarian distance between how things look and the ontological "real," the outward face of the world *should* be questioned. Whilst acknowledging, as ever, the manifold differences be-

---

138. Similar imagery is evoked by Chesterton: "The ordinary man has always been sane because the ordinary man has always been a mystic. He has permitted twilight. He has always had one foot in earth and the other in fairyland." Chesterton, *Orthodoxy*, 46.

139. Berdyaev, *Dream and Reality*, 297.

140. Ibid.

141. Schwab, "Nonsense and Metacommunication," 158.

142. Throughout her adventures Alice finds that things are seldom as they appear, and the more she attempts clarification the more obscure and dreamlike objects be-come. Such as the episode when Alice finds herself in a shop owned by a sheep. "'Things flow about so here!' she said at last in a plaintive tone, after she had spent a minute or so in vainly pursuing a large bright thing that looked sometimes like a doll and sometimes like a work-box and was always in the shelf next above the one she was looking at." Carroll, *LG*, 154–55.

143. Berdyaev, *Freedom and the Spirit*, 31.

tween nonsense and Christianity, the following two quotations testify to the aptness of this association. One quotation describes the anarchic element of literary nonsense; the other presents the anarchic dimension to Christianity. Without consulting the footnotes, it is not at all clear which refers to which:

> [X] sets out to question received wisdom and in the process it stimulates new ways of thinking. This makes it highly effective for writers who want to comment on, and so affect society, and those who propose new ways of representing culture.

> [X provides] liberation from the bonds of the present system of living. [X] takes place by *playing games*. [. . .] We discover with a laugh that things need not at all be as they are and as we have been told they have to be.

The first is a commentary by a secular critic referring to the purpose of non-sense in children's literature;[144] the second is Jürgen Moltmann's description of the Christian attitude to the world in the light of the resurrection claim.[145] In both cases, X could be substituted for either nonsense or Christianity, although neither writer intended to describe the other.

Anarchy and nonsense thus appear to be analogous in the preaching of non-conformity in a non-conformist mode. The correlation between religious faith and the anarchic aspect of the nonsensical imagination ultimately consists in the participant's capacity to think in terms that contradict a secular interpretation of the familiar world. This apparently inadvertent link might tell us something significant about the nature of both nonsense and Christianity. Perhaps literary nonsense could be helpfully used in dialogue between believers and atheists to explain some aspects of Christian faith. Perhaps a more thorough inquiry into the potential ontological significance of nonsense might offer a new and illuminating method of approaching criticism of literary nonsense. I will return to consider these ideas following our examination of the third and final component of the nonsensical imagination namely, the childlike.

144. Reynolds, *Radical Children's Literature*, 45.
145. Moltmann, *Theology and Joy*, 36.

CHAPTER 3

The Childlike _____

NONSENSE AND THE CHILDLIKE

TWENTY YEARS AFTER THE publication of the first *Alice* story in 1865, Carroll reflects in a letter: "The germ of *Alice's Adventures in Wonderland* was an extempore story, told in a boat to 3 children of Dean Liddell: it was afterwards, at the request of Miss Alice Liddell, written out for her."[1] For many literary critics, anxious to unearth Wonderland's hidden meaning, there almost seems to be a disappointment at the story's apparent spontaneity, as if its whimsical origin is somehow problematic for serious study.[2] Juliet Dusinberre believes: "Since Alice has become accepted into the cannon of adult literature it is partly as an excuse for this new attitude that critics have tried so hard to prove that Dodgson meant very much more by his two stories than light-hearted amusement for children."[3] Dusinberre articulates a sense of embarrassment attached to the adult enjoyment of a story meant for children and the need felt by many critics to invest the tale with some deeper significance.

---

1. Letter to E. Gertrude Thomson July 16, 1885, in Carroll, *The Selected Letters of Lewis Carroll*, 149.

2. Marijke Boucherie believes that nonsense writing "bypass[es] the serious effort required by more mainstream poetry to engage in the struggle of 'words and meanings.'" Because of this, she considers that it "occup[ies] a childlike stance outside language." Boucherie here links a disregard of the intentionally serious modes of cognition to the more whimsical, ephemeral stance of the childlike. "Nonsense and Other Senses," 266.

3. Dusinberre, *Alice to the Lighthouse*, 60.

John Pudney, consulting Duckworth's diaries, emphasizes that "Duckworth testified the tale's spontaneity: "I rowed *stroke* and he rowed *bow* [. . .] and the story was actually composed and spoken *over my shoulder* for the benefit of Alice Liddell."[4] Moreover, Duckworth's report coincides with Alice Liddell's own recollection of the event:

> Nearly all of *Alice's Adventures Underground* was told to us on that blazing summer afternoon. [. . .] [O]n the next day I started to pester him to write down the story for me. [. . .] It was due to my 'going on' and importunity that, after saying he would think about it, he eventually gave the hesitating promise which started him writing it down at all. This he referred to in a letter written in 1883 in which he writes of me as the 'one without whose infant patronage it might possibly have never had written at all.'[5]

We have little reason, then, to doubt testimony of the story's "germ," and it is important that we establish this as we approach the third strand of the nonsensical imagination: the childlike. In our treatment of the *Alice* stories so far, we have deduced little from the *fact* of Alice. By this, I mean two things; firstly, as we have seen the creation of Wonderland came about as an attempt to entertain the real Alice. Secondly, the reader experiences the stories *through* Alice—we journey at her pace and witness Wonderland via her thoughts and her encounters.[6] Reflecting on this, Lecercle believes one of the most revolutionary aspects of Victorian nonsense is "not the image of the child the text projects, but [. . .] *how the child herself talks.* Nonsense embodies this new approach to childhood."[7]

Twenty-five years after the famous boating trip and following the immense success of the two *Alice* stories, Carroll *still* thinks the original circumstance important to emphasize. In an article written on the adaptation of *Alice* for the stage, Carroll again recalls the tale's foundation: "And so, to please a child I loved (I don't remember any other motive), I printed in manuscript, and illustrated with my own crude designs."[8] And yet, as

4. Pudney, *Lewis Carroll and His World*, 10.

5. Hargreaves, "Alice's Recollections" in *Norton Critical Edition*, 276–77.

6. The same point is made by Cristopher Hollingsworth; he writes: "The Wonderland story [. . .] opens with Alice's private thoughts, and we immediately experience action *through* her, not from outside her." *Alice Beyond Wonderland*, 28.

7. Lecercle, "Nonsense and Politics," 371.

8. Lewis Carroll, "Alice on Stage," *The Theatre* (1887). The commercial publication of *Alice in Wonderland*, was also inspired by the request of a particular child, George MacDonald's son, Greville. Greville recalls his mother reading *Alice's Adventures Underground*, "When she came to an end I, being aged six, exclaimed that there ought to be sixty thousand volumes of it. Certainly it was our enthusiasm that persuaded our

Michael Hancher observes, "whatever his original intentions, by 1890 Carroll had accepted the fact that adults enjoyed his children's books."[9] Moreover, Hancher emphasizes, "no other children's book has been so thoroughly appropriated by adults."[10] So, without denying that the reader may well be an adult, we still have to deal with the fact that the child is the central character and also the intended audience and ask if this has particular significance for the reader's imagination.

Carroll's acceptance that adults enjoyed his books does nothing to alter the centrality of the child, but, rather, Carroll believes, reveals something childlike in the adult reader. In a letter to a grown-up admirer of the books, Carroll writes: "that children love the book is a very precious thought to me, and next to their love I value the sympathy of those who come with a child's heart to what I have tried to write about a child's thoughts."[11] This allows us legitimately to expand "the *fact* of Alice" to the category of "child."[12] Carroll, after all, refers to Alice as "child of my dreams"[13] and it is this element of child, or the childlikeness of Alice, that Carroll recalls in a letter to the grown-up Alice Liddell. He refers to her as "one who was, through so many years, my ideal child-friend."[14]

Carroll concludes *Wonderland's* prefatory poem by entreating his muse: "*Alice! A childish story take.*"[15] Here, "child" has become an adjective. "A *childish* story" introduces the idea of child, not only as audience and character, but also as a primary descriptor of the story's genre. At this point, we can return to Lecercle, who concludes his *Philosophy of Nonsense* by suggesting that the child is at the core of his theory of nonsense. "It will come as no surprise to the reader if I say that the content of the myth is the figure of the child (nonsense as a genre is a modern version of the great Romantic myth of the child)."[16] The conjunction of the child and nonsense would certainly come as no surprise to Chesterton, who begins his "Defence

---

Uncle Dodgson [. . .] to present the English-speaking world with one of its future classics." MacDonald, *George MacDonald and his Wife*, 342.

9. Hancher, "Alice's Audiences" in Holt McGavran (ed.), *Romanticism and Children's Literature*, 196–97.

10. Ibid., 197.

11. Letter to Mary E. Manners December 5, 1885, in *Selected Letters*, 158.

12. Alice's prominence in the global cannon captures, to some degree, the paradigmatic child of the universal imagination Cohen believes, "Charles, intentionally or not, got at the universal essence of childhood." Cohen, *Lewis Carroll*, 138.

13. Lewis Carroll, *Alice on Stage*.

14. Letter to Alice (Liddell) Hargreaves, March 1, 1885, in *Selected Letters*, 140.

15. Carroll, *AW*, 4.

16. Lecercle, *Philosophy of Nonsense*, 222.

of Nonsense" from the premise that the "sense of the abiding childhood of the world [is found] in the literature of nonsense."[17]

Chesterton describes the world as having the *characteristic* of childhood. Likewise, in offering nonsense as a genre (not merely a word-game) Lecercle introduces the figure of the child as a property of the genre. However, perhaps the most transparent emphasis on the unavoidable connection between nonsense and the child comes from Elizabeth Sewell, who believes: "child shall be that which in each of us, regardless of age, responds to Nonsense verse; Nonsense shall be that to which this child responds."[18] What Sewell is exploring here is the idea that there is something about nonsense that is inherently childlike, that is to say, it is both suitable for children, and exercises some deeper childlike nature in the imagination of the adult. Walter De La Mare identifies this element resonant in Carrollian nonsense, believing that it is in the imagination that the adult reader is able to "come with a child's heart" to experience this story for children. He writes: "It is the child that is left in us who tastes the sweetest honey and laves its imagination in the clearest waters to be found in the Alices."[19]

The aim of this chapter is to discuss the degree to which the presence of the childlike in Carroll's nonsense literature corresponds to Christian conceptions of the childlike. This will be done by identifying four central childlike qualities that Alice displays—simplicity, wonder, trust, and an aptitude for make-believe—and deciding to what extent (if at all) they correlate with religious ideas. In-keeping with the overarching aims of the thesis I am interested in considering the ways in which the reader's encounter with the childlike affects the imagination. Let us commence then, by trying to understand what precisely it means to approach nonsense literature "with a child's heart."

Daniel F. Kirk in his treatise *Charles Dodgson Semiotician* begins from a similar starting point: "In short," he writes, "to visit happily in the land of the Duchess and the Red King, one must surrender the attachments to familiar language thinking patterns he strove so hard to form when he was young, for he must assume, once again, the eager simplicity of a child."[20] In this quotation, we can identify a link between the anarchic element of the nonsensical imagination and the idea of the childlike discussed thus far. Kirk seems to imply that the authority of established patterns of thought

17. Chesterton, "A Defence of Nonsense," in *The Defendant*, 64.

18. Sewell, "Nonsense Verse and the Child," in *Explorations in the Field of Nonsense*, 135.

19. De La Mare, "On the *Alice* books," in Phillips (ed.), *Aspects of Alice*, 97.

20. Kirk, *Charles Dodgson Semiotician*, 68.

need to be overthrown, or at least held in abeyance in order to enter the realm of nonsense. Accordingly, the narrative of nonsensical imagining seems to require an anarchic disturbance of the familiar followed by a child-like re-envisioning of events. This "disturbance" may be equally described as a matter of happily accepting the nonsensical appearance or suggestion of things, but however we interpret the revision of the familiar it is the child within the adult that conducts the imagination when the world is made strange.

Edmund Wilson believes that Carroll understands the child within the adult or "the more primitive elements of the mind of maturity" because "[he] is in touch with the real mind of childhood."[21] Critics have suggested that Carroll's sensitivity to the child's mind is a consequence of his failure to grow-up. Perhaps the capacity for imagining in nonsensical terms, past childhood, is a manifestation of the reader's own resistance to maturity. John Skinner, speaking from a psychoanalytical perspective, proposes that the childlike elements in Carrollian nonsense arise from the fact "that Lewis Carroll remained at a childish level in his emotional life."[22] He concludes, "Charles Lutwidge Dodgson, who did not dare become an adult [. . .] re-mained the eternal child."[23] From this perspective, it would seem that the Alice stories offer adult readers a means of escape from the real world—a retreat into the world of nonsense, the realm of the child. This implies that to think in childlike terms is a turning away from reality.

However, even if this is a correct account of childlike imagining, it does not appear to be an accurate understanding of Carroll's perspective. His biographer Cohen explains: "they [the children] more than any other force, fired his imagination, and he found, like Blake, that they saw into the heart of complex truths more clearly and perceptively than weary adults."[24] Cohen's insight reverses the psychoanalytic position and offers instead the belief that the child opens up (rather than shuts down) our vision of reality.[25]

The suggestion that imagining in childlike terms illumines rather than conceals the real begs certain questions such as; what is unique about the child's mind, and, why place such significance on childlike imagining? If

21. Wilson, "C. L. Dodgson," in Phillips (ed.), *Aspects of Alice*, 247.

22. Skinner, "Lewis Carroll's Adventures in Wonderland," in Phillips (ed.), *Aspects of Alice*, 350.

23. Ibid., 359.

24. Cohen, *Lewis Carroll*, 107.

25. An interesting discussion of this theme can be found in Alison Milbank's book *Chesterton and Tolkien as Theologians*, where she discusses Chesterton's revision of the Romantic association of childhood with imagination "to claim, inversely, that it is chil-dren who are the true realists." Milbank, *Chesterton and Tolkien*, 36.

we look closely at moments where Carroll extols his love of the child, it is noticeable that his adulation is often intriguingly connected to his religious faith: "The why of the books cannot, and need not, be put into words. Those for whom a child's mind is a sealed book, and see no divinity in a child's smile would read such words in vain."[26] Carroll further tells us that "the true child [is] a spirit fresh from God's hands,"[27] "that 'tête-à-tête' intercourse with children [is] very healthy and helpful to one's own spiritual life,"[28] and that the child is in some sense "purer, and nearer to God, than one feels oneself to be."[29]

These quotations indicate that for Carroll there is an important connection between the holy and the child. Although Carroll believes that nonsense should be consciously put *aside* when considering theological matters, if, as Carroll supposes, nonsense and divinity are connected to the child, then it seems legitimate to conceive that nonsense and divinity might be connected *through* the child. If this is the case, then despite Carroll's desire to separate nonsense from theological contemplation, the two may prove to be intimately related. It is this possibility that the chapter will explore.

CHRISTIANITY AND THE CHILDLIKE

The suggestion that religious thinking is childlike might seem like the allegation of the skeptic rather than the viewpoint of the Christian. Alongside associations of purity and innocence, the childlike, as Skinner is keen to observe, has connotations of naivety, immaturity and blinkered idealism. Charles Taylor in *A Secular Age* explains: "A very common objection of unbelief to Christianity has been that it offers a childishly benign view of human life, where everything will come right in the end, something which the really mature person cannot believe, and is willing to do without, having the courage to face reality as it is."[30] Unless, therefore, we can discover a coherent scriptural warrant for confronting the world "with a child's heart," it may be advisable for Christianity to avoid association with the term.

Let us begin with a consideration of the idea of the childlike in Scripture. In each of the Gospels, Jesus calls his disciples to become like a child, and on each occasion, this command is coupled with the doctrine of salvation. In canonical order the references are: Matthew 18:3, "Unless you

26. Quoted by Strony, "Lewis Carroll," in Phillips (ed.), *Aspects of Alice*, 87.

27. Carroll, *Alice's Adventures Under-Ground*, Preface to the 1886 facsimile edition.

28. Letter to Mrs. C. F. Moberly Bell, September 27, 1893, in *Selected Letters*, 247.

29. Ibid.

30. Taylor, *A Secular Age*, 318.

change and become like little children you will never enter the kingdom of heaven." Mark 10:15, "Whoever does not receive the kingdom of God as a little child will never enter it." Luke 8:17, "Truly I tell you, whoever does not receive the kingdom of God as a little child will never receive it." John 3:3, "Very truly, I tell you, no one can see the kingdom of God without being born from above."[31] In each case, the injunction is emphatically expressed as a negative syllogism (if not p then not q). This suggests that the childlike is a more than an analogy of peripheral significance to Christianity.

Nevertheless, it could be argued in his first letter to the Corinthians that Paul gainsays this command to be childlike. Instead, Paul seems to encourage the Corinthians to grow out of their childness and become adults in their faith. He writes: "When I was a child, I spoke like a child, I thought like a child, I reasoned like a child; when I became an adult, I put an end to childish ways."[32] However, Paul's reproach to the Corinthians can only be seen to contradict Christ's commandment if "become like children" is taken to mean "become children." It is necessary for the Christian to observe that Christ instructs his disciples to become "as" or "like" a child. In this sense, John's Gospel helps to qualify the other three references by demonstrating that Jesus is not commanding a physical reversion to childhood, but describing a childlike quality. How essential, though, is such a quality?

In the Gospels, this childlike quality seems to be presented as a prerequisite for salvation. The evidence of its necessity can be found in the connective propositions inherent within the Gospel commands. In the Greek, both Matthew and John use the conditional conjunction εαν, meaning "if." Mark and Luke use αν as an alternative, which, although without a direct English translation, denotes an aspect of contingency, whereby the action of the sentence is similarly dependent upon the circumstance of the verb. In all four cases ου is present, which not only introduces a negative statement, but coupled with μη has the effect of making the negation imperative. This reveals that the childlike cannot be "bracketed-out" from an examination of the Christian faith.

Having accepted the term's significance, it is still not clear what precisely is meant by childlike in either nonsense or faith. The presence of the term has been affirmed in both cases, but the specific characteristics may share little or no resemblance. In order to explore what might be meant by the term from a religious perspective, this chapter will lean on the commentary

---

31. The Greek ανωθεν can be translated as "again" or "anew" in addition to "from above." Although John does not use the word "child," his formula and meaning remains equivalent since he uses the subjunctive tense of begat (γενυηθη) indicating that the seeing of the kingdom of God is conditional on being born.

32. 1 Cor 13:11.

of George MacDonald, who is perhaps the pre-eminent thinker on the relationship between theology and the childlike. In addition, MacDonald was also Carroll's close friend and a writer of children's fairy tales and was instrumental in encouraging Carroll to publish *Alice in Wonderland*.[33] MacDonald insists that his own stories are not written "for children, but for the childlike"[34] and establishes his theology from a simple, overarching principle that "God is child-like."[35] In his *Unspoken Sermons*, MacDonald presents the following deduction: "God is represented in Jesus, for that God is like Jesus: Jesus is represented in the child, for that Jesus is like the child. Therefore, God is represented in the child, for that he is like the child. God is child-like. In the true vision of this fact lies the receiving of God in the child."[36] This implies that the childlike is not just a phase in relationship with God, but is the essential and abiding formula of that relationship.

This initial step in the contemplation of the childlike has reached a similar conclusion to that expressed by Angela-Shier Jones: "for the theologian [. . .] the journey is not optional. In order to obey the biblical imperative to become like a little child [. . .] the richness and complexity of childhood must be explored."[37] However, there are a number of definitional issues to consider concerning the conflating definitions of "child," "childhood," and "childlike." The clarification that the childlike is distinguishable from the child is a helpful observation to prevent the creation of "immaterial fairy-children,"[38] where it is presupposed that children possess inherent childlike qualities. Peter Green admits there has been a tendency, especially in the Victorian era, for "Children [to] become the ideal symbol of their elders' glutinous yearning for purity."[39]

We could perhaps entertain this idea if it were true that all children embody an unreserved purity, in which case the childlike would be translatable with the child. In a letter to Mrs. T. Dyer-Edwards, Carroll expresses indignation at the assumption that he possessed a universal delight in children. "I do *not* (as is popularly supposed of me) take a fancy to *all* children, and instantly: I fear I take *dis*likes to *some*)."[40] Carroll thus accepts, along

33. Carroll's diary entry on May 9th [1863] "Heard from Mrs MacDonald about 'Alice's Adventures Under Ground', which I had lent them to read and which they wish me to publish." *Diaries*.

34. MacDonald, *A Dish of Orts*, 317.

35. MacDonald, *Unspoken Sermons*, 12.

36. Ibid.

37. Shier-Jones, *Children of God*, 183.

38. Knoepflmacher, *Ventures into Childland*, 157.

39. Green, *Kenneth Grahame*, quoted by Dusinberre, in *Alice to the Lighthouse*, 5.

40. Letter to Mrs. T. Dyer-Edwardes, February 12, 1887, in *Selected Letters*, 167.

with MacDonald, that there are children who are not in the least childlike. MacDonald believes: "One of the saddest and not least common sights in the world is the face of a child whose mind is so brimful of worldly wisdom that the human childishness has vanished from it as well as the divine childlikeness."[41] It seems fair to assume that it is the childlike child to whom Carroll was most attracted. In a letter to the mother of Enid Steves he writes, "*many* thanks for lending me Enid. She is one of the dearest of children. It is *good* for one (I mean one's spiritual life, and in the same sense in which reading the Bible is good) to come into contact with such sweetness and innocence."[42] From this comment, we can further distinguish Carroll's belief that the child (that is, the childlike child) reveals some aspect of divinity and speculate that Carroll perceived such qualities in Alice Liddell, his "ideal child-friend" and further, in her literary self, incarnated them.

MacDonald makes a similar observation in his paraphrase of Matthew 18:5 ("whoever welcomes one such child in my name welcomes me"). He writes: "'He that sees the essential in this child, the pure childhood, sees that which is the essence of me,' grace and truth—in a word, childlikeness."[43] MacDonald's contention is not that the particular child in Jesus' teaching is perfected in the image of Christ, but that the child reveals the essential childlikeness of Christ. In his sermon "The Child in the Midst" MacDonald explains, "[Christ] could never have been a child if he would ever have ceased to be a child, for in him the transient found nothing. Childhood belongs to divine nature."[44] In this quotation, MacDonald puts forward the view that Christ is an eternal son since he has an infinite father. In a later sermon, MacDonald develops this idea explaining, "because his father is his father, therefore he will be his child. The truth in Jesus is his relation to his father."[45] The sonhood of Christ is not confined only to his life on earth; it is expressed as a constant mode of interaction, both incarnate and triune: "I came from the Father and have come into the world; again, I am leaving the world and going to the Father."[46] Christ's speech implies that it is his sonhood that is infinite and his personhood (both adult and child) that is conditional.

41. MacDonald, *Unspoken Sermons*, 2.

42. Letter to Mrs. N. H. Stevens, June 1, 1892, in *Selected Letters*, 220.

43. MacDonald, *Unspoken Sermons*, 9.

44. Ibid., 13.

45. Ibid., 422.

46. John 16:28.

For MacDonald, Christ's eternal sonhood authorizes his claim that "childhood belongs to divine nature."[47] However, the usage of the word "childhood" is potentially misleading since it could imply that the Christian cannot enter adulthood and remain a son of God. Although according to the Bible Jesus was incarnate first as a child, the focus of the Gospels is on the adulthood of Jesus; it is in his adult ministry that he is ascribed the titles "Master,"[48] "Teacher,"[49] and "Lord."[50] Whilst this is not disputed, John Milbank argues, "it is Christ the confused child who dies upon the cross."[51] Evidently, Christ was at the peak of his physical maturity at the point of his crucifixion, so if it is at all fitting to refer to him as "child" this must be interwoven with his status as son. MacDonald unpacks this suggestion for us:

> He who is the Unchangeable could never become anything that He was not always, for that would be to change. He is as much a child now as ever he was. When he became a child, it was only to show us by itself, that we might understand it better, what he was always in his deepest nature.[52]

Thus, the definition established here is that Christ participated fully in both childhood and adulthood whilst remaining continuously childlike, and his childlikeness is linked to his sonship.

It seems that we are now able to affirm that sonship is an important aspect of the childlike. However, if sonship was all Christ intended to convey in commanding his disciples to become like little children he could have done so in many other ways, and with much greater clarity by using the word "sonlike," or alternatively, as he does elsewhere, by using the metaphor of man's earthly parents to express that God is *like* a parent.[53] One of the evident distinctions between sonhood and childhood is that the title "son" does not disappear in adulthood.[54] It therefore seems unlikely that the childlike, in the context of the Gospels, means only the sonlike, as there would be no distinction between any human being and the little children. The child-son is not more sonlike than the adult-son; the essence of sonship

---

47. MacDonald, *Unspoken Sermons*, 13.

48. Luke 5:5.

49. Luke 7:40.

50. Luke 9:59.

51. Milbank, "Fictioning Things," 5.

52. MacDonald, *Adela Cathcart*, 19.

53. For example, the Parable of the Prodigal Son.

54. A similar point is made by Guroian in "The Office of Child" where he explains "the office of child does not terminate at puberty [. . .] even at the age of sixty, I am the child, the son, of my father." 106.

is not somehow greater in infancy. Therefore, whilst I recognize that sonship is *part* of the childlike, it is not this quality alone which Christ identifies in the child. It is important, therefore, not to dismiss the child or childhood as irrelevant but to understand that their function is analogical; the childlike is the essential category.

In relation to the wider thesis in this book, we were able to establish paradox and anarchy as thematic elements within the stories. The childlike, however, is more amorphous because the theme is primarily discerned through the character of Alice. Therefore, to structure this chapter I will examine Alice's most prominent childlike qualities individually, considering each in relation to MacDonald's theological writings, specifically his homiletic series *Unspoken Sermons* and *The Hope of the Gospel*. Alice is of course not a perfectly childlike child. Among other fallen traits, Alice displays stubbornness, irritation and pride. Nevertheless, as Carroll recognized in her namesake, she also possesses certain childlike qualities. Most significantly, however, "Alice is the first fictional child to escape from the moral-finder,"[55] and in being stripped of a projected moral or immoral attitude, Carroll is free to present Alice as a *childlike* child as opposed to a "good child" or a "bad child," and she represents a helpful heuristic guide from which to begin deciphering specific characteristics of the childlike.

MacDonald commences his discussion of the childlike from the following premise: "Nothing is required of man that is not first in God."[56] He appeals to Matthew 18:5 to provide evidence for his claim: "Whoever welcomes one such child in my name welcomes me." He explains: "For it is *in my name*. This means *as representing me*; and, therefore, *as being like me*."[57] MacDonald then proposes, "when he tells them to receive *such* a little child in his name, it must surely imply something in common between them all—something in which the child and Jesus meet."[58] This chapter will be concerned with identifying the nature of this "something" and the grounds upon which "the child and Jesus meet."

SIMPLICITY

We will consider Simplicity as the first point of association between Christ and the child. I will draw upon Carroll's direct connection between the child and simplicity as a warrant for proceeding with the subject, and then

---

55. Dusinberre, *Alice to the Lighthouse*, 59.
56. MacDonald, *Unspoken Sermons*, 6.
57. Ibid., 7.
58. Ibid.

explore the biblical relationship between simplicity and faith, consulting MacDonald to see if, and in what sense, he acknowledges simplicity as a childlike attribute. Simplicity has been chosen as an initial childlike quality because Carroll uses the term frequently in his diaries and correspondence to convey his reason for delighting in the company of his child friends.

In a letter describing a photography session with the five-year-old daughter of Dr. Gray, he writes, "she is so perfectly simple and unconscious that it is a matter of entire indifference to her whether she is taken in full dress or nothing."[59] To the mother of another child friend he emphasizes: "I have never seen anything more beautiful in childhood than their *perfect simplicity*."[60] These two letters by no means stand alone in Carroll's use of simplicity as a way of characterizing the child, but they may suffice as a *prima facie* indication of its relevance.

Alice in Wonderland closes with Carroll's contemplation concerning "how she [Alice] would keep, through all her riper years, the simple and loving heart of her childhood, [. . .] how she would feel with all their simple sorrows, and find a pleasure in all their simple joys, remembering her own child-life and the happy summer days."[61] It is not clear from these quotations what exactly Carroll means by "simple" or "simplicity" or if it is very much more than Victorian sentimentality. What *is* a "simple heart" or a "simple sorrow"? In what way might simplicity be related to "indifference" as Carroll's comment above implies? Let us suspend these questions for a moment whilst we look briefly at the biblical usage of the term.

In the New Testament, the word απλους is often translated as "simplicity," although the Greek also denotes singleness and wholeness. Its derivatives απλοτητος and απλοτητι are also interpreted as simplicity and singleness. In Matthew 6:22, for example, Christ declares: "The lamp of the body is the eye. If, then, your eye is απλους [simple, single, undivided] your whole body will be bright." In a like manner Paul articulates his concern for the Corinthians that "as the serpent deceived Eve by its cunning, your thoughts will be led astray from a sincere and απλοτητος [simple, single, whole] devotion to Christ."[62] The New Testament principle of simplicity seems to be concerned with the teaching that the Christian cannot serve two masters, and that to be a true child of God demands undivided or απλους obedience. Theological simplicity thus consists in the ability to give oneself to God, with a whole and undivided will.

59. Letter to Mrs. Chataway October 21, 1876, in *Selected Letters*, 69.
60. Letter to Mrs. Henderson July 20, 1879, in *Selected Letters*, 91.
61. Carroll, *AW*, 99.
62. See also Eph 6:5 and Col 3:22.

MacDonald identifies in Christ this same simplicity or singleness of vision. He writes: "his thought was ever and always his Father. To its home in the heart of the Father his heart was ever turned. [. . .] No vain show could enter at his eyes; neither ambition not disappointment could distort them to his eternal childlike gaze."[63] Perhaps this can help to illuminate Carroll's idea of a "simple sorrow" as a disappointment or misfortune, which, whilst acknowledging the element of sorrow, does not upset the simplicity of the "childlike gaze." If the focus of an individual is truly απλοτητος then "sorrows" and "joys" become illumined by (and do not detract from) such focus. MacDonald explains that "the simple purity of a single affection" enables man's personal vision to become a "willed harmony of dual oneness [. . .] with God."[64] From this it is possible to deduce that Christ's purpose is always απλους, since his mission consists solely in the carrying out of his Father's will. Such a purpose according to MacDonald is childlike because it is perpetually defined within the unity of the relationship between Father and Son.

For MacDonald it is important to affirm that child*like* simplicity is not entirely abstracted from child*hood* simplicity. In direct terms MacDonald writes, "At childhood's heart, the germ of good, lies God's simplicity."[65] Elsewhere he warns against "Forg[etting] the simplicity of childhood in the toil of life,"[66] a simplicity that John Milbank believes allows the child to remain "relatively immune to the goals of ambition, possession and sexual conquest."[67] The idea that children are in some sense removed from the "toil of life" could be connected to their dependence and trust in parental provision, which might indicate that the child's lack of burden reveals something of the simplicity of divine childlikeness.

This belief that the child is liberated from anxiety as a result of parental dependence has a clear connection with Christ's proclamation of God's provision: "do not worry about your life, what you will eat or what you will drink, or about your body what you will wear [. . . ;] your heavenly Father knows that you need all these things."[68] Perhaps Christ appeals to the epithet "Father" because of its metaphorical significance; the true "child" of God is assured that their "Father" will provide for them, and so the disciples who heed this message exhibit the Christian virtue of non-attachment to any-

---

63. MacDonald, *Unspoken Sermons*, 171.

64. Ibid., 101.

65. MacDonald, "To My Sister," in *Poems*, 223.

66. MacDonald, "Wordsworth's Poetry," *A Dish of Orts*, 255.

67. Milbank, "Fictioning Things," 4.

68. Matt 6:25, 32.

thing other than God. The evocation of the parent/child relationship seems to be a practical way of explaining what simplicity achieved *within* the toil of life looks like. Simplicity is manifest as an unburdened attitude to the world, which frees the individual from a consuming attachment to things. "Cast your burdens onto me," declares Christ, "for my yoke is easy and my burden light."[69] Although in a sense the Alice stories are not without darkness, the overarching sentiment remains light: they refuse to mourn; they will not be burdened.

Much literary criticism on the genre of nonsense focuses on its complex and intricate linguistic games.[70] Without denying that much of Carroll's humor relies on semantic puns, the narrative structure of the *Alice* books reveals a radical simplicity as Becker-Lennon observes. She remarks: "the utter simplicity of the opening of Alice is disarming, and no explanations are required [. . .] by paragraph three the rabbit has taken a watch out of its waistcoat pocket and started down the rabbit-hole and in paragraph four Alice is down after it."[71] The lack of logical explanation is a characteristic feature of the nonsense narrative, which lends itself to an extremely simple, paratactic narrative: something happens and then something else happens. As Wim Tigges acknowledges in his definition of the genre: "[nothing] can be obtained by considering connotations or associations because these lead to nothing."[72] Although in some ways this seems like an overstatement by Tigges—there is, for example, a link between the egg in the shop and the egg-shaped Humpty Dumpty, however, it is true that overall there is no progressive linearity to the narratives.

U. C. Knoepflmacher in *Ventures into Childland* explains, "The structure of 'Through the Looking-Glass' relies on what James Kincaid rightly calls 'a series of good-byes' in which the parting from the gnat and the fawn 'are succeeded by the climactic farewell with an old wasp.'"[73] This structural device also seems to be prominent in *Wonderland*, such as the sudden appearing and then vanishing of the Cheshire Cat, or the abrupt transfiguration of characters such as the baby into a pig. The very fact the stories are dream narratives is often a disappointment to the reader, especially the adult, who may be looking for Wonderland as a means of escape, but finds

69. Matt 11:30.

70. For example, Kimberly Reynolds emphasizes that "literary nonsense requires a high degree of technical knowledge and intellectual sophistication for its effects." Reynolds, *Radical Children's Literature*, 47.

71. Becker-Lennon "Escape Through the Looking-Glass," in Phillips (ed.), *Aspects of Alice*, 104–5.

72. Tigges, *Anatomy of Literary Nonsense*, 47.

73. Knoepflmacher, *Ventures into Childland*, 213.

that the tales refuse their entrapment. Alice is not in the least disappointed to find out she was only dreaming, nor is she traumatized from her adventure. She merely expresses "what a curious dream!"

My point here is not that there is any formal theology in the structural lightness of the dream narrative, but that engagement in nonsense literature encourages the reader to imagine in terms of non-attachment. Like Alice, the reader must become accustomed to letting go of expectations and not being weighed down by negative emotions. The reader is expected to approach new situations in the story without the learned anxiety that comes from allowing past traumatic experiences to dictate present attitude. Whether kings, caterpillars, or mad hatters, Alice engages each with the same straightforward simplicity, unfractured by "goals of ambition, possession and sexual conquest." According to W. H. Auden, the simplicity of Alice's character is a symbol of "what, after many years and countless follies and errors, one would like, in the end, to become."[74] Alice draws the reader into an experience of wholeness, which provides (albeit inadvertently) an analogous participation in Christian simplicity.

To refer back to our original question: would it make sense for Christ to say, "unless you change and become *simple* like this little child you will not enter the kingdom of heaven"? It would seem so, *if* Christianity believes in the actual provision of Christ's promise, then the Christian ought to possess a childlike lack of burden, an "unclouded brow," a oneness of will enabling the individual to enter into the same απλους relationship to the Father as Christ. Simplicity thus seems to be one element connecting the Alice stories to a Christian account of the childlike.

WONDER

Following the description of her "pure unclouded brow" in the prefatory poem to *Through the Looking-Glass*, Carroll identifies Alice's "dreaming eyes of wonder." Perhaps the recognition that it is in *Wonder*land that Alice has her adventures, reveals some other aspect of her childlike nature. Elsewhere, Carroll describes Alice as "curious—wildly curious, and with the eager enjoyment of Life that comes only in the happy hours of childhood, when all is new and fair."[75] This abiding sense of newness and curiosity characterizes Carroll's understanding of the child's capacity for wonder. Alice follows the White Rabbit because she is "burning with curiosity"[76] and recalls

74. Auden, *Forewords & Afterwords*, 293.

75. Carroll, "Alice on Stage."

76. Carroll, *AW*, 8.

her adventures as "a wonderful dream."[77] Whilst Alice experiences a range of reactions, wonder seems to be her primary response to the world she encounters.

Virginia Woolf believes that the type of wonder associated with child-hood stems from a literal perception of reality. She explains: "To become a child is to be very literal; to find everything so strange that nothing is surprising. [. . .] It is to be Alice in Wonderland."[78] Woolf puts forward the belief that Alice is not only immersed in a wonder-land, but in a consuming attitude of wonder, whereby "everything" is strange. This idea is supported by the fact that her musing outside Wonderland is equally wonder-filled. Take, for example, her contemplation of nature: "I wonder if the snow *loves* the trees and fields, that it kisses them so gently?"[79] Her wondering at the snow is divorced from the effect it has on her; it is an appreciation of the thing for its own sake. In addition, her animated perception and quasi-personification imbues everyday events in the natural world with a sense of magic.

Alice has no learned immunity to the phenomenon of the natural world for she still exalts in the wonder of the everyday. She delights in the washing habits of her cats as much as she marvels at talking chess pieces or dancing lobsters. This suggests a constant condition of wonderment rather than isolated astonishment. Alice does not experience wonder as aberrant or nonsensical intrusions into "reality." Rather, her constant state of won-der enables her to distinguish between the merely sensational and the truly wondrous. Her sense of wonder is not dependant on, nor radically height-ened by, the extraordinary circumstances because from her perspective, "everything is queer. [. . .] Everything is so out-of-the-way."[80] The important point to observe here is that Alice experiences wonder as a comprehensive vision.

In Ronald Hepburn's essay on "wonder" he draws a distinction be-tween different types of wonder including "surprise wonder" and "existen-tial wonder." "Surprise wonder," he explains is an encounter with something astonishing, which disappears once an explanation has been found or once normalcy resumes. This type of wonder, given its contingency, does not fully represent Alice's consuming attitude of wonderment. Hepburn ac-knowledges that there are "varieties of wonder which are not undermined

---

77. Ibid., 98.
78. Woolf, "Lewis Carroll" in *Aspects of Alice*, 79.
79. Carroll, *LG*, 109.
80. Carroll, *AW*, 18.

by causal explicality,"[81] such as "existential wonder," which he further characterizes as "wonder" at "the sheer existence of a world."[82] This type of wonderment seems more aptly to characterize Alice's manner of perceiving the world. Hepburn's "existential wonder" is closely related to Chesterton's depiction of "spiritual wonder," which, like Alice's condition of wonderment is concerned with an ongoing mode of perception not isolated instances of particular amazement.[83]

Chesterton indicates that the spiritual element present within child-hood wonder is related to an instinct of exaltation and awe.[84] This could be why MacDonald emphasizes: "To cease to wonder is to fall plumb-down from the childlike to the commonplace—the most undivine of all moods in-tellectual. Our nature can never be at home among things that are not won-derful to us."[85] MacDonald believes the unchildlike are not at home, because the unchildlike do not delight in the mundane. They have lost their "simple sense of wonder at the shapes of things,"[86] which for Chesterton and Mac-Donald is vibrantly present in the child. "For grown-up people," explains Chesterton, "are not strong enough to exalt in monotony."[87] He believes that children, on the contrary, "want things repeated and unchanged."[88] Ches-terton concludes that God has the "eternal appetite of infancy; for we have sinned and grown old, and our Father is younger than we."[89] This suggests that the failure to sustain a childlike awed appreciation of the everyday is a characteristic of man's fallen nature.

Assuming, for the moment, that the Christian ought to possess an at-titude of wonder even within the most mundane circumstance, how, then, might a Christian respond to the miraculous? We can draw some insight from Christ's reply to the Pharisees' demand for miracles: "And he sighed deeply in his spirit and said, 'why does this generation seek a sign? Truly, I say to you, no sign will be given to this generation.'"[90] Instead, he blesses

---

81. Hepburn, *Wonder*, 141.

82. Ibid., 140.

83. Chesterton, "A Defence of Nonsense," 70.

84. This attitude is particularly prevalent in the psalms, such as Psalm 45: "On the glorious splendor of your majesty/and on your wondrous works, I will meditate." Ps 145:5.

85. MacDonald, *Hope of the Gospel*, 59.

86. Chesterton, "A Defence of Nonsense," 69.

87. Chesterton, *Orthodoxy*, 55.

88. Ibid.

89. Ibid.

90. Mark 8:12.

the believers "who have not seen and yet have believed."[91] It could be suggested that it is a childlike *unsensational* attitude to wonder that Christ desires in response to his miracles. MacDonald explains: "Those who would not believe without signs and wonders, could never believe worthily with any number of them."[92] This quotation indicates, perhaps surprisingly, that within Christianity, the type of "surprise-wonder" elicited by Christ's miracles is not the essence of wonderment, and in fact, focus on the sensational seems to miss the point entirely.[93]

To support this claim it might be helpful to contrast the varying responses of the chief priests and the children to Christ's miracles. Both parties have witnessed the healing of the blind and the lame:

> When the chief priests and scribes saw the wonderful things that He did, and the children crying out in the temple, 'Hosanna to the Son of David!' they were indignant. And they said to him, 'Do you not hear what they are saying?' And Jesus said to them, 'Yes; have you never read, 'Out of the mouths of infants and nursing babies, you have prepared praise.'[94]

One might assume that the jubilation of the children after seeing the healing is certain indication that religious wonder is deeply connected to astonishment and marvel. Although this is undeniably an aspect of the children's adulation, Christ does not commend them because they are suitably impressed by his miracles; rather, he seems to use them as a point of comparison with the unbelieving scribes. Both parties have seen the miracles and yet the priests and scribes still will not believe even with signs and wonders. Their indignation indicates that a Christian concept of wonder is not located in the sensational because to those without a sense of wonder even the sensational does not appear to be wondrous. This might indicate that "surprise-wonder" is an aspect of "existential wonder" and that to engage in the former one must already possess the latter.

The Christian understanding of wonder seems therefore to be located in an approach to the world and not induced by the miraculous. It is this attitude that Christ both blesses and identifies within the child, and it is here that Jesus and the child meet. Christ's incarnation can be seen as the

91. John 20:29.

92. MacDonald, *Hope of the Gospel*, 73.

93. This may be one reason for Christ's recurring instruction after performing a miracle to keep it secret. For example after the healing of the deaf man in Mark 7:36 "And Jesus charged them to tell no one" or the healing of Jairus' daughter Mark 5:43 "And he strictly charged them than no one should know this."

94. Matt 21:15–16.

embodiment of the miraculous entering the ordinary and his life exemplifies the importance of the ordinary within the miraculous. He subverts the fallen expectation that "wonder" means a sort of gnostic ascent from reality and instead raises reality to the realm of the wondrous. Chesterton echoes this sentiment, suggesting that the function of the religious imagination "is not to make strange things settled, so much as to make settled things strange; not so much to make wonders facts as to make facts wonders."[95] MacDonald, like Carroll, believes this is the natural approach of the child, for whom everyday events are as extraordinary as the uniquely miraculous.

This interpretation of wonder appears compatible with the foregoing category of simplicity, since a sensational construal of wonder does not allow the subject to focus on the miracle *per se*, but is overcome by the individual power associated with the ability to astonish. If such astonishment is not also located in the everyday, relationship with God ceases to be ἁπλοῦς but oscillates and becomes contingent upon sensational circumstances. In his novel, *Phantastes*, MacDonald uses the journey into fairyland to articulate his concept of childlike wonder. He explains that one who travels in fairyland, "takes everything as it comes; like a child, who, being in a chronic condition of wonder, is surprised at nothing."[96] It is the type of wonder that leads to a delight in the object itself, rather than in the sensation generated in the beholder.

To refer back to Carroll's description of Alice, wonder has been described as an ongoing approach to reality rather than a momentary climactic encounter, contingent upon an astounding event. The distinction between "surprise-wonder" and a more enduring type of "existential wonder" was highlighted by considering Christ's reproach to the demand of the Pharisees and the indignation of the scribes even after having witnessed a miracle. We saw how the Bible set these attitudes in contrast to the children's adulation and considered the nature of childlike wonder assisted by MacDonald whose protagonist believes, "the eye of the child, whose every-day life, fearless and unambitious, meets the true import of the wonder-teaming world around him, and rejoices therein without question."[97] The perpetual astonishment at the everyday evidently seems to be an important characteristic of childlike faith, and an attitude naturally assumed in a nonsense world in which "everything is strange."

95. Chesterton, "Defence of China Shepherdesses," in *The Defendant*, 84.

96. MacDonald, *Phantastes*, 47.

97. Ibid., 90.

TRUST

After Carroll defines Alice as "wildly curious," he describes her as "trustful, ready to accept the wildest impossibilities with all that utter trust that only dreamers know."[98] This "utter trust" may be described as "credulity" in the sense that Alice trusts without suspicion or wariness. For example, when she notices a doorway in a tree she acknowledges, "that's very curious!" and then immediately reasons, "But everything's curious to-day. I think I may as well go in at once."[99] Alice's inclination to react with trust rather than fear allows her natural curiosity to be satisfied. Her lack of wariness over unknown consequences is a clear demonstration of her impulsive credulity.

This is compatible with the conclusions drawn from the discussion of wonder in that it keeps open and defends the child's un-delimited sense of the possible. By this, I mean that Alice's trust in some sense safeguards her experience of the incredulous. For example, Alice asks herself: "Would it be of any use [. . .] to speak to this mouse?" She answers, "everything is so out-of-the-way down here, that I should think it very likely it can talk: at any rate, there's no harm in trying."[100] *Because* she trusts, her capacity for wondrous experience increases.

The principle of trust therefore extends the realm of wonder by insisting upon the trustworthiness of the incredulous real, and it is this manner of credulous imagining that Jacqueline Flesher believes is requisite for engaging in nonsense texts. She writes: "Nonsense can be read at different levels. Like most great children's books, it is not simply a book for children. It can be read with the freshness of a child or the critical mind of an adult. Yet, in a way, a full appreciation of nonsense requires "a willing suspension of disbelief."[101] In this quotation, Flesher seems to suggest that trust is the most appropriate mode for interpreting nonsense, indicating that the reader must practice accepting (if only for the sake of story) wild impossibilities. The reader is led by the child in this exercise of credulity, guided by Alice's internal dialogue of curiosity followed by her instinctive trust.

In order to find out if trust, like simplicity and wonder, forms parts of the common ground where "the child and Jesus meet" we need to first identify the concept within scripture before drawing upon MacDonald's theology to explore this union in greater depth. Trust is in many ways the primary seed of faith. Paul communicates this in his letter to the Hebrews: "whoever

98. Carroll, "Alice on Stage."
99. Carroll, *AW*, 61.
100. Ibid., 18.
101. Flesher, "The Language of Nonsense in Alice," 144.

would draw near to God must believe that he exists."[102] Trust seems necessary for any manner of union with God, it is not some superior quality possessed by the learned disciple. Specifically in reference to salvation, John's
Gospel records Christ's emphasis: "Truly, truly, I say to you, whoever hears
my word and believes him who sent me has eternal life."[103] The double use
of the adverb ἀμὴν ἀμὴν makes clear the supreme import Christianity places
on accepting the trustworthiness of the testimony of scripture.

Whilst it is clear that trust is a necessary feature of faith, it is not evident why this is specifically linked to the child. Tolkien's famous essay "On
Fairy Stories" provides some insight. He observes: "A child may well believe
a report that there are ogres in the next county."[104] Tolkien emphasizes that
this is not because the child desires to live in a mythical world, but because
a goblin is in one sense just as plausible as an elephant, and the child, in
general, has an instinctive trust. The child's unadulterated naivety is precisely why Dusinberre believes the child has a noetic advantage over the
adult. She explains in reference to Alice's interaction with the unicorn, "The
child's capacity for belief [. . .] is infinitely greater than the adult's because
every aspect of his experience tests it. He has no ground of acquired knowledge from which to divide the phenomena of the world into the real and
unreal."[105] This helps to address the question of whether trust is a necessary
criterion for a child to "understand." It can be inferred from Dusinberre's
statement that *because* the child's grasp of reality is limited, his verification
must be based upon an intuitive trust rather than some prior belief system.
For Dusinberre this means that the position of skepticism is unnatural to
the child.

In more directly theological terms, Chesterton affirms that a lack of
skepticism is required for a discernment of Christian truth. He writes: "the
degree to which we can perceive [truths] depends strictly upon how far we
have a definite conception inside us of what is truth. It is ludicrous to suppose that the more skeptical we are the more we see good in everything."[106]
Alice seems to possess the type of intuitive trust described by Dusinberre
and Chesterton: her worlds are full of possibility. "'Oh, how I wish I could
shut up like a telescope! I think I could if only I knew how to begin.' For, you

102. Heb 11:6.
103. John 5:24.
104. Tolkien, "On Fairy-Stories," 118.
105. Dusinberre, *Alice to the Lighthouse*, 193.
106. Chesterton, *Heretics*, 159.

see, so many out-of-the way things happened lately, that Alice had begun to think that very few things indeed were really impossible."[107]

Within Carroll's nonsense worlds, fearlessness seems to emerge as an important prerequisite for trust. Donald Rackin ascribes to Alice a type of innocent fearlessness, which he specifically connects with her status as child. He writes: "Alice enters upon her journey underground simply because she is curious with the fearlessness of an innocent child never once considering how in the world she was to get out again."[108] "Is it because Alice is a child," he asks, "that she fails after all this to see Wonderland for what it is? Is it her youthful ignorance that makes her miss the dangerous significance of a grin without a cat?"[109] Alice does not fear the Cheshire Cat because she trusts in the essential goodness of the creature's intent. She acknowledges it has "*very long claws and a great many teeth*,"[110] but still maintains, "it looked good-natured."[111] Despite the Cheshire Cat's flagrant defiance of Alice's normal creaturely expectations, she still thinks the Cat is trustworthy enough to ask for directions.

Alice's fearlessness, based on her instinctive trust, shares an analogous association with the child of God, who is instructed to be ignorant to the fear that comes from insecurity. "Have no fear of them," Christ commands, "for nothing is covered that will not be revealed, or hidden that will not be known."[112] The focus of Christ's teaching is the trustworthiness of God, which overcomes man's fearfulness. MacDonald comments: "It is not alone the first beginnings of religion that are full of fear. So long as love is imperfect, there is room for torment. [. . .] When the conscience is not clear, the anxiety may well amount to terror."[113] This, as MacDonald argues, is a form of superstitious fear which is outside a relationship of trust. MacDonald is adamant that a fearful conscience is the result of "a lack of faith and childlikeness," suggesting that fear comes from a deficiency of trust in the Father's character.[114] MacDonald affirms: "The true son-faith is that which

107. Carroll, *AW*, 10.

108. Rackin, "Alice's Journey to the end of the Night," in *Aspects of Alice*, 454.

109. Ibid., 467.

110. Carroll, *AW*, 51.

111. Ibid.

112. Matt 10:26.

113. MacDonald, *Unspoken Sermons*, 314.

114. I do, more generally, wish to leave room for a positive Christian comprehension of fear, which might help to shape the moral conscience. However, the fear of God prompted by an uncertainty of God's character and lack of assurance of salvation seems to have no place in the Christian message.

comes with boldness, fearless of the Father doing anything but what is right fatherly, patient, and full of loving-kindness."[115]

In his sermon on "The Cause of Spiritual Stupidity" MacDonald declares: "Distrust is atheism, and the barrier to all growth. Lord, we do not understand thee, because we do not trust thy Father."[116] He agrees that trust is attributable to the childlike, and uses the suffering of Job as an example: "The true child, the righteous man, will trust absolutely, against all appearances, the God who has created in him the love of righteousness. God does not, I say, tell Job why he had afflicted him: he rouses his child-heart to trust";[117] and it is trust that MacDonald links to divine illumination.[118] Thus, when Christ asks his disciples to become like children, he is not demanding an epistemological regression. Instead, he uses the child to demonstrate that it is possible to be a part of the world of experience and yet remain one of the "innocently fearless."[119] It is the child, "impregnably fortified in a helpless confidence,"[120] who is able to achieve naturally what the disciples must endeavor to re-learn.

Perhaps this is why in his essay "Fictioning Things," John Milbank writes that the child's "initial imaginative and intuitive response" contains "more authority than the adult reflection."[121] Alice in many crucial ways displays the type of instinctive trust valued by Christian thinkers and we see once more how nonsense might not be the negation of theological truth, but analogous to the type of thinking required for theological insight. One such element is Alice's innocently fearless approach to her adventures, which, considered in conjunction with wonder, suggest that "the child and Jesus meet" in an incredulous reality approached with "helpless confidence"

MAKE-BELIEVE

Trust has been discussed as the natural orientation of the child and a manner of perceiving the world, without which faith is impossible. I suggested

---

115. MacDonald, *Unspoken Sermons*, 237–38.

116. Ibid., 213.

117. Ibid., 353.

118. "He who trusts can understand; he whose mind is set at ease can discover a reason." Ibid., 208.

119. This is attributed to Frances Hodgson Burnett's literary child, Lord Fauntleroy who is described as looking "as if he had never feared or doubted anything in his life." *Little Lord Fauntleroy*, 21.

120. MacDonald, *Phantastes*, 128.

121. Milbank, "Fictioning Things," 4.

that Alice's trusting nature is in some sense responsible for her experience of the wondrous—because she trusts, she increases her engagement with the incredulous. Alice's entrance to Wonderland, for example, is only possible because of her trusting reception of the White Rabbit. However, her entry into Looking-Glass Land is not located in the credulous reception of an extraordinary event, but rather in her own creative appetite for the fantastic: her ability to make-believe. "'Let's pretend there's a way of getting through into it, somehow, Kitty. Let's pretend the glass has gone all soft like gauze, so that we can get through. Why it's turning into a sort of mist now, I declare! It'll be easy enough to get through—.'"[122] And so she does. Here Alice's capacity for make-believe gives way to actual belief.

Carroll describes Alice's make-believe as an ongoing gamelike approach to reality: "'Kitty, dear, let's pretend'—And here I wish I could tell you half the things Alice used to say, beginning with her favourite phrase 'Let's pretend.'"[123] There appears to be a self-referential wink in this reference to Alice's make-believe, for in a sense Carroll, Alice and the reader are all playing the game together. Indeed, the dominance of the theme in *Through the Looking-Glass* is such that not only does Alice make-believe in Looking-Glass Land, but Looking-Glass Land makes-believe in *her*. Tweedledum and Tweedledee explain to Alice: "You're only one of the things in his [the Red King] dream. You know very well you're not real."[124] The unicorn overcomes his doubt at the existence of a human child, ("I always thought they were fabulous monsters") by proposing a game of make-believe ("if you'll believe in me, I'll believe in you."[125])

In order to explore whether make-believe is a theological category connecting Jesus and the child, I want to invoke Catherine Pickstock's concept of liturgical impersonation as a way of explaining the role of make-believe in religious transformation. I will then appeal to C. S. Lewis' concept of "dressing-up as Christ" in which he discerns a strong correlation between mature faith and the imaginative play of childhood.

To begin with, however, it is not immediately clear why make-believe is applicable to a religious conviction, since it carries connotations of frivolity and pretense. Yet Miller, writing from a Christian perspective, puts forward the view that "Faith is make-believe. It is playing as if it were true."[126] Miller goes on to explain that it is not that religion is therefore false, but that faith

122. Carroll, *LG*, 111.
123. Ibid., 110.
124. Ibid., 145.
125. Ibid., 175.
126. Miller, *Gods and Games*, 168.

is acting "as if" the unseen were seen.[127] The biblical outline of faith—the belief of things hoped for, the evidence not seen—indicates how make-believe can become a helpful approach to thinking theologically because it involves a creative abstraction from the seen reality. Not only does the Christian believe that the reality of creation is mysteriously other than how it appears, but that man's apperceptive mode is also fallen. This emerges as a twofold obstruction to true seeing, which accordingly requires a twofold imaginative reversal: a purified vision of the real and a purified visibility by which to perceive this vision.

In reference to liturgy, Pickstock shows how play-acting is entirely necessary for true participation in liturgical transformation. Make-believe, as a mode of imagining, seems to be a prerequisite for traversing two worlds or the "transgressions of domains."[128] Pickstock accepts that the fall has effected a radical disconnection between the divine and the human and emphasizes that "liturgical expression is made 'impossible' by the breach which occurred at the Fall."[129] She calls for a "liturgical reform" that refuses to be "enculturated" into commonplace speech and thought.[130] Pickstock admits a distance between things taken as they appear and the transcendent "real."[131] It is this "admission of distance" that lays the foundation for suggesting that make-believe is required to bridge this transcendental gap.

Pickstock uses the word "impersonation" to signify what I consider to be the presence of make-believe in liturgical theology. She explains: "the Celebrant enacts on our behalf an impersonation of the angels in their perpetual hymn of praise. This would suggest a protean ontology whereby impersonation precedes our 'authentic' voice."[132] We might consider the celebrant's impersonation "make-believe" in the sense that he is acting *as if* he possesses an angelic vision of the real and the ability to break out of the enculturated imagination to perceive this real with the simple vision of the angelic eye. Through the Celebrant's invitation to participate in his impersonation, Pickstock believes that "we *can* enter into purification because we are not simply purified *like* Christ, but, through the gift of the Spirit [. . .] we *put on* Christ's own purity."[133] This putting-on appears as a form

127. The clearly supports and follows on from the discussion of the anarchic imagination, which brings about the disturbance of Caesar through acting "as if" the Spirit is tangibly sovereign.

128. Pickstock, *After Writing*, 212.

129. Ibid., 176.

130. Ibid.

131. Ibid., paraphrased from 178.

132. Ibid., 209.

133. Ibid., 187–89.

of make-believe, which, according the Pickstock is made real through the transformative power of the Spirit.

C. S. Lewis in *Mere Christianity* evokes a similar concept of impersonation or make-believe to bring about the transformation of vision. He entitles a chapter with Alice's reprise "Let's pretend" and puts forward the contention that the words of the Lord's Prayer "Our Father" "mean quite frankly that you are putting yourself in the place of a son of God. To put it bluntly, you are *dressing up as Christ*. If you like, you are pretending."[134] Lewis suggests that Christ encourages his followers to put themselves in the place of Jesus and act as if they were fully obedient to the will of the Father. Lewis continues: "It [the New Testament] talks about Christians 'being born again'; it talks about them 'putting on Christ'; about Christ 'being formed in us'; about our coming to 'have the mind of Christ.'"[135] The command "to become like little children" it would seem, also follows this pattern of make-believe impersonation. The disciple is called to assume the character of Christ "to be conformed to the image of his Son."[136] Alice illustrates the child's natural orientation to make-believe, and it is here that a point of union between the child and Jesus emerges.[137]

For the Christian, make-believe is not about regression but about spiritual growth. Christianity is not endorsing a Peter Pan-like refusal to grow up. On the contrary, the Christian is instructed "to grow up in every way into him who is the head, into Christ."[138] What I am suggesting is that the playful imagination of the child can be an aid to spiritual maturity based on the belief that the act of imitating Christ is itself a sanctifying process. This is radically unlike Peter Pan's play, which is pneumatically static; it does not develop or become more real because there is no ontological substitution; Peter is in effect impersonating his own shadow. Make-believe is not, as Peter believes, about remaining a child, but is in fact about becoming. Lewis agrees that make-believe is a natural aspect of the growth of a child—"that is why children's games are so important," he acknowledges, "the pretence

---

134. Lewis, *Mere Christianity*, 187–88.

135. Ibid., 191.

136. Rom 8:29.

137. It should be acknowledged that from the skeptical perspective, make-believe is the absence of the real, rather than the transformation of the unreal. Likewise, Pickstock accepts that "from a non-liturgical perspective it would seem that nothing really 'happens' in the liturgy" (244). However, for a Christian, make-believe is a relevant theological category because of the conviction of the supreme power of pneumatic transformation.

138. Eph 4:15.

of being grown-up helps them to grow up in earnest."[139] Hence, Christian make-believe, like the child's game, is not about escaping, but, rather, about a fuller mode of becoming. The Christian imitates Christ in order to grow more like Christ, Christian make-believe is therefore fixed on a *telos* outside itself, "Let us pretend" explains Lewis, "in order to make the pretence into a reality."[140]

If make-believe succeeds as a method, then it would seem that there ought to be a terminus to the game. John Milbank, however, disagrees, arguing that play is not something to be grown out of, but a reality into which one continues to grow. "Full mature self-consciousness," he believes, "comes at the point where one half steps *back* into childhood [. . .] back into a flexibility of role-playing in the surer knowledge that one's *unique* character [. . .] will shine through many necessary social disguises."[141] Play is defined here as a fluidity or freedom; it is perichoretic in essence, moving between steadfastness of character and fearlessness of variable circumstance. Meister Eckhart unequivocally champions the perichorectic quality of play in his description of the Trinity: "The Son has eternally been playing before the Father as the Father has before the Son. The playing of the twain is the Holy Ghost in whom they both disport themselves and he disports himself in both."[142] In order for the individual to become like the child, make-believe or impersonation is required to aid the transformation from ideality to reality. He must do his best to be child*like*, until he is fully-grown, that is to say he becomes an unfailing child of God.

To conclude, we can perhaps establish an order emerging between make-believe and play, which would indicate that the end of make-believe is the eternality of play. From Eckhart's depiction of the Trinity, we might venture that the childlike do not stop playing; rather their make-believe is subsumed into the infinite play of the Trinity. This is consistent with Chesterton's eschatological vision, in which he suggests that "the true object of all human life is play. Earth is a task garden; heaven is a playground."[143] And it is here, it seems, that Jesus lifts up the little child and uses him to reveal the reality of heaven, brought closer to those on earth through the imagination of make-believe.

139. Lewis, *Mere Christianity*, 193.

140. Ibid.

141. Milbank, "Fictioning Things," 7–8.

142. Eckhart quoted in Miller, *Gods and Games*, 158.

143. Chesterton, *All Things Considered*, 71. See also Milbank, "Fictioning Things," 10: "And in the end, if the whole of the cosmos has a point, or is its own point, the rituals of play and dance come closer to reality than the solemnities of work, skills, targets and means, so beloved of our current masters."

CONCLUSION: "A CHILDHOOD INTO WHICH WE HAVE TO GROW"

This chapter has been dedicated to charting the significance of the childlike in the *Alice* novels and investigating the specific attributes this entails. At the same time, we have considered the implication of Christ's instruction to become like children, comparing the childlike features exhibited by Alice with the Christian imagination. Reflecting upon the act of reading nonsense literature, we have suggested that while Carrollian nonsense does not offer religious *teaching*, it nevertheless seems to provide a very real way by which to engage in something akin to religious *thinking*. In order to enter the realm of nonsense at all, the reader must exercise a willed lack of skepticism and practice some of the central characteristics of the childlike: simplicity, wonder, trust, and make-believe. When we read a story we engage in a type of play-faith; we pretend as if it were true if only for the sake of the narrative. The content of Wonderland, as Carroll fully intended, is devoid of religious allegory, but there appears to be a likeness between the imagination required for Christian faith and the imagination practiced in reading nonsense.

MacDonald tells us that God "can be revealed only to the child; perfectly, to the pure child only. All the discipline of the world is to make men children, that God may be revealed to them."[144] For MacDonald, then, any act that makes men childlike prepares them for the revelation of God, and a trip down the rabbit hole seems to be one such instance. "There is a childhood into which we have to grow,"[145] writes MacDonald, echoing Wordsworth's radical privileging of the child's perspective. The idea that the child is "the father of the man" suggests that the attunement of the mind to a certain childlikeness is not regressive but integral for Christian maturity. The idea of growing up into a child remains absurd as long as we think in terms of secular development, believing that "grown-up" refers to independence, responsibility and serious endeavor. As we have seen in this chapter, Christianity completely reverses these secular principles of "grown-up," preaching that we must become little children; we must be born again. The mature Christian seeks dependence upon the Father's provision and surrenders the governance of his or her life to God.

A final point I wish to emphasize is that the usage of the Christian concept of the childlike to understand literary nonsense does not limit or skew our interpretation of nonsense. Rather, *because* Christianity believes in the theological significance of the child, it frees nonsense to be nonsensical as

144. MacDonald, *Hope of the Gospel*, 153.

145. MacDonald quoted by Pridmore, "George MacDonald's Estimate of Childhood," 73.

it does not have to apologize for its connection with the child. Tigges inadvertently attests to the fact that without a religious appreciation of the child, literary nonsense cannot express itself as fully childlike. Tigges writes: "that [nonsense] appeals to children does not automatically entitle us to relegate it to an inferior category of literature labelled 'juvenile' or 'trivial.'"[146] In this statement, Tigges, like so many other literary critics refuses to accept nonsense on its own terms; it *is* trivial, but as we have hinted, maybe triviality is itself an encounter with the truly serious. In a world of reversals where the last are first, perhaps the inferior supersedes the superior and maybe that which is juvenile is closer to what is ultimately mature.

146. Tigges, *Anatomy of Literary Nonsense*, 5.

PART II

Celestial Nonsense

CHAPTER 4

Nonsense Theology ⸺

JERUSALEM AND WONDERLAND

Would they not say that you are mad?

1 CORINTHIANS 14:23

THIS BOOK BEGAN BY asking if there is any theological value in venturing the other side of reason and proceeded to discuss parallels between the Christian imagination and certain central features of literary nonsense. Following the confirmation of our initial intuition that these aspects have some religious connotation, it was then asked, can the imagination as it is involved in Christian faith be accurately characterized according to these three features of literary nonsense? This led to the discovery that a significant resemblance exists between the imaginative process of reading nonsense literature and willing assent to the Christian message.

It should be emphasized that the book does not aim to discredit Christian doctrine by likening it to literary nonsense, nor does it attempt to "Christianize" nonsense by showing its likeness to the religious imagination. A study of the two has revealed this intriguing correspondence and we are now in a position to consider the significance of this connection, and ask the fundamental question: what does Wonderland have to do with Jerusalem? I am not the first to have noticed a correspondence. The idea that faith and nonsense are in some way related is alluded to in a selection of theological texts, and to a lesser extent, within the canon of literary nonsense.

The most well known example uniting both nonsense and Christianity is G. K. Chesterton's "Defence of Nonsense." In his brief essay, Chesterton alludes suggestively to the central argument of this book: "the well-meaning person who, by merely studying the logical side of things, has decided that 'faith is nonsense', does not know how truly he speaks; later it may come back to him in the form that nonsense is faith."[1] However, like many of Chesterton's brilliant aphorisms, the idea is not developed. Elizabeth Sewell includes Chesterton's quotation in her own conclusion and believes that faith relates to nonsense, "not as a foreign element but as a necessary extension and completion of our own form of play."[2] Yet it is only at the very end of her argument that she suggests faith might have a place in the study of nonsense and so leaves many questions unanswered and unasked. "For thirteen chapters," Sewell concedes, "we have been logical, only to find at the end that we need an insulation from our own logic which has landed us in the world of magic without telling us what to do there. We need some way of moving from the circle of logic to the world outside the circle, from manipulation to make-believe."[3] This suggestion undercuts most of her previous conclusions, though she does not attempt to explain how it is that "words and play together fringe out into liturgy and magic."[4]

It is therefore unsurprising Tigges believes that Sewell "fails in her attempt to bridge the gap between game and dream at the end of her book, where we are meant to reach 'the world of religion, magic, alchemy, astrology, poetry.'"[5] Most critics of literary nonsense seem to overlook Sewell's last chapter entirely and engage with her work as if the fourteenth chapter had never been written. This appears to be because nonsense criticism, as it currently exists, is essentially a secular enterprise. It is philosophical and psychoanalytical, philological and mathematical; it may be studied from an historical or a cultural perspective, but apparently not a religious one.

There seems to be an unspoken rule that because nonsense literature does not contain explicitly theological language, theology is therefore inappropriate as a means of interacting with the text.[6] Tigges is in a sense correct

---

1. Chesterton, "A Defence of Nonsense," 70.

2. Sewell, *Field of Nonsense*, 184.

3. Ibid., 188.

4. Ibid., 184.

5. Tigges, "An Anatomy of Nonsense," in *Explorations in the Field of Nonsense*, 24.

6. It is at this point where my book diverts from a number of thinkers with whom we have hitherto been in agreement. For example, Jean-Jacques Lecercle to whom we are indebted for his investigation into the contextual, logical, and semantic character of literary nonsense. On the inquiry into the religious, however, Lecercle will not join us. He emphasizes nonsense's lack of the religious and steers well clear of the theological

when he states: "Absolutely forbidden grounds are the themes of sex, feeling or emotion, God and religion, and beauty."[7] However, the prevalence of
psychoanalytical readings of nonsense writing suggests the themes of "sex,
feeling, or emotion" may nonetheless be involved in some less apparent way.
One might therefore wonder if the same may be true of religious themes.
Why, then, is theological inquiry so evidently absent from the canon of nonsense criticism? It may be that the reason rests more with theologians than
with literary critics. Perhaps there is a concern from within theology that
incorporating nonsense into theological discourse would risk characterizing the venture of faith as absurd.

Within theology, generally speaking, there is little formal interaction with nonsense as a possible religious principle, and when the term is
used, it is seldom considered in connection to literary nonsense. Catherine
Pickstock, for example, enlighteningly invokes the language of nonsense to
describe the demarcation in the perspective between believers and atheists. She writes: "Christ is often represented as a madman. The insanity of
the Cross, the non-sense of sacrifice, was a wisdom which drowned in the
'rationality' of the world, and revealed there its non-sense."[8] This shares
something with the writings of Erasmus, the ecstatic and insane elements of
which have helpfully been identified by M. A. Screech:

> The worldly-wise laugh at Christians; human beings laugh at
> real or perceived madness; what the worldly-wise laugh at in
> Jesus—not only as he hung on the Cross—is the sheer lunacy
> they see in him. The world admires money, self-interest, success:
> Christians, insofar as they turn their back on such values and
> hold them to be at best indifferent, are turning the world upside
> down may indeed seem mad.[9]

Although we might be able to see how this equates to earlier definitions of literary nonsense in terms of the anarchic disordering of the familiar, Screech does not employ the word "nonsense" preferring to use
"insanity," "madness" or "upside down." Ronald Hepburn's study *Christianity and Paradox*, however, seems to bring us closer to the location of nonsense within theology. He tells us emphatically "the language of Christianity

---

in his philosophical explorations of nonsense. "No religion is explicitly mentioned, nor
is the text suffused with religiousness, even of the vaguest kind. Alice is not only free
from her family, she is free from the stern God of Protestant extremism." "Nonsense
and Politics," 369.

7. Tigges, "An Anatomy of Nonsense," 80.

8. Pickstock, "Asyndeton" in *The Postmodern God*, 311.

9. Screech, *Laughter at the Foot of the Cross*, 84.

is nonsensical."[10] Yet Hepburn does not offer any further definition of the nonsensical except to assert that the paradoxes within Christianity invite the skeptic's identification of Christianity with nonsense. He uses nonsense in the colloquial sense to mean untenable and not to be taken seriously.

The foregoing examples would seem to indicate that the relationship between theology and literary nonsense is at best strained or tangential and at worst a religious distortion of nonsense literature or an offensive description of Christian faith. However, we have seen from the previous three chapters that there are substantial and significant connections between literary nonsense and religious faith. Furthermore, we have witnessed a number of theologians dealing with nonsensical themes and critics of nonsense describing such literature in ways that recall the language of religious belief. Nevertheless, it is apparent that if nonsense writers see a connection to theology at all, it tends to be as an aside or a local analogy, unrelated to their main treatise. If on the other hand, theologians adopt the language of nonsense, it is generally as an attempt to describe theological principles as they appear *outside* a religious grammar, rather than as a descriptive category *within* religious thought.[11]

There is at present no extended theological study of literary nonsense, nor do we find a sustained "nonsense theology" within the religious corpus. Nevertheless, it appears that theology could bring something vital and original to the appreciation of literary nonsense, and, in turn, that nonsense could assist the communication of theological truths both within a religious context and in dialogue with non-believers. In order to test the plausibility of this contention, Part Two of the book will be dedicated first of all to outlining a theology of nonsense, and, second, to discussing the practical and evangelical implications of this association.

THE LOGIC OF NONSENSE

My heart shall rejoice in your salvation

PSALM 13:5

In adumbrating a theology of nonsense, it will be helpful to begin from within theology and then see if nonsense can assist or deepen our understanding

10. Hepburn, *Christianity and Paradox*, 84.

11. This is Sten Stenson's concern in his study *Sense and Nonsense in Religion*, in which he examines the "absurd locutions" of religious language by measuring them against secular systems of logic. Stenson, *Sense and Nonsense*, 20.

of certain ideas. In order to avoid the accusation that the area of theology examined is arbitrary or peripheral; the doctrine of salvation will provide the theological principles against which we can test whether or not nonsense is a helpful and apposite term. The basic features of soteriology can be extrapolated from the central creeds:

1. Jesus Christ is fully God and fully man.[12]

2. The life, death, and resurrection of Jesus Christ is not a metaphorical event, but actually took place in human history.[13]

3. The purpose of Jesus Christ's life, death, and resurrection was to be the perfect sacrifice for the sin of man, and all who believe in this are forgiven from sin and granted eternal life.[14]

Before constructing a more detailed theology of nonsense, it may be helpful to offer some introductory contextualizing remarks on the apparent connections between Christianity and nonsense more generally, as well as the surprising parallels involved in accepting the doctrine of salvation and in reading nonsense literature. It should be emphasized that these resemblances do not pertain to the level of content, but to the role of the imagination as it engages in the act of reading or believing.

Firstly, addressing the belief that Christ is "fully God and fully man," we can recognize this as a breach with conventional rationality since it goes against the law of non-contradiction. The imagination is involved in the process of holding these dynamic opposites in tension and not seeking to reconcile or collapse the ostensible contradiction. Drawing on the information considered in the chapter on paradox, we acknowledged that belief in Christ requires the ability to imagine in paradoxical terms, to uphold two opposing absolutes in simultaneous harmony. A similar observation, as we have noted, has been made by Wim Tigges, who describes "the strong predilection of nonsense for paradox and dialectic, for a sustained balance between opposites."[15] He explains that this "requires the non-resolution of the tension between the two meanings,"[16] which appears to be the same dy-

---

12. "Furthermore it is necessary to eternal salvation; that he also believe faithfully in the Incarnation of our Lord Jesus Christ [. . .] that our Lord Jesus Christ, the Son of God is God and Man." The Athanasian Creed, c. 600.

13. "God and Man is one Christ; who suffered for our salvation; descended into hell; rose again the third day from the dead." The Athanasian Creed.

14. "We acknowledge one baptism for the forgiveness of sins, we look forward to the resurrection of the dead and the life of the world to come." The Nicene Creed, c. 325.

15. Tigges, *Anatomy of Literary Nonsense*, 56.

16. Ibid., 61.

namic simultaneity that is essential to the imagination of those who would hold that Christ is perfect man and perfect God.

Secondly, the claim that Christ "suffered for our salvation; descended into hell; rose again the third day from the dead" stipulates that these are historical events, which really happened—either Christ was raised or he was not. The importance of considering the historicity of these claims is emphasized by Paul: "if Christ has not been raised then our preaching is in vain."[17] The contravention of common-sense principles is once more apparent; the empirical understanding of the natural cycle of life and death has been overturned and re-envisaged according to religious ideas.

The imagination is involved in the mind's capacity to reconceive reality according to spiritual principles—to accept a distance between how things appear and how they actually are. As we saw in the chapter on anarchy, this requires a re-orientation of customary thinking as the authority of the law of nature is imaginatively overturned. Susan Stewart reflects the essence of this belief in the terms she uses to introduce the character of literary nonsense: "Nonsense is considered as an activity by which the world is disorganized and reorganized."[18] The account of the miraculous within Christian doctrine therefore, in this sense, appears to have more in common with the grammar of the nonsense realm than a world governed by empiricism. Cohen describes Wonderland and the world behind the looking-glass as "mysterious places where characters do not live by conventional rules and that meaning does not play a conventional role. Even the laws of nature, the law of gravity for instance, do not work as they should."[19] As we have seen, Christianity seems to require a similarly "anarchic" act of imagining in relation to the miracles of Christ and his bodily resurrection.

The third aspect of the doctrine of salvation is the conviction that all who believe in the power of Christ's death and resurrection become children of God, who are forgiven of their sin and initiated into an eternal relationship with the Father. From a conventionally rational perspective it would seem that this claim does not correspond to that which is the case: that is to say, believing in God does not appear to alter the believer's mortality; Christians continue to sin, even though it is claimed that Christ has purged them from all sin; and despite the assurance that God is a benevolent and omnipotent Father, Christians are not immune from injustice, illness, or misfortune.

---

17. 1 Cor 14.
18. Stewart, *Aspects of Intertextuality*, vii.
19. Cohen, *Lewis Carroll*, 143.

To maintain a belief in the salvific promises in spite of evidence to the contrary requires an ability to approach the world in a childlike fashion, which as we saw in the previous chapter is characterized by simplicity, wonder, trust, and make-believe. According to Robert Polhemus, nonsense literature offers the reader a similar experience of imaginative transformation:

> [Nonsense] plays with and makes light of some of the central locations of humanity's fear. The intention that comes through in *Through the Looking-Glass* is, in effect, the meaning of mankind's comic capacity, and it is this: I will play with and make ridiculous fear, loneliness, smallness, ignorance, authority, chaos, nihilism, and death; I will transform, for a time, woe to joy.[20]

Having established a tentative link between Christian belief and nonsense literature—based on an analogous breach of quotidian rationality—I want to make it clear that I am not proposing that a nonsensical articulation of faith should replace a more rational apologetic, or that the tradition we have inherited from the Enlightenment is wrong. What I am suggesting is that whilst Christian faith is plausible and cogent, it is also extravagant, playful, and foolish, and that the nonsensical aids the recovery of a number of these currently underemphasized aspects of traditional theology. This is not to say that either system is without coherence or cogency—on the contrary, Christianity and literary nonsense are both systems that possess in different ways deep internal coherence. "Nonsense," as Deleuze argues, is "a word which says its own sense,"[21] thus suggesting that there is not simply one fixed standard of sense but alternative models of sense, which may appear to each other as absurd. Kierkegaard reinforces this point by describing "the inwardness of faith" as "an offense to the Jews, foolishness to the Greeks—and an absurdity to the understanding."[22] To adopt Deleuze's language we might suggest that Christianity "speaks its own sense" in a tongue that is "an absurdity" to those who do not believe.

In offering a working definition of nonsense, it is important—however paradoxical it might seem—to avoid seeing sense as its adversary. Instead, as Deleuze and Tigges have suggested, nonsense involves a balance between meaning and non-meaning, which requires both the disorganization and the reorganization of sense. Literary nonsense *plays* with sense and this often takes the form of reversals and inversions of our fixed expectations of how the world works, which, as we have indicated, parallels certain religious

20. Polhemus, *Comic Faith*, 248.
21. Deleuze, *Logic of Sense*, 78.
22. Kierkegaard, *Concluding Unscientific Postscript*, 213.

ideas such as bodily resurrection. In what follows, I want to investigate the idea that the meaning of literary nonsense is perhaps described most accurately as the inversion of the sensible, not its absence or its destruction.

This is an established definition used by nonsense critics. Tigges, for example, describes the art of "mirroring" as "a prominent stylistic feature,"[23] which he in turn attributes to Susan Stewart's proposal of "reversals and inversions" as a central nonsensical device. Similarly, Deleuze lists "the reversals which constitute Alice's adventures: the reversal of becoming larger and becoming smaller, [. . .] the reversal of more and less, [. . .] the reversal of cause and effect."[24] We have abstracted this more generalized definition from the specific attributes of the nonsensical imagination; paradox, anarchy, and the childlike, all which in their own way reverse common-sense assumptions. In the following section, I want to ask whether a similar pattern of reversals and inversions are present in any significant way in Christian theology. I will consider both views supporting the analogy between Christianity and nonsense and also confront various objections to this hypothesis. G. K. Chesterton's interpretation of the fall will be of particular consequence in this discussion, as will Robert Polhemus' endeavor to construct an atheistic "faith" using comic and nonsensical literature.

THE GREAT REVERSAL

For the trumpet shall sound, and the dead will be raised imperishable, and we shall be changed.

1 CORINTHIANS 15:52

The idea of reversal is a common feature within the *Alice* stories. As one critic observes, "Alice found herself in a world which reversed the patterns of the world, and the story of the looking-glass is a story of complete reversal of the real world."[25] The White Queen explains it to Alice as "the effect of living backwards"[26] where to stay still one needs to keep running and to leave a house one must re-enter it. The idea of reversal is not only present throughout the stories, but also in the titles of the texts:[27] *Through*

---

23. Tigges, *Anatomy of Literary Nonsense*, 56.

24. Deleuze, *Logic of Sense*, 4–5.

25. Skinner "Lewis Carroll's Adventures" in *Aspects of Alice*, 347.

26. Carroll, *AW*, 150.

27. A similar idea is conveyed by Jeffrey Sten in his essay "Lewis Carroll the

the Looking-Glass and *In Wonderland* (or *Under Ground*).[28] Both imply that there are alternative ways of perceiving reality that shatter our common-sense expectations.

Sir Edward Strachey's essay "Nonsense as a Fine Art" (1888) is the first known study of literary nonsense as its own genre. Strachey describes nonsense as the process of reversal and disorder, which he sees as, "not a mere putting forward of incongruities and absurdities but the bringing out a new and deeper harmony of life in and through its contradictions."[29] This is crucial for our investigation, for if nonsense is to be a theologically useful term, it will be necessary to demonstrate that it is not simply a meaningless destruction of order, but rather, as Strachey suggests, it may also function as a means of illumination. He believes that nonsense "bring[s] confusion into order by setting things upside down."[30] The question we need to ask now therefore is whether theology applies a similar method of "setting things upside down" to "bring confusion into order."

Robert Polhemus, whilst a great advocate of the theme of reversal within Carrollian nonsense, believes that the presence of reversal in the text demonstrates the subordination of its religious subject matter. He suggests: "the structure of the game and the plot, as well as the thought and humor of the book, reveal [. . .] Carroll winning out over the Reverend Mr. Dodgson, and comic regression and reversal winning out over orthodox religion."[31] If Polhemus' conclusions are correct, then bringing nonsense into dialogue with theology would not only be a misleading association but would also have an injurious effect on theology. Yet are they correct? Let us consider the assumptions upon which they are based. Firstly, Polhemus assumes that nonsense and Christianity are radically at odds because nonsense is unconventional and Christianity is conventional.[32] Secondly, he claims that the concept of wonder—pervasive in nonsense—has become secularized

---

Surrealist": "For clearly Wonderland and the world through the looking-glass are, even in their names, both vitally concerned with breaking down fences of convention." "Soaring with the Dodo," 133.

28. The original title of the story was *Alice's Adventures under Ground*. Donald Rackin considers "Perhaps even the final version would be more appropriately entitled *Alice's Adventures under Ground*, since, above all else, it embodies a comic horror-vision of the chaotic land beneath the man-made groundwork of western thought and convention." "Alice's Journey to the end of the Night," 452–53.

29. Strachey, "Nonsense as a Fine Art," 515.

30. Ibid.

31. Polhemus, *Comic Faith*, 292.

32. "'Lewis Carroll' chose comedy, not institutional Christianity as his light and his true vocation: but to do so he had to split his identity from his conventional self, the Reverend Charles Dodgson, ordained cleric." Ibid., 247.

and "Carroll is its prophet."[33] Thirdly, Polhemus assumes that religious institutions do not overcome "the limits and terrors of reality."[34] It is worth considering these assumptions in detail, since Polhemus formulates with particular clarity the secular standard that currently dominates criticism of the genre, which views "comic regression and reversal" as manifestly irreconcilable with "orthodox religion."

Standing on one's head

In *Orthodoxy*, Chesterton describes, "conventional" Christianity in terms that call into question Polhemus' depiction of 'orthodox religion": "People have fallen into a foolish habit of speaking of orthodoxy as something heavy, humdrum, and safe. There never was anything so perilous or so exciting as orthodoxy. [. . .] The Orthodox Church never took the tame course or accepted the conventions; the Orthodox Church was never respectable."[35] Cameron Freeman describes how Christ's teachings "perplex and disrupt the history of metaphysics in the West with unexpected reversals that burst through the limits of conventional wisdom."[36] Chesterton would agree with Freeman's stance and point out that orthodox Christianity cannot assume a conventional attitude to the world because it is radically at odds with the conventions of that world. This view is based on the belief that following the fall, humanity is "born upside down." Chesterton writes: "the primary paradox of Christianity is that the ordinary condition of man is not his sane or sensible condition; that the normal itself is an abnormality. This is the inmost philosophy of the fall."[37] Seen in this light, Christianity seems destined to defy common sense or conventional interpretations of the way things are, and as such, "unconventional" begins to seem like it might be a more appropriate description.

33. "Fantasy indicates, however, the secularization of wonder, and Carroll is its prophet. In a large degree, fantasy flourishes and fantasy life looms so large in the modern era because the past two centuries have been a time of religious confusion and doubt." Ibid., 269.

34. Ibid. "People need to believe that the limits and terrors of reality can be changed, that the future can be different and better, that wonderful things can happen; if religious institutions cannot do these things, something else must."

35. Chesterton, *Orthodoxy*, 183.

36. Freeman, *Post-Metaphysics*, 5.

37. Chesterton, *Orthodoxy*, 291–92. A similar point is made by Jean-Yves Lacoste in his essay "Liturgy and Kenosis, from *Expérience et Absolu*," in Ward (ed.), *The Postmodern God*, 249. "No one is born the possessor of what is most proper to him, we do not gain access to ourselves without doing violence to the initial conditions of experiences."

Chesterton's proposal that man is born upside down takes us back to the earlier discussion of Catherine Pickstock's "liturgical stammer," which "bespeaks its admission of distance between itself and the transcendent 'real.'"[38] Like Chesterton, Pickstock identifies the cause of this distance as "the breach which occurred at the Fall."[39] This gap implies that a Christian vision of ultimate reality may contradict our secular sense of things, even though this also corresponds to that which is the case. To be clear: I am not suggesting that reason is always antagonistic to Christian epistemology; on the contrary, we have maintained throughout that Christian faith can be rationally defended. Nonetheless, it seems in-keeping with Christianity's paradoxical core that internal coherence should be balanced against the admission that there are certain Christian beliefs that require a different way of thinking, since they break with conventional systems of reasoning. Pickstock argues in a similar manner that "the insane figure of God incarnate is the wisdom which cannot be understood by empirical or 'logical' investigation, Christ made man, but seen by men as a madman."[40] At this point we are confronted again with the idea that secular rationality is merely one mode of sense and that Christian (ir)rationality "speaks its own sense," which as Pickstock suggests, cannot be interpreted solely through empirical or "logical" methods. This different mode of thinking, required for Christian faith according to Chesterton, "is based on the fact that we do *not* fit in to the world,"[41] and that our natural reasoning is distorted by our fallen condition.

The descriptions of the condition of man given by Chesterton and Pickstock differ of course in a number of ways, though they are both founded on the scriptural account of the same unnatural state of our naturalness and the breach between fallen reason and spiritual truth. Paul explains to the church in Corinth: "The natural person does not accept the things of the Spirit of God, for they are folly to him, and he is not able to understand them because they are spiritually discerned."[42] Paul's contrast between "natural" and "spiritual" evident in the quotation provides biblical support for the claim that the imagination of the believer is attuned to a different manner of acquiring knowledge, which in many instances runs counter to "natural" or conventional habits. The biblical indication that spiritual discernment is a breach with conventional patterns of thought clearly casts doubt on

38. See Pickstock, *After Writing*, 178.

39. Ibid., 177.

40. Pickstock "Asyndeton," 313.

41. Chesterton, *Orthodoxy*, 144.

42. 1 Cor 2:14 ("natural" here is *psychikos*).

Polhemus' contention that Reverend Charles Dodgson had to "split his identity from his conventional self" in order to create a world of nonsense and reversals. Indeed, as Chesterton's account of man's condition might suggest, being a Christian he was always already in a topsy-turvy world.

So far, we have understood the condition of being born upside-down as a charter to seek out alternative ways of knowing, believing natural reasoning to be in some sense distorted by the effects of the fall. Something that is upside down, of course, carries the connotation that there exists a correct way round. Literary nonsense, as we have seen, is only nonsense because the reader recognizes a sensible idea or conventional rule to which it corresponds that has been turned upside-down. Susan Stewart summarizes: "in every case, nonsense depends upon an assumption of sense. Without sense there is no nonsense."[43] From this, it is clear that topsy-turvydom is only topsy-turvy if the reader has a strong sense of the untopsy-turvy. If we apply the same rule to Christianity, the claim that humanity is born upside-down implies that Christianity must be also be able to provide a picture of what the right way up looks like, and that we can expect this to involve a pattern of reversals and contraries.[44] If this were the case, in particular with regard to soteriology, then there would seem to be grounds for challenging Polhemus' contention that the prevalent use of reversal within nonsense "wins out" over orthodox religion.

Noel Malcolm's study *The Origins of English Nonsense* uses the device of reversal to demonstrate the union between modern and early examples of nonsense. Significantly, Malcolm traces the link back to the prophecies in the book of Isaiah:

> The literary device which presents reversals of the natural order of things (known as 'impossibilia' in Latin and 'adynata' in Greek) has a very long history. It can be found [. . .] in some of the best-known prophetic verses of the Bible: 'The wolf shall also dwell with the lamb, and the leopard shall lie down with the kid.'[45]

The prophesies in Isaiah referred to above signal an inversion of the assumed natural pattern of animal behavior, where the lion uncharacteristically eats straw like the ox, instead of devouring the ox, which we may

---

43. Stewart, *Aspects of Intertextuality*, 4.

44. C. S. Lewis applies a similar logic in connection with miracles, he explains: "Nothing can seem extraordinary until you have discovered what is ordinary. Belief in miracles, far from depending on an ignorance of the laws of nature, is only possible in so far as those laws are known." Lewis, *Miracles*, 51.

45. Malcolm, *Origins of English Nonsense*, 78–79.

have expected. We are told by the prophet that leading the revolution of the animal kingdom is a little child,[46] an image that frustrates our expectation of leadership. For the believer, prophetic references to the reversal of natural order have a soteriological function, as they are seen as a reference to the eschaton, when the present (fallen) working order of the natural world will be changed. Since such prophecies tell us something about the nature of the world "the right way up," it will be worth considering some of the particulars.

Death, for instance, is a condition established as a result of the fall: "By the sweat of your face you shall eat bread, till you return to the ground, for out of it you were taken; for you are dust and to dust you shall return."[47] The Old Testament delivers the message that this fallen order is not God's final plan for mankind and this is attested to in the salvific prophesies: "Your dead shall live; their bodies shall rise. You who dwell in the dust, awake and sing for joy."[48] The New Testament reveals Christ as the manifestation of God's promise to reverse the chaotic conditions of the fall. His miracles can be seen as the revelation of a new order and as the counteraction of the curse from Genesis. Such an example might be the raising of Lazarus from the dead,[49] which Isaiah prophesies. However, it is the death and resurrection of Christ himself which is the herald of "the great reversal" when the old order of death and sin is fully and ultimately overturned. Paul expresses this in his letter to the Romans: "Now if we have died with Christ, we believe that we will also live with him. We know that Christ, being raised from the dead, will never die again; death no longer has dominion over him. For the death he died he died to sin, once for all."[50]

The transformation of death into life is just one illustration of the biblical overturning of conventional expectations: ordinary human reasoning tells us that the dead ought to stay dead; that death is the natural and inevitable course. The resurrection is a miraculous event in the sense that it is a breach or interference with the laws of nature—that is, assuming we define "miracle" thus. This traditional definition of the miraculous as the interruption of the regulative principles of nature is not unanimously agreed upon within the Christian tradition. It is, for example, slightly modified by George MacDonald, who acknowledges that Christ's miracles and his resurrection seem *as if* they interfere with the laws of nature, but argues

46. Isa 1:6.
47. Gen 3:19.
48. Isa 26:19.
49. John 11:38–44.
50. Rom 6:8–10.

that "A higher condition of harmony with law may one day enable us to do things which must now *appear* an interruption of law."[51] In other words, Macdonald believes that the miracles of Christ's ministry and pre-eminently of Easter are not the *suspension* of the natural order but the *restoration* of that order. As a result, the supernatural world of healing and resurrection is in a sense more truly "natural" than the fallen conditions of sickness and death.

MacDonald's inversion of the status of the natural helps to shed light on Chesterton's declaration that Christianity emphasizes "the unnatural-ness of everything in light of the supernatural."[52] In the section on anarchy, we witnessed a similar "corrective disordering" and discussed how God's supreme order appears anarchic within a fallen world. In this chapter, we have observed how God's restoration of the natural world seems like a breaking-in of the supernatural or unnatural. What this implies is that to restore something that is upside-down to its right way up requires a radical reversal, and if that something has always been upside-down, it sounds like nonsense to suggest it was the wrong way up in the first place.

It should of course be mentioned that salvation is not *just* a reversal or counteraction—it more than simply returns us to how things were be-fore. The transition from the Garden of Eden to the New Jerusalem is a return with difference. In one sense the New Jerusalem is the reconstitution of Eden with "the tree of life" at the center. But in another sense "the new heaven" and "new earth" reveal something other and there is a transforma-tion that is not merely an edenic replica. In Genesis the overarching imagery depicts the harmony and majesty of the natural world, Revelation, on the other hand speaks of a community of believers, a holy city within which the tree of life is restored. Yet, without losing sight of the idea that transforma-tion is not merely opposition, it still seems useful to draw to the language of reversal in order to illustrate how radically alternative the concept of Eden and the New Jerusalem appear to us within our current fallen world.

To return to MacDonald's inversion of the status of the natural, the point I am trying to establish is that from a Christian perspective, the first place is not the first place, but a post-edenic, unnatural topsy-turvydom. In such a context, to speak of that which is "natural" or "the right way up," it may thus be necessary to speak nonsensically. This may be why a dominant aspect of Christ's ministry is concerned with turning conventional principles upside-down. According to the standards of secular order, the mighty are powerful, the hungry are empty, and the wise govern the foolish. However, the New Testament teaches that "God chose what is foolish in the world to

51. MacDonald, *Miracles of Our Lord*, 53.

52. Chesterton, *Orthodoxy*, 145.

shame the wise,"[53] and that the mighty are brought down from their thrones, whilst the humble are exalted; the hungry are filled and it is the rich who are empty.[54] Cameron Freeman draws the reader's attention to the prevalent pattern of reversals and believes that this awakens in the individual a sense of the absurd. He explains: "in accordance with the paradoxical reversals of meaning and expectation that Jesus used to jolt open the awareness of his audience, then, the truth will strike us as deeply absurd and come to us as something we did not see coming."[55] It is interesting for our project that Freeman draws the same conclusion concerning the absurdity of Christ's message and yet suggests that its very absurdity is—in a counter-intuitive sense—a mark of Christian authenticity.

It might be helpful to describe Jesus' paradoxical teachings as "anastrophic," insofar as the normal, established patterns of society are inverted and re-arranged. Anastrophe is usually classified as a rhetorical device that alters the order of words in a sentence, "a preposterous order, or a backward setting of words,"[56] a device, unsurprisingly, utilized by writers of literary nonsense.[57] However, the Bible uses anastrophe (ἀναστρέφω) to mean to turn upside down, to overturn or to turn back. When Jesus casts the vendors out of the temple, ἀναστρέφω is the word used to describe the overturning of the tables.[58] Its derivative στρέφω is used in connection with conversion, implying that to become a Christian requires a complete overthrowing and turning upside-down of the old self. Matthew's Gospel, for example, uses στρέφω to emphasize the radical nature of conversion: "unless you change [στρέφω] and become like little children you will never enter the kingdom of heaven."

This correspondence between ἀναστρέφω and στρέφω suggests that the overturning of tables can act as both a linguistic and visual metaphor for the overturning of the heart in conversion. This provides strong grounds for maintaining that the language of "upside-down" and "topsy-turvy," traditionally associated with nonsense, is a more accurate description of Christian faith than the common misrepresentation of Christianity as a strictly

53. 1 Cor 1:27.

54. "He has brought down the mighty from their thrones and exalted those of humble estate; he has filled the hungry with good things, and the rich he has sent empty away" (Luke 1:52–53).

55. Freeman, *Post-Metaphysics*, 248.

56. The *OED* provides the following example: *All Italy about I went*, which is contrary to plain order, *I went about all Italy*.

57. For example see Carroll's "Jabberwocky" poem: "Long time the manxome foe he sought. / So rested he by the Tumtum tree." Lewis Carroll, *LG*, 118.

58. John 2:15.

conventional way of thinking and living. So it seems that far from consti-
tuting a threat to theology on account of its frequent use of reversal and
contradiction, the application of the term nonsense could actually prove an
effective tool by which to communicate firstly, the upside-down nature of
man's fallen condition; and secondly, the wholly orthodox sense that to get
the right way up requires a topsy-turvy orientation.

At this point, it may be worth considering Rabkin's description of fantasy as "a quality of astonishment that we feel when the ground rules of a
narrative world are suddenly made to turn about 180 degrees."[59] Tigges has
already commented that "Rabkin's definition of fantasy [...] seem[s] to tally
very well with the 'topsy-turvy' view of nonsense.'"[60] My purpose in also
observing this is to bring to light the potentially hidden union between fantastic nonsense and Christian faith through the principle of reversal. Before
going any further, however, an important caveat must be inserted: whereas
literary nonsense is, in accordance with Rabkin's definition, a 180 degree
turn about, within salvation history there is a double reversal at work—a
360 degree turn, in two halves. In other words, the fall makes things the
wrong way round and salvation flips them back the right way.[61] As such,
nonsense could become a way of describing both man's fallen order from a
heavenly perspective, *and* God's restored order from a human perspective.
To each, the other is upside-down.[62]

This seems a bit like the visual paradox of the mirror, where the image
in the glass is not an identical representation but the reversal of the original
perspective. In fact, it was this peculiarity of the looking-glass that prompted
Carroll to write the sequel to Wonderland: *Alice through the Looking-Glass.*[63]

---

59. Rabkin, *The Fantastic in Literature*, 41.

60. Tigges, *Anatomy of Literary Nonsense*, 108.

61. Although as we have mentioned, salvation does not simply return us to the old
Eden, rather it is transformed into the New Jerusalem. Yet, the conditions of the New
Jerusalem, like those of the Garden of Eden are radically unlike the experience of living
in a fallen world, so it is helpful to speak of topsy-turvy realities, but it needs to be
remembered that the return, though to an upside-down kingdom, is not a strict reversion to the original.

62. Gavin Hopps makes a similar observation in reference to liturgical expression.
He writes, "From a quotidian perspective, such radically uneconomic caesuras will
obviously seem mad or embarrassing and like standing on one's head. Yet in this way,
liturgical semiotics hold out a challenge to that perspective—reminding it of, by speaking from within and seeking proleptically to give form to, another world and an alternative perspective, from which *quotidian* behaviour seems like madness and standing on
one's head." "Romantic Invocation," 49.

63. "When Dodgson was in London, he met a little girl, Alice Raikes. He invited her
indoors, put an orange in her right hand and asked her in which hand she was holding
it. Then, he put her in front of a mirror, and asked which hand the child in the mirror

The logical puzzle that Carroll turned into a brilliant nonsense story is, in a metaphorical sense, the same problem that Chesterton confronts when dealing with Christian truth from a fallen viewpoint. "All the real argument about religion," he writes, "turns on the question of whether a man who was born upside down can tell when he comes the right way up."[64] This is an invitation to question on which side of the looking-glass we are—the side which seems sensible or the side that appears nonsensical.

If salvation history is indeed a story of double reversal, then it seems more likely that Christianity would join the talking flowers in the impossible dimensions of Looking-Glass Land than side with the rationalists who reduce heaven and Wonderland alike to a whimsical dream. Chesterton, who finds deep religious truth within MacDonald's fairy tales, praises this kind of fantastic imagining as an orthodox defiance of the sensible, joyless limitations of a postlapsarian world where flowers cannot talk and dead men cannot rise. Chesterton writes:

> It is not that he [MacDonald] dresses men and movements as knights and dragons, but that he thinks that knights and dragons, really existing in the eternal world, are dressed up here as men and movements. It is not that the crown, the helmet or the aureole that are to him the fancy dress; it is the top hat and the frock coat that it are, as it were, the disguise of the terrestrial stage of conspirators. His allegoric tales of gnomes and griffins do not lower a veil but rend it.[65]

For this reason, Chesterton describes MacDonald's fairy-tales as "celestial nonsense," a mode of creative thinking that seeks to reveal man's upside-down predicament and to bring him the right way round by treating the supernatural as natural.

So it seems that for Christianity, in light of the fall, *all* theology is in some sense "looking-glass theology," requiring an anastrophic act of imagination, such as is common practice to readers of nonsense. On this basis, then, it is possible to refute Polhemus' contention that nonsense and Christianity are at odds because nonsense is unconventional and Christianity is conventional. A world in which flowers can talk bears a closer resemblance

was holding the orange in. Alice told him that it was in her left hand. When he asked her for an explanation, she answered:—'Supposing I was on the other side of the glass, wouldn't the orange still be in my right hand?' He was delighted with her answer and decided that his new book would be about the world on the other side of the looking glass." Graham, *Writing of Looking Glass*, xxxviii.

64. Chesterton, *Orthodoxy*, 291.

65. Chesterton, "George MacDonald and His Work," *The Daily News*, June 11th 1901.

to a world in which stones can cry out than the conventional realm where both must remain silent.

The secularization of wonder

A second reason given by Polhemus for believing that Carroll's nonsense is subversive of religious belief relates to the concept of wonder. Polhemus writes, "Fantasy indicates [. . .] the secularization of wonder, and Carroll is its prophet. In large degree, fantasy flourishes and fantasy life looms so large in the modern era because the past two centuries have been a time of religious confusion and doubt."[66] This suggests two things: firstly, that wonder is an important element within nonsense literature; and secondly, that this type of nonsensical wonder is opposed to the religious.

We have already considered wonder as a childlike attribute, but we have not yet addressed the possibility that an aspect of nonsensical wonder might in fact be hostile towards religion. Polhemus is not alone this contention. Certain religious believers would caution against the reading of nonmoral nonsensical fiction for exactly this reason. In Carroll's own culture, for instance, child educators such as Mrs. Trimmer expressed the dangers of subjecting children to fairy tales, because they were concerned that children would be unable to distinguish between religious truth and fantastic fiction.

Although Polhemus is writing in support of literary nonsense, he essentially puts forward the same case as Mrs. Trimmer, in arguing that the type of wonder presented in Carrollian nonsense is antagonistic towards a religious truth. As we have already observed in the chapter on the childlike, both nonsense and religion offer an experience of wonder in the sense that they contain ideas that generate astonishment.[67] The crowds are "astonished" at Jesus' teachings and miracles,[68] just as Alice is continually astonished at the unfolding events in Wonderland. The potential theological problem is that the wondrous activities of Wonderland evidently have nothing to do with God's power. Moreover, in some instances, wonder seems to be a device used in nonsense literature as a way of mocking things of theological gravity.

For example, Genesis depicts man as the pinnacle of God's creation, made in the image of God, revealing the solemn dignity of each human life.

---

66. Polhemus, *Comic Faith*, 269.

67. The *OED* offers a neutral definition of "wonder" as "something that causes astonishment."

68. Matt 7:28.

Psalm 8 emphasizes that wonder is the appropriate response to the majesty of creation:

> When I look at your heavens, the work
>
> Of your fingers,
>
> The moon and the stars that you
>
> Have established;
>
> What are human beings that you are
>
> Mindful of them,
>
> Mortals that you care for them?
>
> Yet you have made them a little lower
>
> Than God,
>
> And crowned them with glory and
>
> Honor.

This finds a comic corollary in Carroll's nonsensical world where the creatures of Looking-Glass land meet the pinnacle of God's creation:

> 'What-is-this?' he said at last.
>
> 'This is a child!' Haigha replied eagerly, coming in front of Alice to introduce her, and spreading out both his hands towards her in an Anglo-Saxon attitude.
>
> 'We only found it to-day. It's as large as life, and twice as natural!'
>
> 'I always thought they were fabulous monsters!' said the Unicorn. 'Is it alive?'
>
> 'It can talk,' said Haigha solemnly.
>
> The Unicorn looked dreamily at Alice, and said 'Talk, child.'[69]

This seems to be the kind of nonsensical wonder to which Polhemus draws our attention as being subversive of religious sentiment, since it appears to laugh at and make light of a subject of theological seriousness. This is a true and valid point as long as we insist on seriousness as the only proper Christian response to God's majestic creation. If we look again at Psalm 8, the emphasis does not seem to be on man's *solemn* dignity but rather, on his undeserved and almost ludicrous dignity: "*What* are human beings that you are mindful of them?" In fact, wonderment or the quality of astonishment can only be extracted from this psalm if it is a surprise that God should care

---

69. Lewis Carroll, *LG*, 139.

for human beings. It is for this reason that Chesterton believes nonsense can help rather than hinder the presentation of Christian truth. He writes:

> Religion has for centuries been trying to make men exult in the 'wonders' of creation, but it has forgotten that a thing cannot be completely wonderful so long as it remains sensible. So long as we regard a tree as an obvious thing [. . .] we cannot properly wonder at it. And here we fancy that nonsense will, in a very unexpected way come to the aid of the spiritual view of things.[70]

The unicorn regards Alice as thoroughly unobvious, and as a result is astonished at her basic humanity. In this sense, the unicorn displays a similar attitude to the wonderment at creation presented in Psalm 8. Nonsense in this light both disturbs a purely rationalistic explanation of man and provides an account that is at once both more humble and more exalted. We laugh at the unicorn because he regards an ordinary thing as something extraordinary; but the unicorn, like the psalmist, is perfectly serious: there *is* something fearful and wonderful about human beings.[71] In his defense of "baby worship," Chesterton seems to adopt a similar attitude to that of Carroll's unicorn. He writes:

> We do actually treat talking in children as marvellous, walking in children as marvellous, common intelligence in children as marvellous. [. . .] Any words and antics in a lump of clay are wonderful, the child's words and antics are wonderful, and it is only fair to say that the philosopher's words and antics are equally wonderful. We should probably come nearer to the true conception of things if we treated all grown-up persons, of all titles and types, with precisely that dark affection and dazed respect with which we treat infantile limitations.[72]

It is of course comical to suggest that we should clap the politician on the back for simply managing to get dressed in the morning, but there is a certain sense in which a deep humility would be born from introducing nonsensical wonder to everyday events, chiefly because the response of astonishment refuses to take accomplishment for granted (in the instance of Psalm 8 the remarkable creation of human beings and God's love for each individual). This suggests that theological wonder is not exactly a matter of taking things seriously, but rather, as we discussed in the previous chapter, it concerns a perpetual childlike astonishment at God's love, grace and power.

---

70. Chesterton, "A Defence of Nonsense," 69.

71. Ps 139:14.

72. Chesterton, "A Defence of Baby Worship," in *The Defendant*, 150–51.

This is magnified, rather than subverted, by nonsensical wonder because the subjects of wonder are mundane objects that are made wonderful by the spirit of nonsense comedy.

Sewell is keen to emphasize nonsense's strong predilection for the ordinary;[73] she comments on Carroll's re-writing of the well-known poem, "The Star"[74] and observes that its absurdity is located not only in the incongruous association of bats and tea-trays, but also in the substitution of the ethereal (star, diamond) for the ordinary and earthly. The act of making commonplace things extraordinary is, as Chesterton has indicated, an excellent expression of theological wonder. For the Christian, as long as God's love for man remains an astonishing fact, man himself remains humble and gracious.

The limits and terrors of reality

Polhemus' third reason for seeking to divorce theology from nonsense is that he believes the latter, unlike religion, has the ability to traverse "the limits and terrors of reality." Polhemus explains: "People need to believe that the limits and terrors of reality can be changed, that the future can be different and better, that wonderful things can happen; if religious institutions cannot do these things, something else must."[75] He believes nonsense can do this for a variety of reasons, but primarily because nonsense plays with and imaginatively breaches the boundaries of human experience.

Polhemus sees humor as the tool by which humanity has the power to transform an attitude of fear, and argues that this institutes a secular faith in the place of a religious one. "It isn't God," Polhemus stresses, "but the power of humor that takes away death's sting."[76] He offers the following example from *Through the Looking-Glass*:

> 'You may observe a Bread-and-butter-fly'
> 'And what does *it* live on?'
> 'Weak tea with cream in it.'

---

73. Sewell asks, "What is there about bats and tea-trays that makes them more suitable for Nonsense than stars and diamonds? [. . .] The other subtraction, that of a tea-tray for a diamond, works on much the same principles, abandoning beauty, rarity, preciousness and attraction for ordinariness." Sewell, *Field of Nonsense*, 100–101.

74. The version offered by the Mad Hatter follows thus: "Twinkle, twinkle, little bat!/How I wonder what you're at!/Up above the world you fly,/Like a tea-tray in the sky." Carroll, *AW*, 57.

75. Polhemus, *Comic Faith*, 269.

76. Ibid., 271.

> A new difficulty came into Alice's head. 'Supposing it
> couldn't find any?' she suggested.
> 'Then it would die, of course.'
> 'But that must happen very often,' Alice remarked
> thoughtfully.
> 'It always happens,' said the Gnat.[77]

From this passage, Polhemus describes an experience of the unseriousness
of death, a sensation that he cannot seem to articulate without using religious language:

> Death jokes are actually resurrection jokes, they announce that
> there is nothing which the life-force of the mind can't transform
> into vital pleasure. [. . .] We cannot understand the prevalence
> of black humor—any more than we can understand the belief
> in hell—without seeing that it performs a kind of theological
> function. Joking about death is one of the most sophisticated
> ways that we have of combating its menace—of accepting it and
> defying it at the same time.[78]

Polhemus' ability to transform the darkness of death into something
lighter via nonsense humor seems to be an excellent, if unwitting, demonstration of the religious potential of nonsense. It is true that within nonsense
worlds, everyday limitations upon reality are frequently traversed and undercut. It is also true that "terrors" within nonsense tend to be short lasting
and quickly forgotten. Neither of these tendencies is necessarily religious.
However, the idea that the reader's imaginative experience underground or
through the looking-glass can overcome the horrors of real life *is* a theological statement and this is attested to by Polhemus' inability to disassociate his
secular belief from religious language.

Polhemus makes a vital theological statement: death jokes *are* resurrection jokes and they serve "a kind of theological function." One could
go further though and suggest that death can only be seen as a sort of joke
because of the resurrection.[79] Martin Luther describes salvation as Christ's

---

77. Lewis Carroll, *LG*, 134.

78. Polhemus, *Comic Faith*, 272.

79. Catherine Pickstock proposes a similar idea, except her focus is on story rather
than humor. Just as Polhemus suggests all death jokes are resurrection jokes, Pickstock
describes all stories as resurrection stories: "For, on the one hand, 'death' construed as
a nihilistic dereliction might be the end of every story; on the other hand, it ends the
possibility of story. And so every story is by definition a resurrection story, and it is thus
that we can read the Gospel stories as narrating the story which sets out the transcendental condition for every story. Yet, since the resurrection ensures that there is no final
death to end the story, Jesus' story is at once the story which makes stories possible, and

usurpation of the "rights" and "power" of death. He writes: "it was a strange battle where death and life struggled. Life won the victory, it has swallowed up death [. . . ;] death has become a mockery."[80] Given that Christianity describes Christ's victory as enduring, there are grounds for suggesting that even apparently non-religious "death jokes" may participate in the ultimate mockery of death: the resurrection. The earlier reflection on miracles led to the conclusion that *if* Christianity is true, it could overcome the limits and terrors of this-worldly reality, because it is subversive to those limits and ontologically opposed to those terrors, as they are post-edenic without being pre-parousia.

It would seem, then, that there are two conclusions we can draw from this: firstly, that if there is a god, who has a plan for human salvation, where the future really is radically different and the limits of reality are altered, then nonsense can in some analogous sense participate in this celebration of redemption. Alternatively, if there is no god, or if that deity does not grant human salvation, either because he is unable or unwilling, then nonsense cannot bring the reader any closer to overcoming terrors or limits of reality, except as a temporary measure in the form of mental escape from that reality. In suggesting that nonsense literature provides an imaginative basis for transforming humanity's attitude of fear, Polhemus unwittingly advances a theological statement and offers valuable evidence that the non-believer may be able to participate in a religious experience through engaging with literary nonsense.

SALVIFIC EXTRAVAGANCE

In him was life, and the life was the light of men.

JOHN 1:4

Having considered some of the potential difficulties that might be encountered in drawing an analogy between religious belief and literary nonsense, I want in this section to examine the ways that literary nonsense can offer a true and helpful method for interacting with Christian theology, with particular emphasis on the doctrine of Salvation. Any exploration of soteriology involves the balancing of future promise with present experience and to

---

the impossible story which never ends." Pickstock, *After Writing*, 265–66.

80. Francis Browne's translation of Martin Luther's words as set by Bach in Cantana 4.

this extent it is true to say that soteriology is always concerned with an end beyond what is possible now.

The Bible likewise situates salvation in the present as well as the future. Paul preaches, "now is the day of salvation"[81] whilst Peter tells us salvation is "kept in heaven for you [. . .] ready to be revealed in the last time."[82] By acknowledging that both are correct Christianity disturbs our conventional understanding of temporality, as it preaches a paradoxical both/and time frame. Giving equal emphasis to both teachings allows soteriology to speak in its own terms, although these are terms which stray outside quotidian conceptions of the possible. In this sense, then, salvation can be described as "extravagant,"[83] insofar as it is *extra-vagant* and involves wandering beyond the given, and straying outside the possible.

If nonsense is a discourse that can help to express what it means to live in accordance with the promise and actuality of salvation, we need to locate within nonsense moments that not only go beyond purely rational limitations of experience but also in some sense correspond to a "salvific extravagance." It would be of limited value to theology if nonsense simply broke down present conditions without opening up an analogous participation in something outside the everyday. This is not to say that literary nonsense *does* provide an exhaustive eschatological analogy—as we have mentioned soteriology is not a simple looking-glass reversal—however, I do wish to argue that nonsense literature contains within its structure some important ways of engaging the imagination, which closely identify with a Christian attitude to living in the light of salvation.

Final seriousness

We have already looked at the idea that salvation involves passing from the state of deadness in sin to new life in Christ. This new life is described in the Gospels as "abundant life," expressing a sense of extravagant vitality—a life that experiences God's over-generous love and his excessive gesture of grace. This new life in Christ also calls the individual to live on the margins of society, always in part oriented elsewhere, already assuming a "citizenship

---

81. 2 Cor 6:2.

82. 1 Pet 1:4–5.

83. Salvation can also be defined as extravagant under the more common interpretation of extravagant as over-generous, excessive, abundant or extreme. God's love is over-abundant for humanity; the sending of Himself in Christ to die on the cross can be seen as an extravagant gesture of grace.

in heaven."[84] Among other consequences, living life abundantly seems to involve the Christian assuming two particular roles: the child of God and the fool for Christ. Both have an extravagant dimension: the child of God knows he is fully provided for and lives amidst extravagant love and joy. He is carefree and light-hearted. The fool for Christ lives an *extra-vagant* lifestyle, straying beyond the boundaries of respectability never fully centered in the world, heeding a wisdom that comes from elsewhere. Both of these roles crucially involve an anti-serious element, not because they are dissociated from realities that we may consider "serious," such as hard work, suffering and death, but because they interpret God's reality as far more serious than any worldly *telos*.

Karl Barth in *Ethics* maintains that an important effect of salvation upon the believer is the understanding that "ultimately, in the last resort, our life is truly only a game."[85] Barth explains this is a direct result of believing that the only truly "serious" event in history was (and is) Jesus Christ's life, death, and resurrection. Accepting this, Barth says, "we cannot allot final seriousness to what we do here and now. We do it under the divine patience which gives us time, but not with the significance of eternal action."[86] In this, we find a suggestion, from an orthodox theologian not noted for his levity, that believing in salvation encourages a response to the world and an individual's place in it, which is freed from ultimate seriousness by approaching life as a game.

Nonsense has as curious relationship to seriousness. Carroll's cast of absurd creatures all take themselves and their business seriously. In fact, it is often the sombre and earnest devotion to their cause that creates the nonsense humor. Take for example Tweedledum's anguish at his spoilt rattle:

> 'Do you see *that?*' he said, in a voice choking with passion, and his eyes grew large and yellow all in a moment, as he pointed with a trembling finger at a small white thing. [. . .] Tweedledum cried in a greater fury than ever. 'It's *new*, I tell you—I bought it yesterday—my nice NEW RATTLE!' and his voice rose to a perfect scream.[87]

The reader of course is not encouraged to pity Tweedledum but to laugh at his outrage. However, if the rattle were substituted for an expensive car then we might be expected to respond with a degree of empathy, but given

---

84. Phil 3:20.
85. Barth, *Ethics*, 504.
86. Ibid., 505.
87. Carroll, *LG*, 146.

the context, the reader is not meant to take Tweedledum's reaction seriously. The scene progresses and he prepares to fight his brother insisting that Alice deck him out in "bolsters, blankets, hearth-rugs, table-cloths, dish-covers and coal-scuttles."[88] In this scene Carroll takes what actually is a serious situation (a fight between two brothers) and makes light of it by overemphasizing its solemnity: "'You know,' he [Tweedledum] added very gravely, 'it's one of the most serious things that can possible happen to one in a battle—to get one's head cut off.' Alice laughed loud: but she managed to turn it into a cough, for fear of hurting his feelings."[89] Tweedledum actually makes a perfectly reasonable statement, it is of course one of the worst possible eventualities of a battle. However, picturing the scene (perhaps with the aid of Tenniel's drawing) of an oversized schoolboy, padded out with cloth and saucepans, preparing to duel over a rattle, the reader is encouraged to laugh along with Alice at the ridiculous solemnity displayed by Tweedledum. When we close the book, I wonder, if there any case for suggesting that laughing at nonsensical situations translates to the ability to take lightly our own anguish? Both the child and the fool embody this making light of seriousness in different ways, and both occupy central positions in nonsense literature. What I want to consider in the rest of this section is whether the foolish wit and childish play of nonsense share any likeness with the attitudes of God's child and Christ's fool.

The child of God

Barth's interpretation of Christian living as breaking free from seriousness participates in the biblical message that salvation involves becoming God's child: "we now start with the fact that the divine command is also that of the Father whose children we are."[90] We concluded the previous chapter on the childlike by accepting that a prerequisite of salvation involves assuming a childlike status before God. We have similarly found that in the practice of reading nonsense, there is a shift away from adult thinking to a childlike imagining, and this is one of the foremost reasons that nonsense, like Christianity, breaks away from seriousness.

The theme of regression dominates Polhemus' attempt to establish a "secular faith" derived from Carroll's nonsense. "In all comedy," he writes, "there is something regressive that takes us back to the world of play that we first knew as children. And if all comic literature somehow involves

88. Ibid., 147.
89. Ibid.
90. Barth, *Ethics*, 497.

regression, many will naturally find it frivolous."[91] Barth describes a similar "frivolity" that ought to be identifiable in the redemptive play of the children of God. He writes, "we should not fail to say that as God's children we are in fact released from the seriousness of life and can and should simply play before God."[92] Christianity, properly understood, does not advocate regressive infantilism, but reverses the idea that mature adult seriousness is more "grown up" than childlike playfulness. This corresponds with Eckhart's expression of the eternal play of the Trinity and seems to call for our participation in that infinite expression of joyfulness. Barth expresses that this invitation to play is in fact the one vital and emphatic mode of Christian being:

> We are not only permitted but commanded to find the concept of our essential relationship to God in the promise that we are his children in the sense of his *little* children. [. . .] We must not play the part, then, of adult sons and daughters of God who gradually come to be on a level with their father. [. . .] We are always, in fact, his *little* children.[93]

Barth seems to be adamant that the childlike is not merely a helpful mode for certain individuals to think theologically. He accepts that no ultimate seriousness can be allotted to anything accomplished here and now, believing everything has been (and will be) accomplished on the cross and at the parousia. "From this angle," explains Barth, "we can regard our action only as play. [. . .] We have simply to realize that we are children, and will be so to the very end."[94]

For all their differences, Polhemus and Barth use very similar language. They both tell us there is a specific connection between play and being like children and both indicate that this makes the activity free from seriousness and can have the appearance of frivolity. Barth describes this mode of frivolity as "Christian relaxation": "relaxation of man as such, of his whole present being as a creature."[95] By adopting this attitude to the world, the child of God—assured of Christ's victory and trustful of God's promises—is reborn *beyond* seriousness, and even *amidst* suffering and sorrow, he is called to embody a joyous frivolity. Barth explains: "in the present we are still sick and frail. We are still imprisoned, bound and confined. [. . .]

91. Polhemus, *Comic Faith*, 248.
92. Barth, *Ethics*, 504.
93. Ibid.
94. Ibid.
95. Ibid., 503.

Nevertheless—here is the point—there is a release and relaxation even in this sighing."[96] This suggests that living an extravagant life of joy and trust is not a matter of pretending that there is no suffering, but rather entails approaching experiences with a certain degree of detachment enabled by an eschatological perspective.

The imagination of the child of God possesses the capacity to overturn and break down obstacles that appear to demand a more serious response. So, for example, the preoccupation with economic success and worldly status, or the fear of death, illness, and failure are "serious" concerns that disturb what according to Barth should be the *gamelike* quality of life lived in the conviction of salvation. *Seriousness* for Barth comes into operation when the eschatological imagination is in some way hindered. Literary nonsense seems to encourage a similar imaginative suspension of the serious. The worlds of nonsense fiction are of course far from utopic and terrible things happen to characters. However, as Sewell explains, this is all done with a "detachment of those involved [. . .] and so it does not matter if they meet with dreadful fates."[97] Several good examples of this aspect of literary nonsense are found in the limericks of Edward Lear:

> There was an Old Man of the Nile,
>
> Who sharpened his nails with a file,
>
> Till he cut off his thumbs, and said calmly, 'This comes
>
> Of sharpening one's nails with a file!'[98]

Lear's character shows a remarkable detachment to his physical anguish emphasized by the calm manner with which he articulates his predicament. Sewell describes this manner of detachment as a "robust carelessness towards characters and objects."[99] Of course, there is a crucial distinction here: nonsense can take these things lightly because it is a purely fictional world with a cartoon ontology. By contrast, from a Christian perspective, whilst on the one hand there is no diminution of the immediate suffering, Christians are at the same time enjoined to see it in a wider perspective from

---

96. Ibid., 102.

97. Sewell, *Field of Nonsense*, 141.

98. Lear, *Complete Nonsense*, 49.

99. Sewell, *Field of Nonsense*, 138.

which suffering is not ultimate.[100] "We cannot," as Barth says, "be totally serious as the children of God."[101]

In other words, both nonsense and Christianity demand a degree of imaginative frivolity to enter into difficult experiences with an attitude of childlike play. On this matter, Barth is resolute: "you live in and by the fact that you are the child of God, that you already stand at his side, triumphing over the contradiction and the limits of your existence. [. . .] Act as one who lives in and by this gift."[102] To act and live in the belief that God has already triumphed over every cause for sorrow suggests that Christianity has an ontological warrant for thinking and acting in a manner of extravagant frivolity.

It is worth remarking that without the conviction that the non-serious may be a religious posture many nonsense critics seem to feel it necessary to temper or defend the frivolity of the fiction, as if nonsense in itself is not serious enough to warrant intellectual study. Polhemus admits that literary nonsense *seems* frivolous but qualifies that although *some* find comic regression frivolous, "I see the comic regression in *Through the Looking-Glass* as profound."[103] Polhemus has to claim that nonsense humor is not mere frivolity because otherwise he cannot draw meaning from it. Nonsense thus becomes a pseudo-frivolity since it is covertly transformed into something else in an attempt to save its significance.

A *theology* of nonsense, by contrast is possible precisely because nonsense is not a pseudo-frivolity, it actually *is* a frivolous activity. From a theological perspective, nonsense is not an extravagant frivolity if there is an underlying expectation of "profound" thought. Barth tells us that "art is always play,"[104] and this is because "in art we venture not to take present reality with final seriousness."[105] For the Christian it is a duty not to take reality too seriously, but from a secular point of view, deconstructing the seriousness of a subject could be seen as a devaluation of meaning. This is

100. This is, of course, a very difficult subject to write about since suffering is extremely delicate and problematic territory. One way of addressing the problem might be to suggest that there is a discrepancy between what we tell ourselves and how we act pastorally. The Bible does invite the individual to take his own suffering lightly (such an example is found in 2 Cor 4:14 "for this slight momentary affliction is preparing us for an eternal weight of glory beyond all comparison"), but how we communicate this to another person in the face of their suffering requires a deep empathy and sensitivity.

101. Barth, *Ethics*, 511.

102. See ibid., 501.

103. Polhemus, *Comic Faith*, 248.

104. Barth, *Ethics*, 509.

105. Ibid., 508.

particularly problematic for Polhemus, as he not only wants to use art to say something meaningful about the world, but also wants to construct a secular faith by showing that there is something more profound to art than just play. For Barth, it is precisely *because* there is nothing more to art than just play that it is profound, and also religious.[106]

At this point, we might pause and reflect that in attempting to outline how literary nonsense is relevant to faith, we have ended up describing how the categories of faith feed into the study of nonsense. This seems to be a natural consequence of defining humor and childlike play as discourses that carry with them ontological implications. Because the secular critic is without an ontological understanding of the non-serious, they are often forced to distort the genre in order to defend their study of it. We observed a similar misrepresentative defense of nonsense in the conclusion to the chapter on the childlike. Tigges found he could not let the juvenile remain juvenile because this would apparently relegate his study to a similar status. By contrast, Barth's non-serious theology of the child calls for the embrace of light-hearted modes such as nonsense play, due to the conviction that light-heartedness has intrinsic worth.

The fool for Christ

We have already commented on the frequent practice of reversal within scripture, including the election of the foolish "to shame the wise."[107] This does not seem to be a passing comment, but a consistent and central emphasis.[108] It is not with hesitation but with "boasting" that Paul describes his status as a fool to the Corinthians: "But whatever anyone else dares to boast of—I am speaking as a fool—I also dare to boast of that."[109] Erasmus celebrates Paul's teaching as "a high praise of folly from a high authority"[110] and describes folly as "a valuable and necessary quality of mind."[111] This suggests that folly (or foolishness) is not an optional but a *necessary* attitude for the Christian to assume. It is not, however, immediately evident what

---

106. Cf. Ibid., 504: "our work in relation to his is more play than work, obedient play, play in the peace of the father's house that is waiting for us, yet still play."

107. 1 Cor 1:27–28.

108. Erasmus tells us that folly is not just an obscure strand of the Christian tradition, but rather, "the entire Christian religion seems to bear a certain natural affinity to folly and to relate far less clearly to wisdom." Erasmus, *Praise of Folly*, 82.

109. 2 Cor 11:21.

110. Erasmus, *Praise of Folly*, 80.

111. Ibid.

precisely either Paul or Erasmus mean by "fool," nor why they depict folly as an important Christian quality, since "fool" also has biblical connotations of being impious and spiritually blind.[112]

In seeking to define the term, Jean-Yves Lacoste makes a helpful distinction between the fool and the lunatic; he explains: "The fool denies his belonging to the world, while the lunatic's insanity prevents him from joining happily in human society, and the denial is not the same thing as the prevention."[113] Lacoste maintains that *intention* drives folly, whereas he sees lunacy as distinctly lacking pre-meditation. Significantly, Lacoste also situates folly within the context of salvation, he observes that "The fool's experience has an eschatological horizon—otherwise we could not account for it—while the lunatic's experience is obviously devoid of such a horizon."[114] Here, Lacoste identifies folly's *extra-vagant* dimension, an otherworldly focus that is orientated towards the not-yet aspect of God's kingdom, appearing topsy-turvy to those upside-down.[115]

The tradition of Christian folly seems thus to involve the overthrowing of quotidian principles in a manner which sets the fool apart from society. Such an understanding leads the Christian theologian John Saward to remark: "if the world does not regard us as foolish it is probable that we are conformed to it."[116] Accordingly, being seen as a fool is an important statement of the believer's genuine attachment to a reality elsewhere. Saward describes Paul's instruction "be transformed by the renewal of your mind"[117] as "a precept which necessarily entails non-conformity to the world and thus to its wisdom."[118] Folly in a Christian context is therefore used to call into question the certainty of our *a priori* rational assumptions and the significance we attach to worldly standards and endeavors.

Robert Polhemus' interpretation of foolishness in Carroll's nonsense seems to strongly accord with this religious characterization of folly.

112. "The fool says in his heart 'there is no God'" Prov 14:1. See also The Parable of the Rich Fool (Luke 12:20).

113. Lacoste, "Liturgy and Kenosis," 251.

114. Ibid.

115. We are reminded of Shakespeare's portrayal of the wise fool, which plays around with our pre-conceptions of power and intelligence. His fools often speak the strongest wisdom (such as The Fool (*King Lear*), Feste (*Twelfth Night*), and Touchstone (*As You Like It*) "The Fool knows that the only true madness is to recognize this world as rational. The feudal order is absurd and can be described only in terms of the absurd. The world stands upside down." Kott, *Shakespeare*, 136.

116. Saward, *Perfect Fools*, 214.

117. Rom 12:2.

118. Saward, *Perfect Fools*, 212.

Polhemus claims that nonsensical folly prompts us to consider whether our attitude towards a particular convention or idea is unnecessarily solemn. He writes:

> Victorian intellectual life was filled with the self-important voices of sages who professed to speak in the name of science, poetry, and nature. Assuming roles, they identified their egos with cosmic intentions. Carroll['s] [. . .] weapon is *reductio ad absurdum*: seizing on an authority figure's grandiose words, he takes them literally, like a child, and imagines their full implications to show how ridiculous they are.[119]

Almost all the characters Alice meets take themselves very seriously (like the Victorian intellectuals) but Carroll makes them ridiculous by their words and actions. For example, the White Queen's boast to Alice: "I'll tell you a secret—I can read words of one letter! Isn't *that* grand? However, don't be discouraged. You'll come to it in time."[120] Kings, Queens, courts, judgment, death, war, learnedness, rank, and authority in Carroll's worlds are all dealt with in a manner that gives emphasis to their foolish sides.[121] Through nonsense literature, the reader is able to laugh at and ridicule institutions that he may normally revere. Nonsense takes a grave theme (like war) and depicts it in such a way that diminishes its fearful and horrific quality by turning that which is threatening into something small and comic. Polhemus elaborates upon this idea with reference to the episode with Tweedledee and Tweedledum: "The comedy controls for the moment the potential horror of battle by putting it in a context of play asserting from a dispassionate point of view, which we have the power to assume, war means the ridiculous behavior of Tweedledee and Tweedledum."[122]

Barth, without any reference to the art of literary nonsense, provides us with a similar theological interpretation of this particular venture of folly. He writes, "like art, humor undoubtedly means that we do not take the present with ultimate seriousness, not because it is not serious enough in itself, but because God's future, which breaks into the present, is more serious.

---

119. Polhemus, *Comic Faith*, 225.

120. Carroll, *LG*, 195.

121. To this extent, Carroll's world's are *excessively* foolish, since almost all of his characters display extensive foolish tendencies. This is an interesting inversion of the traditional position of the fool, who is normally the odd one out (consider the court fool, and Shakespeare's dramatic institution of the fool). In Carroll's world Alice alone embodies a rational outlook and there is a reversal of the common dramatic troupe since in the nonsense worlds all the characters are fools (or as the Cheshire Cat remarks, "We're all mad here"). Carroll, *AW*, 51.

122. Polhemus, *Comic Faith*, 260.

Humor means the placing of a big bracket around the seriousness of the present."[123] As we can see, without any consideration of literary nonsense, Barth has informed us of nonsense's deeply theological core, nonsense is nonsense as long as it brackets out the seriousness of the present, and insofar as the reader must surrender his seriousness in order to engage in literary nonsense, he shares an analogous participation in the Christian practice of faithful folly. Barth emphasizes that God's future is "more serious" than any worldly situation, including our own physical or psychological problems. Humor, he believes, is a way in which we can implement this perspective and aim towards the "eschatological horizon" just like Lacoste's fool.

Literary nonsense thus not only offers a respite from "the age of *dignity*,"[124] but also an active rebuttal of its over-solemnized values. Carroll's nonsense can help us to see the vanity of those things we are tempted to take most seriously: death, power, and the self. It should be stressed that I am by no means claiming that nonsense *intends* to present a theological message through folly; I am suggesting, rather, that nonsense cannot help it. As we have seen, for Barth, the theological significance of humor relates to moving beyond seriousness to a position of humility before God. He explains, "When we have first laughed at ourselves we can then laugh at others, and we can stand cheerfully the final test of being laughed at by them."[125]

There is, of course, a significant distinction between Christian folly and nonsensical folly. Being a fool for Christ, as Lacoste observes, is premeditated and involves having one's eyes set on an "eschatological horizon"; the foolish wit in Carroll's nonsense does not have such an ultimate goal or purpose. However, simply by being the other of common sense, nonsense folly resists and challenges the certainty of man's *a priori* rational assumptions. Lacoste indicates how this can be interpreted as a theological activity: "A human being cannot confront God without first ridding himself of the *a priori* dominion exercised by the world, no one is born the possessor of what is most proper to him; we do not gain access to ourselves without doing violence to the initial conditions of experience."[126] These conditions include our intuition of the possible and the plausible. Hence, the foolish comedy of nonsense provides a comic relief from human wisdom and in so doing, participates in the activity of mental *extra-vagance*, which is akin to an eschatological faith. Lacoste speaks of the necessity of breaking down the

123. Barth, *Ethics*, 511.
124. Balthasar, *The Glory of the Lord*, 22.
125. Barth, *Ethics*, 511.
126. Lacoste, "Liturgy and Kenosis," 249.

a priori dominion of worldly wisdom, and this is what Christ's fool tries to bring about, and what literary nonsense inadvertently does.

EVANGELIZING NONSENSE

These men who have turned the world upside down have come here also.

ACTS 17:6

So far, the investigation has been predominantly theoretical. I have addressed the principal structural devices of literary nonsense, the character of the religious imagination and identified a correlation between the two in terms of an *extra-vagant* and non-serious comportment. We can now use this information to investigate whether there are any peculiar advantages for theology in discovering an analogy with nonsense. We have established that there *is* a connection; I now want to explore the evangelical and practical associations.

It tends to be assumed that nonsense means a detour or lack of communication. I want to argue instead that nonsense may be both an appropriate and helpful way to speak about the divine. The relationship between theology and nonsense has been articulated by way of analogy, and to this extent, we have established a metaphorical association. It will be helpful to begin by considering the broader application of metaphor in theology and then proceed to examine the particular suitability of nonsense as a theological analogy.

The initial question I want to ask concerns *when* (if at all) metaphorical speech might be relevant in theological discourse. Perhaps the most obvious instance is in the conveyance of mystical experience. Janet Martin Soskice in her seminal work *Metaphor and Religious Language* writes that the mystic "often feels a crisis of descriptive language because there do not seem to be words and concepts in the common stock adequate to his or her experience."[127] Soskice remarks that this leads to a heavy reliance on metaphor to communicate what appears to the individual as an ineffable experience. The use of metaphor is a commonly accepted form of communicating mystical encounters; but there is often an assumption that everyday occurrences can be vocalized without resort to metaphor.

---

127. Soskice, *Metaphor*, 151.

Christians, however, are in some sense involved in a daily mystical experience, and face the task of communicating an ongoing, everyday, relationship with a transcendent deity. Soskice's study reveals the mystical dimension present in all theological statements and accounts for this by drawing a distinction between "referral" and "definition," maintaining that God can always be referred to without ever being exhaustively defined. For this reason, she argues, metaphorical speech lies at the heart of all theological expression: "in our stammering after a transcendent God we must speak, for the most part, metaphorically or not at all."[128]

This observation certainly seems to be in-keeping with biblical language, as Chesterton reminds us: "the diction used by Christ is quite curiously gigantesque; it is full of camels leaping though needles and mountains hurled into the sea."[129] Certainly metaphor is a consistent mode of communication in scripture, to the extent, Sallie McFague argues, that it is correct to assert that all theology is rooted in biblical metaphor. Metaphor, she insists, is primary to theology: "We are never given a theology of the kingdom," she explains, "but we are told stories about it [. . .] we are shown metaphors—pearls, seeds, camels and needles, children, hungry and thirsty strangers, maidens and a bridegroom, and so on—which image it forth."[130] If we accept that metaphor is not simply a helpful tool, but forms the basis of all religious communication then we need to consider what implication this has for our analogy with literary nonsense. Is it merely a species of metaphor that works like any other? Or is there anything about it that makes literary nonsense particularly significant in the conveyance of Christian truth?

Embracing atheism

In colloquial usage, when nonsense is applied to faith, the intention is almost always pejorative. It might seem that the implications of the term are thoroughly detrimental to the religious cause, as the label "nonsense" suggests those who hold a religious conviction are deluded. On the other hand, the established existence of the term could provide a possible point of entrance into religious discourse for the non-believer in terms they are likely to have already accepted. I want to propose that bringing nonsense into a theological grammar offers a non-threatening linguistic basis by which a theist can interact with a strong evidentialist such as A. J. Ayer. Take for example Ayer's following statement:

128. Ibid., 140.
129. Chesterton, *Orthodoxy*, 270.
130. McFague, *Speaking in Parables*, 40.

> To say that something transcends the human understanding is to say that it is unintelligible. And what is unintelligible cannot be significantly described. [. . .] If one allows that it is impossible to define God in intelligible terms, then one is allowing that it is impossible for a sentence both to be significant and to be about God. If a mystic admits that the object of his vision cannot be described, then *he must also admit that he is bound to talk nonsense when he describes it.*[131]

What would happen if the same believer whom Ayer is attempting to trap in his verificationist rhetoric *conceded* Ayer's point? Admittedly, in doing so, the believer would be playing a language game with Ayer, for the theist would be accepting nonsense as an analogy, in accordance with literary nonsense, rather than Ayer's intended meaning. However, the believer would thereby have avoided Ayer's language trap, and instead established nonsense as a common ground.

By discussing nonsense and faith analogously, we are thus effectively able to agree with the empiricist *and* affirm a religious conviction. The believer is then poised to offer the empiricist a new interpretation of nonsense, and stipulate that nonsense does not necessarily make a statement redundant or untrue, but calls for a different type of logic. As he divulges his reasons for agreeing with the empiricist, the believer has found he is engaged in a type of apologetics originating from the terms offered by atheism. If it is recognized that from the perspective of empiricism certain aspects of Christian faith are nonsensical, then the first practical implication we can draw from the association between faith and nonsense is an increased potential to avoid unprofitable conflict in evangelical discussion, chiefly because the apologist begins by embracing the complaints of atheism in the sphere of logical unfeasibility.

Another important consequence of exhibiting a relationship between nonsense and religion is revealed within the context of postmodern theology. John Milbank believes "The end of modernity [. . .] means the end of a single system of truth based on universal reason, which tells us what reality is like."[132] He goes on to explain, "with this ending, there ends also the modern predicament of theology. It no longer has to measure up to accepted secular standards of scientific truth or normative rationality."[133] This is the crucial message of postmodern theology: the "Enlightenment critique of religion

131. From Ayer, *Language, Truth and Logic*, 156, quoted in Soskice, *Metaphor*, 144. My emphasis.

132. Milbank, "Postmodern Critical Augustinianism," in *God, the Gift and Postmodernism*, 265.

133. Ibid.

boomerangs back against itself."[134] There seems to be a certain metaphysical boldness encouraged by postmodernity; the "boomerang" effect has turned staunch rationalism (not theism) into an outmoded and blinkered position, the outcome of which means theology no longer has to apologize for, or suppress the fact that it does not harmonize with "normative rationality," something that is now being celebrated rather than concealed.

Such developments in postmodern thinking have unquestionably made possible a theological exploration into nonsense, and yet, whilst revelling in the spirit of postmodernity it is unwise to fall into the trap of "defending religion by attacking the Enlightenment."[135] There have been a number of apt critical responses to the postmodern tendency to demonize Enlightenment principles, failing to recognize the self-evident goods that weave similar threads. John Cottingham, for example, offers an important qualification of Caputo's rejection of Enlightenment values and discusses how certain postmodern positions are themselves indebted to modernity. "The values of the Enlightenment," Cottingham explains, "are part of the long journey of the human mind towards an ever fuller and more accurate understanding of the natural order."[136]

Perhaps it is true that postmodern theology goes too far in its condemnation of Enlightenment thought, but its attempt to establish faith as a sufficient epistemological basis sends out a clear and important message that religion should not apologize for its lack of conformity to secular standards of reason. In a similar way, acknowledging a congruity between nonsense and theology is an unashamed recognition of the scandal of faith. This idea of awakening a sense of scandal seems to be the second practical implication we can draw from considering nonsense literature as a theological analogue.

It is worth remembering that a bold or scandalous declaration of faith is prevalent throughout the New Testament, Paul asks the Ephesians to pray that he may "boldly proclaim the mystery of the gospel."[137] This prayer can be seen as a biblical invitation to be bold about the mysterious core of Christianity, to declare there is something inexplicable and unreasonable about the good news of Christ, and to *expect* the message to be perceived with skepticism and even ridicule. In order to *"boldly* proclaim the *mystery* of the gospel," Christianity needs to find a way to reassert the mystery, or make the word strange again in order that it may be boldly declared. By unearthing an analogy with literary nonsense, Christianity can disturb the placid ac-

---

134. Robins, Introduction, *After the Death of God*, 19.

135. Cottingham, *Spiritual Dimension*, 115.

136. Ibid.

137. Eph 6:19–20.

ceptance of the gospel as a "nice story" and reawaken the strangeness of the faith: it is, in short, a way of recovering the scandal of the gospel.

The virtue of the non-moral

The next practical strength prominent in using the term "nonsense" to describe faith is that it can help correct the common misapprehension that Christianity is exclusively concerned with observing a moral code. Atheists and agnostics will often concede that although Christianity's *metaphysical* claims are nonsense, it is still a good way to live because of its positive *ethical* standards. To seek deliberately to undercut this message therefore has the potential to sound offensive to Christianity, where Christianity has been accepted primarily for its ethical merit. However, C. S. Lewis, in his humorous collection of letters from a senior devil to a junior devil, describes the reduction of Christianity to its ethical function as a "devilish" technique:

> We thus distract men's minds from Who He is, and What He did. We first make Him solely a teacher. [. . .] [W]e want very much to make men treat Christianity as a means; preferably, of course, as a means to their advancement, but failing that, as a means to anything—even to social justice. The thing to do is to get a man at first to value social justice as a thing which the Enemy [God] demands, and then work on him to the stage at which he values Christianity because it may produce social justice.[138]

In this text, (with the devil as a mouthpiece) Lewis expresses the supreme error of placing the advantage of an ethical code above Christianity's theological truths. The point Lewis conveys is that ethics, isolated from faith, is not a different expression of the same belief, but an outright rejection of the Christian message. A sole emphasis on the morality of Christianity, as Screwtape tells us, "distracts men's minds from Who He is, and What He did." Instead, Paul explains to the Romans, justification comes about through faith "apart from works of the law."[139] Of course, morality *is* an important demonstration of God's supreme goodness, but, as Paul teaches, "the righteousness of God has been manifested *apart from the law,* although the Law and the Prophets bear witness to it—the Righteousness of God through faith in Jesus Christ for all who believe."[140] To suggest, as Paul does that both God's goodness and man's justification are manifest outside

---

138. Lewis, *Screwtape Letters*, 118–19.

139. Rom 3:28.

140. Rom 3:21 (my emphasis).

the moral law argues against the assumption that Christianity is a narrowly "moral" religion.

The advantage of comparing nonsense literature to religion is that the genre is distinctly disassociated from the moral tale. Carroll's stories were revolutionary as they initiated the break with the conventions of children's literature by refusing to offer moral homilies. Jack Zipes explains, "Carroll made one of the most radical statements on behalf of the fairy tales and the child's perspective by conceiving a fantastic plot without an ostensible moral purpose."[141] Although there were several earlier diversions from the moral tale,[142] Zipes is accurate in his contention that the stories, poems and novels written for children during the time of the publication of *Alice* were predominantly intended as religious instruction. "If literary fairytales were written and published," Zipes explains, "they were transformed into didactic tales preaching hard work and pious behaviour."[143] Carroll not only refused to present a moral resolution but also blatantly mocked this Victorian pre-occupation, evidenced in the exchange between the Duchess and Alice:

> 'You're thinking about something, my dear, and that makes you forget to talk. I ca'n't tell you just now what the moral of that is, but I shall remember it in a bit.'
> 'Perhaps it hasn't one,' Alice ventured to remark.
> 'Thu, tut, child!' said the Duchess. 'Everything's got a moral if only you can find it.'[144]

The Duchess proceeds to describe to Alice the moral value of "mustard mines" and croquet games. By suggesting the moral qualities of such ludicrous ideas (especially given the dominant context of the moral tale), Carroll invites his readers to laugh at the fixation upon morality. To use a distinctly amoral fiction to propose a point of analogue with Christianity could thus be an effective method of shifting the primary focus off moral behavior and instead prompting an individual to reconsider their diagnosis of Christianity as either oppressively legislative or simply a nice code by which to live. Rather, Christianity looks beyond the moral realm and fixes on the ultimate source of goodness, which is another type of goodness altogether. C. S. Lewis sums up the position thus:

141. Zipes quoted in Mickenburg and Nel (eds.), *Tales for Little Rebels*, foreword, xxii.

142. For an overview of the history of the dissent from the moral tale see Jeanie Watson's "Coleridge and the Fairy Tale Controversy," in Holt McGavran (ed.), *Romanticism and Children's Literature*, 14–31.

143. Jack Zipes quoted in *Tales for Little Rebels*, xiv.

144. Carroll, *AW*, 71.

> I think all Christians would agree with me if I said that though
> Christianity seems at first to be all about morality, all about du-
> ties and rules and guilt and virtue, yet it leads you on, out of
> all that into something beyond. One has a glimpse of a country
> where they do not talk of those things, except perhaps as a joke.
> Every one there is filled full with what we should call goodness
> as a mirror is filled with light. But they do not call it goodness.
> They do not call it anything. They are not thinking of it. They are
> too busy looking at the source from which it comes.[145]

Lewis' suggestion—that from an ultimate perspective preoccupation
with morality might be joked about—intimates that associating Christianity
with nonsense is not irreligious, but could be a positive way of confronting unhelpful assumptions about the religion. Rather like Lewis' method
of teaching Christian truths through the mouth of a devil, the analogy with
nonsense is an apology for Christianity that recommends it by means of its
opposite. Suggesting that Christianity is nonsense is really a way of commenting on the nonsense of the world and the uprightness of the upside-
down kingdom.

The purpose of the non-useful

In addition to not offering a moral homily, any literature wishing to be defined as nonsense must avoid concluding with any meaningful objective.
Lecercle recognizes this as an important feature of nonsense and believes
this is why nonsense literature can never have a political agenda "because
the texts constitutionally lack a point."[146] Other nonsense theorists also acknowledge the lack of utility as an essential attribute of the genre. Tigges, for
example, states: "the game of nonsense by is played for its own sake rather
than with a transcendent aim."[147] Stewart likewise describes nonsense as "an
activity where means become more important than ends."[148] Carroll is often
quoted for his own admission that the Alice stories "do not teach anything
at all."[149] It might seem strange to recommend nonsense as a Christian analogue on account of its apparent pointlessness.

---

145. Lewis, *Mere Christianity*, 118.

146. Lecercle "Nonsense and Politics," 359.

147. Tigges, *Anatomy of Literary Nonsense*, 55.

148. Stewart, *Aspects of Intertextuality*, 119.

149. Lewis Carroll to the Lowrie children, August 18, 1884, cited in *Selected Letters*,
136.

In his work *Theology and Joy*, Jürgen Moltmann speaks out against valuing the church "only on the basis of *its usefulness,* [. . .] [where] its ends are determined by morality and politics."[150] He works from the central premise that "man is trapped in usefulness."[151] Moltmann calls for a means of approaching Christianity without considering its utility. He writes: "Those who try to defend religion by establishing its external usefulness and necessity turn out to be its worst enemies in the long run."[152] Moltmann substitutes utility for play and presents a theology of play, stemming from the conviction that games interrupt the focus on goal and "serve as temporary suspensions of the normal state of affairs."[153]

Theories of play often tend to emphasize that whilst games must appear purposeless from an external viewpoint, "a game is meaningful within itself."[154] This suggests that within even the most basic game, strategy is important, tasks have an end, costumes serve a purpose and props are functional. However, nonsensical play seems to be an interesting exception to this rule because it refuses meaning even *within* the context of its own play. For example, at the mad tea party the Hatter instigates a game of riddles: "Why is a raven like a writing-desk?"[155] The point of this game is to guess the correct answer. Alice experiences frustration, not because she fails to work out the solution, but because there isn't one:

> 'Have you guessed the riddle yet?' the Hatter said, turning to Alice again.
> 'No, I give it up,' Alice replied: 'what's the answer?'
> 'I haven't the slightest idea,' said the Hatter.
> 'Nor I,' said the March Hare.
> Alice sighed wearily. 'I think you might do something better with the time,' she said, 'than waste it in asking riddles that have no answers.'[156]

Alice does not enjoy the game of nonsense and finds it tiresome because she has learned that all things have a purpose, even games. The problem that confronts Alice, as Tigges puts it, is that "the 'pointe' is essentially lacking

---

150. Moltmann, *Theology and Joy*, 78.

151. Jenkins, Introduction to *Theology and Joy*, 11.

152. Moltmann, *Theology and Joy*, 79.

153. Ibid., 33.

154. Ibid., 30–31: "All theories about play make the point that a game is meaningful within itself but that it must appear useless and purposeless from an outside point of view."

155. Carroll, *AW*, 55.

156. Ibid., 56.

in nonsense."[157] This reveals a potential danger with the game analogy; winning can easily become the purpose of the game and can in effect become a shadow version of the professional world. An ideal game metaphor would therefore need to produce new standards of game playing that are divorced from the traditional patterns of winning and losing. Whilst all play appears to be composed for its own sake, nonsense play is perhaps unique because it is supremely subversive to purpose; it does not even "play" at being useful.

Carroll's absurd Caucus Race promotes a method of play which through nonsense refuses to conform to established patterns: "There was no 'One, two, three, and away,' Alice reports, 'but they began running when they liked, and left off when they liked, so that it was not easy to know when the race was over.'"[158] When the contestants inquire as to the winner, the Dodo announces, "*Everybody* has won and *all* must have prizes." This nonsense game radically diverts from the normal condition of winning where there is often a fixation on coming first or being the best.[159] Rather, the absurd Caucus Race is in a sense closer to "the game of grace" where, as Moltmann tells us, "the loser wins."[160] Nonsense play therefore through rejecting purpose and end allows for the temporary suspension of achievement measured by a secular standard of accomplishment.

By introducing "grace" into the system of "game," it becomes once again apparent that nonsense is only conceivable as a theological analogy due to the doctrine of salvation. Moltmann explains: "Easter opens up the boundary-crossing freedom to play the game of the new creation. [. . .] The cross of Christ therefore does not belong to the game itself, but it makes possible the new game of freedom. He suffered that we may laugh again."[161] This is an important qualification to highlight because it emphasizes that the playful transcendence of purpose is only possible because Christ embodies and satisfies supreme purpose. "For this purpose I was born," Christ states, "and for this purpose I have come into the world—to bear witness to the truth."[162] God's incarnation in Christ is understood as the manifestation of

---

157. Tigges, *Anatomy of Literary Nonsense*, 257.

158. Carroll, *AW*, 23.

159. See Deleuze, *Logic of Sense*, 69. "Not only does Lewis Carroll invent games, or transform the rules of known games (tennis, croquet), but he invokes a sort of ideal game. [. . .] These games, [the caucus race and the croquet match] have the following in common: they have a great deal of movement, they seem to have no precise rules, and they permit neither winner nor loser. We are not 'acquainted' with such games which seem to contradict themselves."

160. Moltmann, *Theology and Joy*, 47.

161. Ibid., 53.

162. John 18:37.

ultimate purpose and by seeing his purpose through to the end, God effectively concludes all worldly *telos*, and as such, ushers in an eternal playtime.

Perhaps, even more so than a general analogy with play, the association with nonsense subverts the categories of purpose and necessity on a
grand scale. Moltmann asserts: "Religion refuses to answer questions concerning its practical social value and its moral usefulness. Its dignity lies
precisely in that it compels us to abandon this greedy and selfish line of
questioning if we are to understand religion."[163] The colloquial connotations
of the term "nonsense" as "futile" or "pointless" together with the refusal of
the literary genre to offer a significant meaning could thus prove beneficial
in the communication of Moltmann's message and the wider mission of
the church, that God's purpose is greater than any social utility or personal
accomplishment.

CONCLUSION: THE LUNATIC'S RISK

We were fools for Christ's sake

1 CORINTHIANS 4:10

Pausing for a moment, before we come to a final conclusion, this project
has, in a sense, been a long response to Martin Heidegger's question: "will
Christian theology one day resolve to take seriously the world of the apostle
and thus also the conception of philosophy as foolishness?"[164] This volume
has suggested that while faith is a solemn and sensible matter, it is also extravagant, playful, and foolish, and that the category of the nonsensical aids
the recovery of a number of these underemphasized aspects of traditional
theology.

We have looked at some of the reasons why using literary nonsense
as a theological analogue is accurate and helpful—firstly, for the believer,
it preserves a biblical sense of scandal and secondly, it makes faith more
presentable to the atheist. This project has suggested that literary nonsense
can serve—albeit imperfectly—as a cosmic allegory of both man's fall and
his salvation. I have described the structural principles of literary nonsense
as replicating the shape of the salvific imagination. Experiencing God *can*
be likened to falling down the rabbit hole—all manner of things become be-
lievable which were previously thought impossible. Certain aspects of faith

163. Moltmann, *Theology and Joy*, 79.
164. Heidegger, *Pathmarks*, 288.

seem like nonsense when the individual's dominant method of assessment is rationalistic. This is why the imagination is so vital to Christian faith, because if our inherited *a priori* faculties are upside-down then we require a radically alternative way of thinking in order to begin the process of approaching God's topsy-turvy kingdom.

Moreover, this type of imagining might also be a useful exercise for the Christian for whom religious faith makes obvious sense. Because nonsense is a looking-glass analogy, it confronts not only the self, but also the reverse image of the self, and can therefore become a useful symbol for reminding Christians about the strangeness of their message. As such, making a connection with literary nonsense could also be beneficial for the believer who cannot understand why Christianity is often incomprehensible to an atheist.

Perhaps, above all, what the analogy between faith and nonsense reminds us, is that faith is a risk. Kierkegaard reaches a similar conclusion and invokes the language of absurdity in order to highlight the risk entailed in religious belief. "Someone," he writes, "'a serious man,' may say, 'But is it certain and definite that there is such a good, is it certain and definite that there is an eternal happiness in store?—because in that case I surely would aspire to it; otherwise, I would be lunatic to risk everything for it.'"[165] Kierkegaard frustrates the serious man's desire for epistemic certainty because of his conviction that "the absurd is precisely the object of faith and only that can be believed."[166] Kierkegaard wants to separate faith from the language of logical probability as he sees this thirst for assurance as a barrier to religious belief. Faith is a risk precisely *because* of its noetic uncertainty and at any point an individual could come to the conclusion that it may not be true.

The suggestion that certain aspects of Christian faith are rationally indefensible thus draws attention to the daily risk involved in believing in God, which according to Richard Kropf is vital for spiritual integrity and growth: "We cannot advance spiritually," Kropf states, "unless we are willing to let go of the *security* that so often binds us to what is familiar or comfortable. In other words, faith involves risk."[167] A heavily rationalized apologetic can often give the illusion that the "risk" content of faith has been greatly reduced. The reduction of risk may, for many, seem appealing, and it is often the precondition of the atheist's conversion: "I would believe in God if only I could be assured of His existence." Yet, for others, the reduction of risk leads to an impoverished version of faith. Matthew Bagger describes the action of ironing out moments of logical absurdity in religion as "making

165. Kierkgaard, *Concluding Unscientific Postscript*, 422.

166. Ibid., 211.

167. Kropf, *Faith, Security and Risk*, 2.

faith too easy" and "depriv[ing] the individual of the 'fear and trembling' accompanying the leap of faith."[168] What an association with nonsense brings to the fore is that the risk involved in religious belief is immense.

Hugo Meynell tells us, "the true scandal of faith is its insistence that man should surrender his illusion of self-sufficiency."[169] Part of the problem, we have discovered, with overemphasizing the logical credibility of faith is that the individual is more susceptible to sustaining the "illusion of self-sufficiency."[170] Take, for example, Wolterstorff's introduction to *Faith and Rationality* in which he describes reason as "something that each of us possesses intrinsically. [. . .] Thus, to follow the voice of Reason is not to submit to some new external authority. It is to follow *one's own* voice."[171] In this thesis we have adopted Chesterton's description of the topsy-turvy condition of man and therefore encounter a theological problem with Wolterstorff's dictum, since, if our inner voice of reason is upside-down then following it, as he recommends, will not deliver us the right way up. The language Wolterstorff uses promotes the sufficiency of our internal powers of reasoning and so in this sense disguises the "scandal of faith" and the inherent risk.

Does the believer then live in constant fear of the instability of his belief? Does faith bring with it a desperate insecurity? The assurance from the Bible is that faith is an unveiling of knowledge not previously known, which brings with it a restoration and transformation of the individual. It is in this purified state that the risk of faith is calmed: "blessed are the pure in heart, for they will see God."[172] It is not that faith, once entered into, ceases to involve any uncertainty, but that in the venture of faith, as the individual struggles against his desire for security, a new standard of assurance is revealed to the believer, although it may not seem any less certain to the atheist.

The description of faith as a risk may help to illuminate the purpose of this project; we have drawn an analogy with nonsense because it seems to be a true characterization of aspects of Christian belief, not because we wanted to say something controversial about faith or because it seems bold and counter-intuitive. In fact, what we have described as the nonsensical component of religious belief is, viewed from the believer's perspective, simply the most accurate description of reality. For all his famous statements

---

168. Bagger, *Uses of Paradox*, 28.

169. Meynell, *Sense and Nonsense*, 253.

170. See also Bagger's reflection of Kierkegaard and the paradoxical: "Christian paradox forces the understanding to step aside and thereby roots out the final illusions of self-sufficiency." *Uses of Paradox*, 39.

171. Wolterstorff, *Faith and Rationality*, 5.

172. Matt 5:8.

on the lunacy and incredulous nature of faith, Kierkegaard also reflects that "when the believer has faith, the absurd is not the absurd—faith transforms it, but in every weak moment it is again more or less absurd to him. The passion of faith is the only thing which masters the absurd."[173] In agreement with Kierkegaard, I have not sought to promote nonsense as some eternal or superior category, but used the term to aid the passage to the other side of reason where nonsense can reveal its hidden sense. Coleridge describes this idea beautifully in his *Biographia Literaria*:

> the scheme of Christianity [. . .] though not discoverable by human reason, is yet in accordance with it; that link follows link by necessary consequence; that religion passes out of the ken of reason only where the eye of reason has reached its own horizon; and that faith is then but its continuation: even as the day softens away into the sweet twilight.[174]

So too as we have seen with nonsense, it is but the re-awakening of sense, at the dawn of the upside-down kingdom.

173. Kierkegaard, *Journals and Papers*, 7.
174. Coleridge, *Biographia Literaria*, 247.

Bibliography

Agamben, Giorgio *The Time That Remains*. Translated by Patricia Dailey. Palo Alto, CA: Stanford University Press, 2005.

Allison, C. FitzSimons. *The Cruelty of Heresies*. Harrisburg, PA: Moorehouse, 2002.

Anderson, James. *Paradox in Christian Theology*. Paternoster Theological Monographs. Milton Keynes, UK: Paternoster, 2007.

Anselm. *The Major Works*. Edited by Brian Davies and G. R. Evans. Oxford: Oxford University Press, 1998.

Aquinas, Thomas, *Summa Theologia*. Translated by Timothy McDermott. London: Methuen, 1991.

———. *Super Boethium de Trinitate*. Translated by Rose E. Brennan. S.H.N. New York: Herder, 1946.

Aristotle. *Metaphysics*. Translated by Christopher Kirwan. Oxford: Clarendon, 1993.

Armstrong, A. H. *The Cambridge History of Latin, Greek and Early Medieval Philosophy*. Cambridge: Cambridge University Press, 1967.

Auden, W. H. *Forewords & Afterwords*. New York: Vintage, 1974.

Augustine. *City of God*. Translated by Henry Bettenson. London: Penguin, 2003.

———. *On Free Choice of the Will*. Translated by Thomas Williams. Indianapolis: Hackett, 1993.

———. *Sermons: On the Liturgical Seasons*. Edited by John E. Rotelle. Translated by Edmund Hill. New York: City, 1993.

———. *De Trinitate*. Translated by Edmund Hill in *The Major Works*. Oxford: Oxford University Press, 1998.

Bagger, Matthew C. *The Uses of Paradox: Religion, Self-transformation, and the Absurd*. New York: Columbia University Press, 2007.

Balthasar, Hans Urs von. *The Glory of the Lord*. Translated by Erasmo Leiva-Merikakis. San Francisco: Ignatius, 1982.

Barth, Karl. *Church Dogmatics 4.1*. Edited by T. F. Torrance and G. W. Bromiley. Edinburgh: T. & T. Clark, 1956.

———. *Ethics*. Edinburgh: T. & T. Clark, 1981.

Bartley, Jonathan. *Faith and Politics After Christendom: The Church as a Movement for Anarchy*. Milton Keynes, UK: Paternoster, 2006.

Baurman, Zygmunt. "Postmodern Ethics." In *The New Social Theory Reader*, edited by Stephen Seidman and Jeffrey C. Alexander, 138–47. London: Routledge, 2001.

Begbie, Jeremy. *Beholding the Glory*. Grand Rapids: Baker, 2001.

Bencivenga, Ermanno. *Logic and Other Nonsense: The Case of Anselm and His God*. Princeton: Princeton University Press, 1993.

Berdyaev, Nicolas. *The Beginning and the End*. Translated by R. M. French. London: Bles, 1952.

———. *The Destiny of Man*. Translated by N. Duddington. London: Bles, 1937.

———. *Dream and Reality*. Translated by Katherine Lampert. London: Bles, 1950.

———. *Freedom and the Spirit*. Translated by Oliver Fielding Clarke. London: Bles, 1935.

———. *The Realm of Spirit and the Realm of Caesar*. Translated by Donald A. Lowrie. London: Gollanez, 1952.

———. *The Russian Idea*. Translated by R. M. French. London: Bles, 1947.

———. *Self-cognition*. Translated by Dimitri Lisin. Moscow: Kniga, 1991.

———. *Truth and Revelation*. Translated by R. M. French. London: Bles, 1953.

———. *The Meaning of the Creative Act*. Translated by Donald A. Lowrie. New York: Collier, 1962.

Berlin, Isaiah. *Three Critics of the Enlightenment: Vico, Hamann, Herder*. Princeton: Princeton University Press, 2000.

Binski, Paul. *Medieval Death*. London: British Museum, 1996.

Boff, Leonardo. *Jesus Christ Liberator*. Translated by Patrick Hughes. New York: Orbis, 1979.

Boucherie, Marijke. "Nonsense and Other Senses." In *Nonsense and Other Senses: Regulated Absurdity in Literature*, edited by Elisabetta Tarantino, 259–74. Newcastle, UK: Cambridge Scholars, 2009.

Boyne, Rob. *Foucault and Derrida: The Other Side of Reason*. London: Routledge, 1990.

Bradley, Ian. *Colonies of Heaven*. London: Darton, Longman and Todd, 2000.

Brizer, David, and Ricardo Castaneda, eds. *Clinical Addiction Psychiatry*. Cambridge: Cambridge University Press, 2010.

Brown, Frank M. *Boolean Reasoning: The Logic of Boolean Equations*. New York: Dover, 2003.

Bruce, F. F. *The Epistle of Paul to the Romans: An Introduction and Commentary*. London: Tyndale, 1963.

Burnett, Frances Hodgson. *Little Lord Fauntleroy*. Mineola, NY: Dover, 2002.

Calian, Carnegie Samuel. *The Significance of Eschatology in the Thoughts of Nicolas Berdyaev*. Leiden: Brill, 1965.

Calvin, John. *Institutes of Christian Religion, Volume II*. Edited by John T. McNeil. London: Westminster, 1960.

Caputo, John D. *The Prayers and Tears of Jacques Derrida: Religion without Religion*. Bloomington: Indiana University Press, 1997.

Caputo, John D., and Michael J. Scanlon, eds. *God, the Gift and Postmodernism*. Bloomington, IN: Indiana University Press, 1999.

Caputo, John D., and Gianni Vattimo. *After the Death of God*. Edited by Jefferey Robins. New York: Columbia University Press, 2007.

Caraher, Brian G., ed. *Contradiction in Literary and Philosophical Discourse*. Albany, NY: State University of New York Press, 1992.

Carroll, Lewis, *Alice's Adventures in Wonderland*. Edited by Donald Grey. London: Norton, 1992.

―――. *Alice's Adventures Underground*. London: MacMillan, 1886.

―――. *Alice Through the Looking-Glass*. Edited by Donald Grey. London: Norton, 1992.

―――. *Diaries*. Bedford, UK: The Lewis Carroll Society, 1993.

―――. *The Selected Letters of Lewis Carroll*. Edited by Morton N. Cohen. London: Macmillan, 1989.

―――. *Sylvie and Bruno Concluded* in *The Complete Illustrated Lewis Carroll*. Ware, UK: Wordsworth Editions, 1996.

Chesterton, G. K. *All Things Considered*. Fairfield, IA: First World, 2008.

―――. "Both Sides of the Looking-Glass." In *The Spice of Life and Other Essays*. London: Cox and Wyman, 1964.

―――. *The Defendant*. London: Dent & Sons, 1901.

―――. *Heretics*. Mineola, NY: Dover, 2006.

―――. *Orthodoxy*. London: Cloves and Sons, 1927.

―――. *St Thomas Aquinas*. London: Hodder and Stroughton, 1933.

―――. *What's Wrong with the World*. London: Cassell, 1910.

Cohen, Morton N. *Lewis Carroll: A Biography*. London: Papermac, 1995.

Coleridge, Samuel Taylor. *The Collected Works of Samuel Taylor Coleridge, Volume 7: Biographia Literaria*. Princeton: Princeton University Press, 1983.

Cottingham, John. *The Spiritual Dimension: Religion, Philosophy and Human Value*. Cambridge: Cambridge University Press, 2005.

Cox, Harvey. *The Feast of Fools*. Cambridge: Harvard University Press, 1969.

Cusa, Nicholas. *Nicholas of Cusa: Selected Spiritual Writings*. Translated by H. Lawrence Bond. New York: Paulist, 1997.

Damico, Linda H. *The Anarchist Dimension of Liberation Theology*. New York: Lang, 1987.

Dancy, R. M. *Sense and Contradiction: A Study in Aristotle*. Dordrecht: Reidel, 1975.

Davidson, Andrew, ed. *Imaginative Apologetics: Theology, Philosophy and the Catholic Tradition*. London: SCM, 2011.

Davies, Brian. *The Thought of Thomas Aquinas*. Oxford: Oxford University Press, 1992.

Deane, David. *Nietzsche and Theology: Nietzschean Thought in Christological Anthropology*. Farnham, UK: Ashgate, 2006.

De Lubac, Henri. *Paradoxes of Faith*. Translated by Sadie Kreilkamp. San Francisco: Ignatius, 1987.

Deleuze, Gilles. *Desert Islands and Other Texts, 1953–1974*. Translated by Michael Taormina. New York: Semiotext(e), 2004.

―――. *The Logic of Sense*. Translated by Mark Lester. London: Continuum, 2004.

―――. *Negotiations 1972–1990*. Translated by Martin Joughin. New York: Columbia University Press, 1997.

Derrida, Jacques. *Aporias*. Translated by Thomas Dutoit. Palo Alto, CA: Stanford University Press, 1993.

―――. *The Beast and the Sovereign*, Vol. 1. Translated by Geoffrey Bennington Chicago: Chicago University Press, 2009.

―――. *Dissemination*. Translated by Barbara Johnson. Chicago: University of Chicago Press, 1981.

———. *The Gift of Death*. Translated by David Wills. Chicago: Chicago University Press, 1996.

———. *Of Grammatology*. Translated by Gayatri Chakravorty Spivak. London: John Hopkins University Press, 1998.

———. *Paper Machine*. Translated by Rachel Bowlby. Palo Alto, CA: Stanford University Press, 2005.

———. *Writing and Difference*. Translated by Alan Bass. London: Routledge, 2001.

Dickson, Keith A. *Towards Utopia: A Study of Brecht*. Oxford: Clarendon, 1978.

Dusinberre, Juliet. *Alice to the Lighthouse*. London: Macmillan, 1987.

Edwards, Ian. "Derrida's Ir(religion): A Theology of Differéènce." *Janus Head* 6.1 (2003) 142–53.

Eller, Vernard. *Kierkegaard and Radical Discipleship*. Princeton: Princeton University Press, 1968.

Ellul, Jacques. *Anarchy and Christianity*. Translated by Geoffrey W. Bromley. Grand Rapids: Eerdmans, 1991.

———. *The Subversion of Christianity*. Grand Rapids: Eerdmans, 1986.

Erasmus, Desiderius. *The Praise of Folly*. Edited by Robert M. Adams. New York: Norton, 1989.

Evagrius of Pontus. "Praktikos." In *The Greek Ascetic Corpus*, translated by Robert E. Sinkewicz, 91–115. Oxford: Oxford University Press, 2006.

Flesher, Jaqueline. "The Language of Nonsense in Alice." In *Yale French Studies*, 43 (1969) 128–44.

Foucault, Michel. *Madness and Civilisation*. Translated by Richard Howard. London: Tavistock, 1967.

Freeman, Cameron. *Post-Metaphysics and the Paradoxical Teachings of Jesus: The Structure of the Real*. New York: Lang, 2010.

Freud, Sigmund. *The Psychopathology of Everyday Life*. Translated by James Strachey. London: Hogarth, 1973.

Fronda, Earl Stanley B. *Wittgenstein's (Misunderstood) Religious Thought*. Leiden: Brill, 2010.

Gardner, Helen, ed. *The Metaphysical Poets*. Harmondsworth, UK: Penguin, 1957.

Geisler, Norman L., and Ronald M. Brooks., eds. *Come, Let Us Reason: An Introduction to Logical Thinking*. Ada, MI: Baker Book House, 1990.

Gill, Jerry H. *Essays on Kierkegaard*. Minneapolis: Burgess, 1969.

Gordon D. Kaufman. *The Theological Imagination*. Philadelphia: Westminster, 1981.

Goulder, Michael. *Incarnation and Myth*. London, SCM, 1979.

Graham, Eleanor. *Lewis Carroll and the Writing of Through the Looking Glass*. London: Puffin, 1981.

Green, Garrett. *Imagining God: Theology and the Religious Imagination*. Philadelphia: Fortress, 1987.

———. *A Kingdom Not of this World*. Palo Alto, CA: Stanford University Press, 1964.

Green, Michael Steven. *Nietzsche and the Transcendental Tradition*. Champaign, IL: University of Illinois Press, 2002.

Guroian, Vigen. "The Office of Child in the Christian Faith: A Theology of Childhood." In *The Vocation of the Child*, edited by Patrick McKinley Brennan, 104–24. Grand Rapids: Eerdmans, 2008.

Hamann, Johann Georg. *Writings on Philosophy and Language*. Edited by Kenneth Haynes. Cambridge: Cambridge University Press, 2007.

Hart, Trevor. "Through the Arts: Hearing, Seeing and Touching the Truth." In *Beholding the Glory: Incarnation through the Art*, edited by Jeremy Begbie, 1–26. London: Darton, Longmann & Todd, 2000.

Hart, W. D. *The Evolution of Logic*. Cambridge: Cambridge University Press, 2010.

Hasker, William. *God, Time and Knowledge*. Ithaca, NY: Cornell University Press, 1998.

———. *Providence, Evil and the Openness of God*. London: Routledge, 2004.

Heath, Peter. *The Philosopher's Alice*. New York: St. Martin's, 1974.

Helm, Paul, ed. *Faith and Reason*. Oxford: Oxford University Press, 1999.

Heidegger, Martin. *Pathmarks*. Edited and Translated by William McNeill. Cambridge: Cambridge University Press, 1998.

Hepburn, Ronald W. *Christianity and Paradox*. London: Watts, 1958.

———. *"Wonder" and Other Essays*. Edinburgh: Edinburgh University Press, 1984.

Herbert, R. T. *Paradox and Identity in Theology*. New York: Cornell University Press, 1979.

Hiebert, Ted. *In Praise of Nonsense: Aesthetics, Uncertainty, and Postmodern Identity*. Quebec: Mcgill-Queen's University Press, 2012.

Hobson, Marian. *Jacques Derrida: Opening Lines*. London: Routledge, 1998.

Hollingsworth, Cristopher, ed. *Alice Beyond Wonderland: Essays for the Twenty-first Century*. Iowa City: Iowa University Press, 2009.

Holt McGavran, James, ed. *Romanticism and Children's Literature in Nineteenth-Century England*. Athens, GA: University of Georgia Press, 1991.

Hopkins, Gerald Manley. *The Poems of Gerald Manley Hopkins*. Edited by W. H. Gardner and N. H. MacKenzie. Oxford: Oxford University Press, 1967.

Hopps, Gavin. "Romantic Invocation: A Form of Impossibility." In *Romanticism and Form*, edited by Alan Rawes, 40–59. Basingstoke, UK: Palgrave Macmillan, 2007.

Huxley, Thomas Henry. *Hume*. London: Macmillan, 1879.

Hyman, Gavin. *A Short History of Atheism*. London: I. B. Tauris, 2010.

Janaway, Christopher, ed. *The Cambridge Companion to Schopenhauer*. Cambridge, Cambridge University Press, 1999.

Kainz, Howard P. *Five Metaphysical Paradoxes*. Milwaukee: Marquette University Press, 2006.

Kant, Immanuel. "An Answer to the Question: What is Enlightenment?" In *What is Enlightenment?* edited and translated by James Schmidt, 58–64. Berkeley, CA: University of California Press, 1996.

Kenny, Anthony. *Faith and Reason*. New York: Columbia University Press, 1983.

Kierkegaard, Søren. *The Concept of Anxiety*. Princeton: Princeton University Press, 1980.

———. *Concluding Unscientific Postscript Volume 1*. Translated by Howard V. Hong and Edna H. Hong. Princeton: Princeton University Press, 1992.

———. *Journals and Papers A–E, Vo1. 1*. Translated by Howard V. Hong and Edna H. Hong. Bloomington, IN: Indiana University Press, 1967.

Kincaird, James R., and Edward Guiliano, eds. *Soaring with the Dodo: Essays on Lewis Carroll's Life and Art* in *English Language Notes*. Charlottesville, VA: University Press of Virginia, 1982.

Kirk, Daniel, F. *Charles Dodgson Semiotician*. Gainesville, FL: University of Florida Press, 1963.

Knoepflmacher, U. C. *Ventures into Childland*. Chicago: University of Chicago Press, 1998.

Kott, Jan. *Shakespeare our Contemporary*. London: Methuen, 1964.

Kropf, Richard W. *Faith, Security and Risk*. Mahwah, NJ: Paulist, 1990.

Lakoff, Robin Tolmach. "Lewis Carroll: Subversive Pragmatists." *Pragmatics 3* (1993) 367–85.

Lawlor, Leonard. *Thinking through French Philosophy: The Being of the Question.* Bloomington, IN: Indiana University Press, 2003.

Lear, Edward. *Complete Nonsense*. Ware, UK: Wordsworth Editions, 1994.

Lecercle, Jean-Jacques. *Deleuze and Language*. Baisingstoke, UK: Palgrave Macmillan, 2002.

———. *Philosophy of Nonsense*. London: Routledge, 1994.

———. *Philosophy through the Looking-Glass: Language, Nonsense, Desire*. London: Hutchinson, 1985.

Lewis, C. S. *The Chronicles of Narnia*. Grand Rapids: Zondervan, 2004.

———. *God in the Docks*. Grand Rapids: Eerdmans, 2014.

———. *Mere Christianity*. London: HarperCollins, 2002.

———. *Miracles*. New York: HarperCollins, 2001.

———. *The Screwtape Letters*. Glasgow: Collins, 1984.

———. *Surprised by Joy*. London: Bles, 1955.

Lewis, John Michael. *Galileo in France: French Reactions to the Theories and Trial of Galileo*. New York: Lang, 2007.

Llewelyn, John. *Margins of Religions: Between Kierkegaard and Derrida*. Bloomington, IN: Indiana University Press, 2009.

Locke, John. *An Essay Concerning Human Understanding*. London: Tegg and Son, 1836.

Lopez, Alan. "Deleuze with Carroll." *Angelaki: Journal of the Theoretical Humanities* 9.3 (2004) 101–20.

Lowrie, Donald A., trans. *Christian Existentialism: A Berdyaev Anthology*. London: George Allen and Unwin, 1965.

Luther, Martin. *Bondage of the Will*. Translated by Henry Cole. Digireads.com, 2009.

———. *A Commentary on Saint Paul's Epistle to the Galatians*. Translated by J. Duncan. London: Duncan, 1830.

———. "Second Sunday in Epiphany." 17th January 1546, *Dr Martin Luther's Werke: Kritische Gesantausgabe*, Vol. 51, translated by H. G. Ganss. Weimar: Boehlaus Nachfolger, 1914.

MacDonald, George. *Adela Cathart*. Whitehorn, CA: Johannesen, 2000.

———. *A Dish of Orts*. Whitehorn, CA: Johannesen, 1996.

———. *The Hope of the Gospel*. Whitehorn, CA: Johannesen, 2000.

———. *Miracles of our Lord*. Whitehorn, CA: Johannesen, 2000.

———. *The Gifts of the Child Christ*. Edited by Glenn Edward Sadler. Oxford: Mowbray, 1973.

———. *Phantastes*. Whitehorn, CA: Johannesen, 2000.

———. *Poems*. London: Longman, Brown, Green and Roberts, 1857.

———. *Unspoken Sermons I, II, III*. Whitehorn, CA: Johannesen, 1999.

Macdonald, Greville. *George MacDonald and His Wife*. London: Allen & Unwin, 1924.

Malcolm, Noel. *The Origins of English Nonsense*. London: HarperCollins, 1997.

Manlove, C. N. *The Impulse of Fantasy Literature*. London: Macmillan, 1983.

Marshall, Peter. *Demanding the Impossible: A History of Anarchism*. London: Fontana, 1993.

McFague, Sallie. *Speaking in Parables: A Study in Metaphor and Theology.* Philadelphia: Fortress, 1975.

McGrath, Alister. E. *Christian Theology: An Introduction.* Oxford: Blackwell, 1997.

———. *Reformation Thought.* Oxford: Wiley-Blackwell, 2012.

McIntosh, Mark A. *Mystical Theology.* Oxford: Blackwell, 1998.

McKim, Donald K., ed. *The Cambridge Companion to Martin Luther.* Cambridge: Cambridge University Press, 2003.

Menninghaus, Winfried. *In Praise of Nonsense: Kant and Bluebeard.* Palo Alto, CA: Stanford University Press, 1999.

Meynell, Hugo. *Sense and Nonsense in Christianity.* London: Sheed and Ward, 1964.

Mickenburg, Julia L., and Philip Nel, eds. *Tales for Little Rebels.* New York: New York University Press, 2008.

Milbank, Alison. *Chesterton and Tolkien as Theologians.* London: T. & T. Clark, 2007.

Milbank, John. "Fictioning Things: Gift and Narrative." *Religion and Literature* 37.3 (2005) 1–37.

———. *Theology and Social Theory.* Oxford: Blackwell, 2006.

———. "Paul against Biopolitical." *Theory, Culture and Society* 25.7–8 (2008) 125–72.

———. *The Suspended Middle.* London: SCM, 2005.

———. *Truth in Aquinas.* New York: Routledge, 2001.

Milbank, John, and Slavoj Žižek. *The Monstrosity of Christ: Paradox or Dialectic.* Edited by Creston Davies. Cambridge: MIT Press, 2009.

Miller, David. *Gods and Games: Toward a Theology of Play.* New York: World, 1969.

Milton, John. *Paradise Lost.* Edited by Christopher Ricks. New York: Penguin, 1968.

Moltmann, Jürgen. *Theology and Joy.* Translated by Reinhard Ulrich. London: SCM, 1973.

———. *The Way of Jesus Christ.* Translated by Margaret Kohl. Minneapolis: Fortress, 1990.

Mullarkey, John. *Post-Continental Philosophy: An Outline.* New York: Continuum, 2006.

Nash, Ronald H. *Faith and Reason: Searching for a Rational Faith.* Grand Rapids: Zondervan, 1988.

Newman, John Henry. *An Essay in Aid of a Grammar of Assent.* New York: The Catholic Publication Society, 1870.

Nietzsche, Friedrich. *The Will to Power*, Vol II. Translated by Anthony M. Ludovici. Edinburgh: Foulis, 1910.

Norris, Christopher. *Derrida.* Cambridge: Harvard University Press, 1987.

Nucho, Fuad. *Berdyaev's Philosophy.* London: Gollancz, 1967.

O'Neil, Mary Kay, and Salman Alchtar, eds. *On Freud's "The Future of an Illusion."* London: Karnac, 2009.

Otto, Rudolph. *The Idea of the Holy.* Translated by John W. Harvey. Oxford: Oxford University Press, 1950.

Palamas, Gregory. *The Triads.* Translated by Nicholas Gendle. Mahwah, NJ: Paulist, 1983.

Parsons, Marnie *Touch Monkeys: Nonsense Strategies for Reading Twentieth-Century Poetry.* Toronto: Toronto University Press, 1994.

Phillips, D. Z. *Faith After Foundationalism.* London: Routledge, 1988.

Phillips, Robert, ed. *Aspects of Alice.* Harmondsworth, UK: Penguin, 1974.

Pickstock, Catherine. *After Writing.* Oxford: Blackwell, 2000.

Plantinga, Alvin, and Nicholas Wolterstorff, eds. *Faith and Rationality: Reason and Belief in God.* Notre Dame, IN: University of Notre Dame Press, 1983.

Plato. *The Republic.* Translated by Tom Griffith. Cambridge: Cambridge University Press, 2000.

Polhemus, Robert. *Comic Faith: The Great Tradition from Austen to Joyce.* Chicago: University of Chicago Press, 1980.

Pridmore, J. "George MacDonald's Estimate of Childhood." *International Journal of Children's Spirituality* 12.1 (2007) 61–74.

Priest, J. C. Beall, and Bradley Armour-Gard. *The Law of Non-Contradiction.* Oxford: Clarendon, 2004.

Pseudo-Dionysius. *Pseudo-Dionysius: The Complete Works.* Translated by Colm Luibheid. Mahwah, NJ: Paulist, 1987.

Pudney, John. *Lewis Carroll and His World.* London: Thames and Hudson, 1976.

Quash, Ben, and Michael Ward, eds. *Heresies and How to Avoid Them.* London: SPCK, 2007.

Quine, W. V. *The Ways of Paradox and Other Essays.* MA thesis, Harvard University Press, 1976.

Rabkin, Eric S. *The Fantastic in Literature.* Princeton: Princeton University Press, 1976.

Rahner, Karl. "The Problem of the Concept of the Person." In *The Trinity*, translated by J. Donceel, 103–14. New York: Sunbury, 1974.

Reynolds, Jack. *Merleau-Ponty and Derrida: Intertwining Embodiment and Alterity.* Athens, OH: Ohio University Press, 2004.

Reynolds, Kimberly. *Radical Children's Literature: Future Visions and Aesthetic Transformations in Juvenile Fiction.* Baisingstoke, UK: MacMillan, 2007.

Riasanovsky, Nicholas V. *A History of Russia.* Oxford: Oxford University Press, 2000.

Richard of St. Victor. *The Complete Works.* Translated by Grover A. Zinn. London: SPCK, 1979.

Robinson, Edward. *The Language of Mystery.* London: SCM, 1987.

Robinson, Guy. *Philosophy and Mystification: A Reflection on Nonsense and Clarity.* London: Routledge, 1998.

Saward, John. *Perfect Fools: Folly for Christ's Sake in Catholic and Orthodox Spirituality.* Oxford: Oxford University Press, 1980.

Schopenhauer, Arthur. *On the Basis of Morality.* Translated by E. F. J. Payne. Indianapolis: Hackett, 1998.

Screech, M. A. *Laughter at the Foot of the Cross.* London: Penguin, 1997.

Schwab, Gabriele. "Nonsense and Metacommunication: Reflections on Lewis Carrol." In *The Play of the Self*, edited by R. Bogue and M. Spariosu, 157–80. New York: State University of New York Press, 1994

Sewell, Elizabeth. *The Field of Nonsense.* London: Chetto and Windus, 1952.

Shakespeare, William. *The Complete Works.* London: Really Useful Company, 2006.

Shier-Jones, Angela., ed. *Children of God: Towards a Theology of Childhood.* Beccles, UK: Clowes, 2007.

Soskice, Janet Martin. *Metaphor and Religious Language.* Oxford: Clarendon, 1985.

Stenson, Sten H. *Sense and Nonsense in Religion: An Essay on the Language and Phenomenology of Religion.* Nashville: Abingdon, 1969.

Stewart, Susan. *Aspects of Intertextuality in Folklore and Literature.* Baltimore: The John Hopkins University Press, 1979.

Strachey, Sir Edmund. "Nonsense as a Fine Art." *The Quarterly Review* 167 (1888) 335–65.

Stern, Jeffrey. "Lewis Carroll the Surrealist." In *Lewis Carroll: A Celebration*, edited by E. Guiliano, 132–53. New York: Potter, 1982.

Taylor, Charles. *A Secular Age*. London: Harvard University Press, 2007.

———. *Sources of the Self: The Making of the Modern Identity*. Cambridge: Harvard University Press, 1989.

Taylor, Mark C. *Erring: A Postmodern A/theology*. Chicago: The University of Chicago Press, 1987.

Tieck, Ludwig. *The Land of Upside Down*. Translated by Oscar Mandel. Madison, NJ: Fairleigh Dickinson University Press, 1978.

Tigges, Wim. *An Anatomy of Literary Nonsense*. Amsterdam: Rodopi, 1988.

———, ed. *Explorations in the Field of Nonsense*. Amsterdam: Rodopi, 1987.

Tolkien, J. R. R. "On Fairy-Stories." In *A Tolkien Miscellany*, 97–148. New York: SFBC, 2002.

Viladesau, Richard. *Theology and the Arts: Encountering God through Music, Art, and Rhetoric*. Mahwah, NJ: Paulist, 2000.

Ward, Graham, ed. *The Postmodern God: A Theological Reader*. Oxford: Blackwell 1997.

———. *Theology and Contemporary Critical Theory*. London: Macmillan, 2000.

Ward, Michael. "The Good Serves the Better and Both the Best: C. S. Lewis on Imagination and Reason in Apologetics." In *Imaginative Apologetics*, edited by Andrew Davidson, 59–78. London: SCM, 2010.

Waugh, Evelyn. *Brideshead Revisited*. London: Penguin Classics, 2000.

Weber, B. N., and Hubert Heinen, eds. *Bertolt Brecht: Political Theory and Literary Practice*. Athens, GA: University of Georgia Press, 1980.

Wells, Samuel. *Improvisation: The Drama of Christian Ethics*. London: SPCK, 2004.

Williams, Rowan. *The Wound of Knowledge*. London: Darton, Longman and Todd, 1990.

Williams, S. H. *The Lewis Carroll Handbook*. Northamptonshire: Dawsons, 1962.

Wippel, John F. *Mediaeval Reactions to the Encounter between Faith and Reason*. Milwaukee: Marquette University Press, 1995.

Yerxa, Donald A. *Recent Themes in Historical Conversation*. Columbia: University of South Carolina Press, 2008.

Zipes, Jack., ed. *Victorian Fairy Tales: The Revolt of Fairies and Elves*. New York: Routledge, 1991.

Index

220   INDEX

negative theology. *See* apophaticism
Newman, John Henry, 19
Nicholas of Cusa. *See* Cusa, Nicholas of
Nietzsche, Friedrich, 17–18, 25
nihilism, 29, 115, 167
non-contradiction, law of, 5–9, 10–11,
      15n55, 17, 22–24, 28–29, 40–43,
      64–65, 90–92
nonsense, passim
   absurdity within literary, 40, 43, 89,
      91n202, 96–97, 169, 181, 192,
      202
   anarchic aspects of, 92–95
   child, role of within, 131–34, 145,
      149–51, 153, 158
   childlike aspects of, 130–35
   criticism, 129, 130, 134, 143, 158,
      162–63, 170, 189
   death, depiction of, 167, 182,
      192–93
   faith, relationship with, 39, 101, 129,
      161–69, 190, 195–98, 203–6
   games, 40, 94, 153, 162, 200–202
   imagination, effect on, 39–40, 46,
      129, 131, 161, 168
   play, 45, 89, 95, 128, 162, 167,
      192–96
   paradoxical aspects of, 39–46
   postmodernity and, 32–33, 46
   evangelical implication of, 194–203

open theism, 72–73
orthodoxy, 2, 28, 29, 49, 52, 57, 61, 64,
      66, 71, 89, 97, 116, 123, 169–70

Palamas, Gregory, 66–70
paradox, 2n3, 8–9, 18–19, 29–32, 39–91
      passim, 165, 175–76
Paul, St,
   anarchism and, 100, 112–15, 120–22
   on the child, 136
   on divine space, 81–82
   as a fool, 190–91
   justification and, 198
   on the incarnation, 58, 62
   nonsense and, 166, 171, 173
   paradox of free will in, 74–77
   on reason and folly, 6–7

Peter Pan, 155
Pickstock, Catherine, 80, 83–84, 153–
      55, 163, 171, 182n79
Plato, 6, 22
play
   childlike, 153–57, 186–90
   nonsensical, 45, 89, 95, 128, 162,
      167, 192–96
   theological, 154–57, 186–90,
      200–203
Phillips, D. Z., 34
Polhemus, Robert, 94, 95, 167, 169–70,
      172, 177–80, 181–83, 186–87,
      189, 190–92
postmodernity
   Derrida and, 21, 25, 27
   nonsense and, 32–33, 46
   within theology, 18, 31, 33, 46n28,
      196–97,
pretence, 153–57
Priest, Graham, 28, 29n7
Pseudo-Dionysius, 8–9, 68–71

Quash, Ben, 49

Rabkin, Eric S., 176,
Rackin, Donald, 93, 94, 151, 169n28
Rahner, Karl, 57
reason
   faith and, 5–25 passim, 28–36,
      70–72, 163, 171, 205, 206
   paradoxical construal of, 42–45
repentance, 72, 74
resurrection, 33, 113, 128, 129, 165–66,
      168, 173–74, 182–83
reversal, 46, 128, 154, 158, 168–83
      passim
revolution
   secular, 110, 120–21
   spiritual, 98, 99, 107, 110, 113,
      120–21, 124–25
Richard of St. Victor, 53–57
risk, 17, 203–5

salvation, 61, 71, 73–76, 87, 102–4, 115,
      135–36, 150, 165–67, 174–77,
      182–88, 191
satire, 108–10

Lightning Source UK Ltd.
Milton Keynes UK
UKOW06f1221101016

284885UK00003B/570/P